A Continuous State of War

SERIES EDITORS

Stephen Berry
University of Georgia

Amy Murrell Taylor
University of Kentucky

ADVISORY BOARD

Edward L. Ayers
University of Richmond
Catherine Clinton
*University of Texas at
San Antonio*
J. Matthew Gallman
University of Florida
Elizabeth Leonard
Colby College

James Marten
Marquette University
Scott Nelson
University of Georgia
Daniel E. Sutherland
University of Arkansas
Elizabeth Varon
University of Virginia

A Continuous State of War

*Empire Building and Race Making
in the Civil War–Era Gulf South*

MARIA ANGELA DIAZ

The University of Georgia Press   *Athens*

© 2024 by the University of Georgia Press
Athens, Georgia 30602
www.ugapress.org
All rights reserved
Set in Adobe Caslon Pro 10.5 / 13 by Rebecca A. Norton

Most University of Georgia Press titles are
available from popular e-book vendors.

Printed digitally

Library of Congress Cataloging-in-Publication Data

Names: Diaz, Maria Angela, author.
Title: A continuous state of war : empire building
    and race making in the Civil War–era Gulf South / Maria Angela Diaz.
Other titles: Empire building and race making in the Civil War-era Gulf South | Uncivil wars.
Description: Athens : The University of Georgia Press, [2024] | Series: Uncivil wars |
    Includes bibliographical references and index.
Identifiers: LCCN 2023049036 | ISBN 9780820366487 (hardback) | ISBN 9780820366494
    (paperback) | ISBN 9780820366500 (epub) | ISBN 9780820366517 (adobe pdf)
Subjects: LCSH: Imperialism. | Gulf Coast (U.S.)—History. | Southern States—
    History—1775–1865. | Southern States—Race relations—History—19th century. |
    United States—Territorial expansion—History.
Classification: LCC E415.7 .D53 2024 | DDC 976/.03—dc23/eng/20231108
LC record available at https://lccn.loc.gov/2023049036

For My Family

CONTENTS

ACKNOWLEDGMENTS ix

INTRODUCTION
Wanting a Southern Empire 1

CHAPTER 1.
The Possibilities of Texas 9

CHAPTER 2.
The Possibilities of Pensacola 36

CHAPTER 3.
Making Meaning of the U.S.-Mexican War 56

CHAPTER 4.
Annexing the Gem of the Antilles 81

CHAPTER 5.
Galveston and the Fight for the Texas Borderlands 105

CHAPTER 6.
Launching a New Nation 129

CHAPTER 7.
Empire on the Run 155

CONCLUSION.
What Comes after Southern Imperialism? 179

NOTES 183

BIBLIOGRAPHY 201

INDEX 221

ACKNOWLEDGMENTS

Many people and institutions helped me throughout my time researching and writing this book. First, I would like to thank my parents, Jose M. Diaz and Francisca Diaz, my brother, Joe Anthony Diaz, and my entire family for their constant encouragement and support. Without their unwavering belief in my abilities this would not have been possible. I love them all more than I can say. My dear friend Autumn L. Hanna read various drafts and always offered a clear perspective. She was also one of my loudest cheerleaders. She made me laugh when I really needed it. I am also indebted to many other friends and colleagues who read different parts of this book and offered valuable critiques. These include but are not limited to, Allison Fredette, Timothy Fritz, Andrea Ferreira, Roberto Chauca, Aurélia Aubert, R. Scott Huffard, and James J. Broomall. Peter Carmichael and Watson Jennison were two of my favorite professors at the University of North Carolina at Greensboro, and they both played a crucial part in helping me to realize my goal of obtaining my PhD.

The History Department at the University of Florida provided an ideal environment to write my dissertation. It provided me with the support I needed to produce what became the first draft of this book. I would like to thank my advisors, William A. Link and J. Matthew Gallman, for their guidance, patience, and kindness. Bill Link answered every question and every late-night email with thoughtful suggestions. His generosity as a mentor is extraordinary, and I hope to be as good a mentor to my students as he was to me. I still seek his guidance and am honored to count him as a friend and colleague. Matt Gallman pushed me to think more creatively about my work and our many discussions over coffee and lunches led me to consider this project in new and different ways. It would not be the study it is today without his guidance. Both of these amazing historians have taught me what it means to be a scholar. I would like to thank Paul Ortiz, who helped me to begin thinking about the important connections between Latino and Southern history. I would like to thank my dissertation committee, Sean

Adams, Leah Rosenberg, and Paul Ortiz, for their thoughtful critiques and questions.

After two years at my first job, I was unceremoniously let go. It was a nightmare scenario for which I was unprepared. It caused me to question everything about my life as a historian. At a time in my life when I desperately needed to make a change, I received a postdoctoral fellowship in Texas history at Texas Tech University. It was there that I was able to regroup, re-envision my book project, and complete my research. I am forever indebted to the wonderful scholars of the TTU History Department for their unending encouragement. Miguel Antonio Levario became a dear friend and mentor. He believed in me at time when I needed it most. I thank Sean P. Cunningham for offering a friendly ear and constant commitment to support my work on this project. Emily Skidmore, Jacob M. Baum, Sarah Keyes, and Catharine R. Franklin, and Erin-Marie Legacey all read parts of this book and provided helpful critiques. Our daily discussions about each other's work allowed me space to imagine this book and its completion.

I found a wonderful home in the History Department at Utah State University. Many of my colleagues provided guidance and thoughtful critiques during the final stages of revisions. I am particularly thankful to the folks in the Works in Progress writing group: James E. Sanders, Julia M. Gossard, Tammy M. Proctor, Christopher Babits, Lawrence Culver, and Seth Archer. Colleen O'Neill, Kyle M. Bulthuis, and Kerin Holt provided me with advice on the publication process. Thank you to Mick Gusinde-Duffy and the University of Georgia Press. Thank you to the UnCivil Wars series editors, Stephen Berry and Amy Murrell Taylor. A special thanks to Amy, who worked closely with me on revising every part of the manuscript with immense patience and a careful eye.

I am indebted to the archivists such as Jim Cusick at the Special and Area Studies Collections, George A. Smathers Libraries, University of Florida; the Dolph Briscoe Center for American History and the Nettie Lee Benson Latin American Collection at the University of Texas; the Southern Historical Collection at the Louis Round Wilson Library at the University of North Carolina; Archives and Special Collections at Tulane University; the Historical New Orleans Collection; the Hill Memorial Library at Louisiana State University; the Galveston and Texas History Center at the Rosenberg Library; and the University Archives and West Florida History Center at the John C. Pace Library, University of West Florida. Lastly, if there is anyone that I forgot in this short statement, please know that I thank you as well.

A Continuous State of War

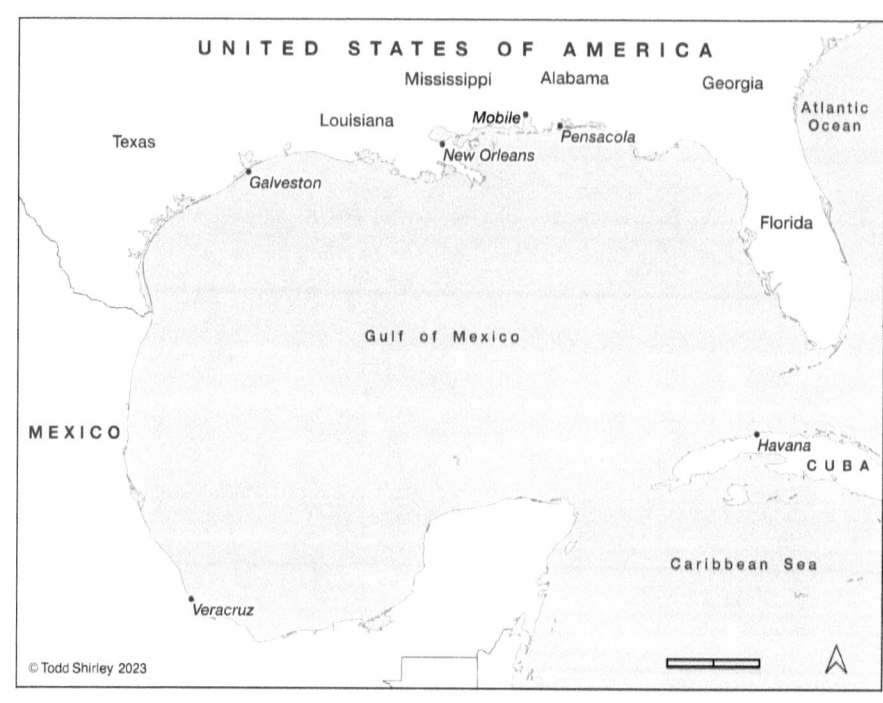

INTRODUCTION

Wanting a Southern Empire

In 1853 Frederick Law Olmsted, then primarily known for his travel writing traveled to Texas. Long before he became one of the nation's most famous landscape architects, Frederick and his brother, John Hull Olmsted, crossed the Red River on horseback into the state. For months they lived in the saddle, making note of the vast landscape through which they passed and encountering the state's various inhabitants, including white slaveholders, working-class and poor whites, enslaved African Americans, wealthy, and working-class Mexican Texans. As they wound their way through Texas's cotton lands, Olmsted observed that "whenever slavery in Texas has been carried in a wholesale way, into the neighborhood of Mexicans, it has been found necessary to treat them [Mexicans] as outlaws ... and forbidden, on pain of no less punishment than instant death, to return to the vicinity of the plantations."[1] Olmsted's observations hinted not only at the contest over territory between Anglo Americans and Mexicans but also at the racist views of white enslavers who were suspicious of Mexican Texans. It also reflected the way such views were applied to a variety of peoples of color in the Gulf South region throughout the mid-nineteenth century. Olmsted's experiences in Texas revealed the contestation over slavery's expansion that would draw the communities of the Gulf South into the tumult of the American Civil War.

Throughout the Civil War era, the Gulf South was in a continuous state of conflict. War existed in the far-flung borders of the Gulf of Mexico and affected communities large and small throughout the entire Southern coastal region. From the 1840s to the 1880s, white Southerners in the Gulf South fought with Native Americans, Mexicans, Cubans, the Spanish, and finally, when Americans went to war with each other, white Northerners and free and enslaved African Americans. These conflicts placed the Gulf of Mexico at the center of Southern expansionism and were an important part of expansionists' efforts to construct a race-based imperialist fantasy that justified and perpetuated territorial conquest in Latin America. Coastal print culture engaged in a regional and national production of ideas of empire, race, and Manifest Destiny, while coastal communities hoped to benefit from this hunger for more territory. This collection of ideas and efforts framed the Gulf of Mexico and Latin America as an essential part of Southern expansion.

A Continuous State of War examines the central role of Gulf South communities in Southerners' attempts to grab territory in Mexico and the Caribbean and the effects that this process had on those communities. I argue that Gulf Coast communities facilitated both the physical efforts to seize territory and the construction of the highly racialized imperialist ideas that imagined Latin America as a region that could secure the South's future. Yet the pursuit of that territory created a fluctuating and uncertain situation that shaped the choices of the diverse peoples who lived along the upper rim of the Gulf of Mexico. White Southern concepts of race became more rigidly fixed through the wars chronicled here. The fantasies of expansion were not snuffed out at the Civil War's end but persisted in the attempts of former Confederates to resettle in Latin America in the postwar period. By studying expansionist wars and the ideas used to promote them, this book traces the ways that ideas about Latin America and its peoples took shape within the complex port communities of the Gulf Coast as well as within the nation at large.

Throughout its early history, the United States obtained through war and negotiation different parts of the upper rim of the Gulf Coast. American control over the region continued to be contested even as it served as a launching pad for further expansionist projects. Indeed, the wars of expansion that occurred around the Gulf of Mexico during the mid-nineteenth century were as much about achieving authority over the region as they were about using those communities as staging grounds for conquest elsewhere. The United States may have laid claim to Florida, Alabama, Mississippi, and Louisiana by 1820, but conflict still raged across these states and then continued into Texas in the 1840s. This unending conflict and the militarization of the region continued right into 1861, when the Confederate States of America attempted to exert their own control over the Gulf South.

Many different worlds collided in the Gulf of Mexico. The history of expansion in the United States is usually presented as the story of westward movement. However, from the perspective of those living in the Gulf Coast, expansion happened west *and* south.[2] Placing different parts of the Gulf

Coast in conversation with one another draws attention to the fact that the whole Gulf of Mexico was affected by the various conflicts of the mid-nineteenth century. Expansionists such as John Quitman, Sam Houston, and Albert Sidney Johnston, also saw the borderlands of the U.S. South, Mexico, and the Caribbean as a connected whole. The Gulf South evolved into a center for trade and cultural and political exchange between the Atlantic World, the Caribbean, the U.S.-Mexico borderlands, and the U.S. South. It was also buffeted by a multitude of local, regional, national, and transnational forces. Gulf communities large and small continually angled for more military protection, more of the share of trade in cotton and enslaved African Americans, more access to better shipping methods, to the agricultural hinterlands, and more input into the visions that drove expansion.

The way that white Southerners constructed ideas about expansion was drawn from some of the most fundamental and far-reaching aspects of Southern society, namely race and slavery. To that end, the inclusion of Texas broadens this study for two main reasons. First, Texas was one of the main sites of expansion in the antebellum period. Second, many of the ideas about race that concerned Latin American peoples were, in part, formulated through the colonization, settlement, and annexation of Texas. For white Southerners, the annexation of Texas, and later the U.S.-Mexican War, served as prime examples of what territorial expansion could accomplish in terms of economic prosperity and the protection and spread of slavery.

As this book reveals, examining expansion's effects on different parts of the Gulf South simultaneously makes plain that, despite the tendency in American history to separate the stories of violent conquest against Mexicans and other Latin Americans and Native Americans from that of antebellum slavery these stories are deeply connected. White Southerners dreamed of them as connected, not only to each other but to what lay even further south; they dreamed of these spaces and the peoples that inhabited them as coming under their mastery. They feared these connections as much as they fantasized about them. They feared that the failure to extend white American authority would let loose the fulfillment of other fears, such as slave rebellions, and upend the carefully constructed world around them. Territorial expansion was ultimately about the future. Americans were interested in these territories not just because they could obtain more physical land but because they were enamored with the potential of that land. That is what expansion was all about: potential. Potential could be either positive or negative, and expansionists saw both kinds of potential in the land they coveted.

I have chosen to focus primarily on American expansionist efforts in Mexico and Cuba. The combination of efforts in Mexico and Cuba shed light on how Southern slave society's Black-white racial binary was used to shape the racism of Southern imperialism and territorial expansion and vice versa. Within this vision, Mexico with its mixed-race population would be conquered. Meanwhile, Cuba, with its slaveholding Cuban elite, could be annexed as a new state. Although Cuba's population was just as complex as Mexico's, the presence of slavery within that society meant that it was often viewed by white Southerners as similar to their own. Thus, while Latin American societies were far more complex than the Southern imaginary depicted, this vision helped to justify the mode of territorial expansion in the Gulf, giving meaning to Southern imperialism and later giving rise to the methods Southerners used to pursue the Civil War in this region. Eventually these early imaginings formed the basis for how the United States would engage with Latin American countries and Latin American peoples.

Figures such as rough-hewn Texan soldiers, Indian fighters, the great volunteer army of the U.S.-Mexican War, a protective navy, and rebellious filibusters all peopled the discourse of antebellum Southern expansionism as the slave states' heroes. In doing so they fought against a variety of enemies, most of them peoples of color. They went to war with Native Americans such as the Comanche, the Creek, and the Seminole, Mexicans, the Spanish colonial authority, Cubans, all the while exerting their brutal authority over enslaved and free African Americans. And they were thwarted by many of these foes in a variety of ways that undermined the efficacy of white Southern violence. Where I felt I could, I have inserted the voices and stories of those who pushed back against Southern imperialism. Where I could, I have inserted the voices of the oppressed, the overlooked, the displaced, and the disrupted who were forced to do the work of expansion or were forced to get out of its way.[3]

In many ways this is a book about failure. It is about the failure of Southern imperialism and the failure of white Southerners' attempts to steer American expansion southward into Latin America. Southern imperialism started out successfully but ultimately hit the disaster of the filibuster craze that began a decline that evolved all the way through the Civil War and finally ended during Reconstruction. This book brings into sharp relief white Southerners' frustration with the fact that their lived realities often failed to measure up to the fantasies they created; it is also about the failure of the Confederacy to salvage those fantasies once it became evident that the United States federal government and army no longer cared to prop them up.[4] During and after the Civil War, the national project of expansion persisted and grew into the imperialism of the late nineteenth century, but it did so without Southern fantasies of a slave power dominant in the hemisphere. Even objections to a slave empire that stretched into Latin America, however, were based in racist notions regarding the peoples that lived there. Whether it was an empire based in free labor or slave labor, it was still an empire determined to take things from people of color and give them to white Americans.[5]

The work found here speaks to the "transnational turn" in Civil War–era and Southern studies. The work of historians to place the American South in a broader context and in conversation with other nations and spaces provides a lens through which to understand the Gulf South during the nineteenth century.[6] A significant part of this historiography concerns the study of the efforts of Southern slaveholders in the United States to create for themselves a transnational empire based on slave labor and cotton production. Southern historians continue to make important connections and comparisons between the slave societies of the U.S. South and Latin American nations and colonies. This book builds on this important work by addressing the manner in which the region's imperialist inclinations shaped how Southern whites related to and understood Latin American people as a race.[7] Justifications of slavery not only racialized African American people, they were also part of how and why white Americans constructed racist images of Latin American people. Therefore, if there was any kind of kinship to be had between the slaveholding South and the slaveholding societies of Latin America, the relationship was never perceived as equal. Southern whites did not necessarily seek unification between these worlds. Rather, they fought for control and dominance over those they viewed as racially questionable or altogether inferior. Furthermore, the drive for empire and racial supremacy was also motivated by the fear of being eclipsed within the nation as well as on the world's stage. Historians studying the creators of Southern imperialism often cast them as self-confident men—and it was especially men—leading the nation's expansion with a cosmopolitan outlook on the world and a singular vision. However, a study of both the words of Southern imperialists and the ways that the ideas they promoted played out on the ground demonstrates that they were as much reactionary as they were visionary. They articulated nightmares as much as they did dreams, and the Civil War was born of both.[8] Studying how white Southerners interacted with and conceived of Latin American societies in the mid-nineteenth century uncovers as much about Southern society as it does about their conception of others. As the decades passed from the thirties to the fifties, and challenges to slavery mounted, they defined themselves against the outside world as much as they did against the North. Southerners criticized the classed societies of Europe as well as those to be found in Latin American nations, especially Mexico. In so doing, white Southern critics revealed much not only about their constructions and understanding of race but also their understanding of class.[9]

In recent years work in transnational history has demonstrated that debates concerning secession were not only battles to determine the fate of the nation; they also concerned the goals of the United States in terms of its position in the hemisphere.[10] This book is a reminder that the Civil War, in part, answered these questions of empire. Much work that has been done on the transnational connections of the Civil War focuses either on the level of the wealthy planter class or that of government officials and diplomats. The U.S. federal government laid out a plan for westward settlement and colonization even as its armies marched on Southern locales and men died by the hundreds of thousands. Historians have understood these policies as efforts on the part of politicians in the Republican Party to gain during the war what they failed to attain in the antebellum years. These policies also reflected a decision concerning the process of expansion that veered away from more Southern attitudes toward empire. Centering Gulf South communities gives us a window into how local communities dealt with these same connections throughout this period in U.S. history.[11]

Borderlands history and its unique perspective proves essential for understanding the Gulf South in the nineteenth century. The Gulf South is usually treated as a borderland during its colonial period, when French, Spanish, and English colonial authorities tried to exert their power over the region, often times against Native American nations and enslaved African Americans. As Samuel Truett and Pekka Hämäläinen noted in their essay "On Borderlands," this perspective speaks to the promise and the challenges of exploring nontraditional borderlands such as bodies of water. Viewing the mid-nineteenth century Gulf South through a borderlands lens highlights the complex and often interwoven nature of cultures, races, and violence in these communities. It also highlights the fact that though a large swath of the Gulf South had come under U.S. authority during the first half of the nineteenth century, that authority was still heavily contested and fragile. Additionally, examining the manner in which members of these communities helped to construct racism as it pertained to Latin American peoples demonstrates that it was not just Anglos in the southwest who were doing this work. It occurred in multiple spaces along the borders of the United States simultaneously, as the nation pushed west and south.[12]

The Civil War, though seemingly outside of this story must be situated within it. Even with the transnational interventions, it is often still largely understood as a different kind of war than those that came before or after it in the nineteenth century. Examining the experiences of communities in the

Gulf South helps to put the pieces together. While the war was a fight over the fate of slavery and the nation, it was also about the way that the nation would expand in the West as well as its imperialist interests in Latin America. Recentering the region puts these complex aspects of the war's central narrative in focus. We see the way that the South's imperialism split from the larger story of American expansion by examining how these communities were shaped by both sets of ideas.[13]

A Continuous State of War begins with the Texas Republic just after its establishment as an independent nation in 1836 and examines the different sides of the annexation debate within Texas. It explores the way that violent conflicts in the Texas Republic shaped ideas about statehood, independence, and race. The process of annexation stalled before President John Tyler's administration and this encouraged those in Texas who sought independence. Annexationists concocted a powerful story of an imperiled Texas engaged in fighting off Mexicans and Native Americans that galvanized support for their side and helped bolster the eventual outcome of statehood. Chapter 2 examines Pensacola and West Florida and that territory's parallels with the violent tensions that existed in Texas. It explores the ways that Pensacolians used a similar discourse to advocate for improvements made to coastal defenses in West Florida amid the continued resistance to Indian Removal, the Second Seminole War, a Creek rebellion, and the outbreak of the Mexican War.

Chapter 3 focuses entirely on the U.S.-Mexican War and traces several key aspects of the discourse associated with that conflict. At the end of the chapter the words of soldiers and sailors are used to understand how expansionism shaped their experiences. What comes out of an examination of the war is an image of Mexico and Mexicans as a people who required violent control both in the United States and Mexico.

These ideas about both race and class would be used in the filibustering craze that took over after the war and is discussed in chapter 4. The U.S.-Mexican War was followed by a rash of filibuster expeditions and increased efforts to obtain further Latin American territory. This chapter addresses the Narciso López expeditions to achieve Cuban annexation and focuses on New Orleans as a point of connection between the Caribbean and the Gulf Coast communities. After serving as the major jumping-off point for thousands of soldiers headed for Mexico, New Orleans became a hotbed of filibustering and a growing Cuban exile community. An analysis of the ideas used to justify the filibusters reveals that white Southerners' imagining of Cuban society was framed against the backdrop of both the U.S.-Mexican War and Southerners' past relationship with white and Black

Creoles in the Gulf South. The failure of both Cuban expeditions as well as the failed attempt to negotiate with Spain over Cuba revealed chinks in the armor of Southern expansionism.

As white Southerners in New Orleans pushed for Cuban annexation, city boosters in communities along the Texas coast, especially in Galveston, the state's largest port city, sought to encourage the influx of settlers into the Texas hinterlands. Accordingly, chapter 5 revisits the area covered in chapter 1 on the eve of the Civil War. It examines the rising tensions between Anglos and Mexicans in the years following the U.S.-Mexican War and suggests that the war actually settled very little for Texans. This chapter also covers the way that city officials in Galveston proceeded to make their city an important site of trade, both of slaves and cotton, and immigration for Texas.

Chapter 6 examines the outbreak of the Civil War and its effects on the Gulf Coast. Southern interests in Latin America evolved with the creation of the Confederacy. Though most secessionist discourse focused on the North, the Republican Party, and the threat Lincoln posed to slavery, the imagery of Latin American nations and peoples that expansionists cultivated was also deployed to articulate the hopes and anxieties connected to secession and the Confederacy. Secessionists used ideas about the African slave trade in Cuba and "bandits" in Mexico to emphasize the necessity of separation. When the war began, coastal communities, especially Mobile, served as important sites of blockade running to the Caribbean to retrieve supplies in an effort to sustain the infant Confederacy.

The final chapter explores the transformation of connections between the Gulf South and Latin American nations. After the fall of New Orleans to Union hands in 1862, the Gulf South became a center for white refugees, both Confederate and Unionist, as well as to "refugeed" enslaved African Americans. In the aftermath of the Civil War, many Southerners fled to Latin American countries such as Brazil, Cuba, and Mexico. In a dramatic end of a long period of expansionist fantasies, Confederates did not arrive as leaders but as refugees, desperate to escape a failed South. Ideas about Latin America again changed during the debate that ensued over the movement of ex-confederates to these nations. In examining these ideas, chapter 7 links the efforts of the colonies of Southerners with developments in the South during Reconstruction. But even here they could not escape the forces of emancipation. In the end, Southern imperialism died in the spaces that Southern whites thought would sustain it in perpetuity.

CHAPTER 1

The Possibilities of Texas

In June 1844 the New Orleans *Daily Picayune* published a satirical letter by a fictional character invented by the humorist C. M. Haile, named Pardon Jones. Jones declared, "I'm for annexation, only conditionally. If Texas wants to come to us (and I know she duz) we'd ought to take her. If Texas would strengthen the South, (and I know she would,) she'd strengthen the Union, and we'd ought to have her . . . if England wants to abolish the niggers in Texas, (and I know she duz,) then she wants to abolish 'em in the South, and to abolish our Glorious Union." "As to Santy Anny and Mexico," he added, "we can't wait a hundred years for them to whip Texas, and you know, as well as I do, that they can't du it, no how."[1] Jones's letter touched on several different elements that summed up expansion in the 1840s. It reflected the complex geopolitical contest over Texan annexation and recalled the string of conflicts that existed between the Republic of Texas and Mexico in 1830s and 1840s.

As a slaveholding republic, Texas stood between the United States, another slaveholding republic, and Mexico, an antislavery republic far larger than the United States. References to Antonio López de Santa Anna (Santy Anny) recalled the Texas Revolution in 1836 in which Anglos and Mexicans in Texas gained their independence; they also touched on the continued tensions between these two groups of Texans. Mentions of Britain as an abolitionist country signaled its continued presence in the Gulf of Mexico and in Latin American politics and the danger it posed to the United States and the Southern slaveholding states in particular. Indeed, Jones's conflating the interests of the nation and the interests of the South recalled the history of U.S. expansion into the Lower South along the Gulf Coast that preceded the fight for Texas annexation. In the antebellum era, the fight for Texas statehood linked between this older history of expansion and the newer efforts at gaining more territory for both the slaveholding states and the larger United States.

For Texans the road toward annexation was full of uncertainty and violence. From the end of the Texas Revolution in 1836 to the annexation of Texas by the United States in 1845, the Texas Republic navigated a series of geopolitical conflicts while also being embroiled in the debate over annexation and independence. Annexation was the culmination of a dream, but it was also insurance against the threat of a world increasingly at odds with Southern chattel slavery. Leaders such as Samuel Houston aimed through statehood to protect Texas from what they viewed as economic and political disaster, while others such as Mirabeau Bonaparte Lamar favored independence as the best method of protection and prosperity. Public discourse in Texas and Southern communities along the Gulf Coast fixated on events such as the invasion of Texas by Comanche warriors, known as the Great Raid in 1840, and the Mexican invasion of 1842. Events like these were used to demonstrate why Texas annexation was important to American sovereignty and the security of Texas' interior and coastal parts. Understanding the reaction of those living in the Gulf ports, as well as those in the Texas interior, provides a much fuller picture of what was at stake for both Texans and Anglos living in the U.S. South. Texas annexation often is explained as an act of westward expansion, but it was also, as this chapter demonstrates, about securing the Gulf of Mexico under American control.

With a coastline that spanned over three hundred miles, the Republic of Texas stood at an important geographical location. By 1840 Great Britain's interest in Texas and Mexico gave proslavery annexationists in the United States a new sense of urgency when it came to securing U.S. authority within the Gulf of Mexico. Texas was a fertile territory ripe for Southern cotton and the growing sugar industry and was important for both its ports and its lands. The machinations of British abolitionists endangered its great promise, as did an unstable and vulnerable Mexico.[2]

The way that annexationists and independence-minded expansionists framed Texas's situation depended as much on the production of racialized fantasies concerning Mexicans and Native Americans as it did on the republic's geopolitical position. When a coalition of Anglos and Tejanos won the Texas Revolution, the republic they created altered the geopolitical landscape of North America in a way that heightened the anxieties of slave-owning whites in the South and their kin in Texas. The annexation of Texas marked a transition from earlier American expansionism and what was to come in the Civil War era. Annexation took place within hardening partisan and sectional lines in the United States and in Texas that influenced the ways that Anglo Texans and white Southerners spoke and thought about the events leading up to statehood.[3]

There was a tension between ideas about expansion and the lived realities of Texans during the period between independence and annexation. Though the story of annexation is often depicted as a triumphant aspect of American expansionism, and Southern imperialism, in reality the joint resolution that finally brought Texas into the United States was a last-ditch effort that barely succeeded. Anglo Texans emphasized their superiority as a fact, peppering their discourse with racist notions of Tejanos, African Americans, and Native Americans, all while constantly having to fight their supposed inferiors. As Anglo Texans battled against both these various forms of resistance and foreign nations, they used the debate concerning annexation as a way to maintain their enthusiasm for American, southern, and Texan interests.

From the perspective of white Southerners who supported annexation, an independent and ultimately vulnerable Texas was cause for alarm. Anglo Texans who supported annexation tended to do so because of the reasons often cited by individuals such as Robert J. Walker, the pro-annexationist senator from Mississippi. The expansion of slavery had been at the heart of Anglo American settlement in Texas throughout the early 1830s, and protecting it created an array of concerns for white Texans and slaveholders in the American South once it became independent in 1836. For the Gulf South, other troubles might plague them if Texas was left on her own, such as added competition for a developing export and import trade; the region also risked losing out on the growing cotton trade in Texas. Over the course of the early nineteenth century an intimate relationship developed between Gulf Coast communities of the United States and those living in Coauhila y Tejas. During the Texas Revolution in 1836 merchants, bankers, politicians, and slaveholders used those established connections to involve themselves in the war, many with an eye toward eventually annexing Texas, and Texas's political leaders sought aid in the cities of the Gulf South.[4]

In addition to the connections of Gulf ports, many Texan leaders held up Texas as a kind of Southern promised land with the power to banish white Southerners' worries concerning land, the growing population of enslaved people, and the financial calamities that had befallen them during the 1830s. Pro-annexationist Texans were certainly obliged to fulfill that image:

they promoted their republic as a space populated by intensely militaristic white people, ferocious fighters, which proved to be popular among white Southerners in the United States. To promote annexation, Anglo Texans also encouraged evolving racist ideas about Mexicans and Mexico that already existed among Americans. Early depictions of Mexicans as being duplicitous and lacking in the capabilities necessary to govern the expanse of Texas were rooted in both the Texas Revolution and the following years of Anglo settlement. These images worked to enhance the idea of Anglo rule and the "rightness" of a society based in slavery. As a result, white Texans and Southerners outside of Texas began painting much stronger lines of division between themselves and Mexicans than they had during the years before the Texas Revolution.[5]

When Texas became a state, it helped set the stage for years of interactions between white Southerners and Latin American people that echoed those initial fantasies and fears. Those fears, in turn, themselves echoed the early nineteenth-century history of the Gulf South in which Anglos clashed with Europeans and Native Americans in the states that became the Deep South. In addition to American expansion into Spanish-controlled West Florida at the beginning of the nineteenth century, the annexation of Texas provides a bridge that joins two forms of Americans expansionism—the earlier expansion in which white Southerners migrated into the lower South, and the subsequent expansion in which white Americans began edging into Mexican territory.[6]

WHAT COMES AFTER A REVOLUTION?

Frederic Leclerc, a French physician, arrived in Texas in 1838. He remained for only a few months, but the country made such an impression on him that he felt the need to write *Texas and Its Revolution*. Part history and part travelogue, Leclerc's book portrayed Southern fears concerning the growing population of slaves and the need to obtain new territory as the main impetus for settlement and annexation. Texas, he wrote, "offered an almost limitless field to slave-labor, one practically boundless both in area and in the types of agriculture." Florida, Louisiana, and Alabama had been described similarly as places where surplus slaves could be sold and surplus whites could move.[7] Leclerc traveled into eastern Texas, the center of the republic's plantation agriculture. He marveled at the experience of floating down the San Jacinto River and thought about the final battle of the Texas Revolution that had been fought there. He characterized the appeal of the region as lying in "the natural resources of the country, the beauty of its climate, the possibility of establishing steamboat navigation on its rivers."[8]

Texas held out the possibility of abundance as had other frontiers before it, and Anglos hoped that capitalize on that allure. Attracting sufficient numbers of settlers to the Republic of Texas was actually an inherited problem. Like the Spanish and the Mexicans before them they now had to figure out how to bring Texas under their control.

As Anglo and Mexican Texans fought for independence from Mexico in 1836, the question of annexation to the United States was already a part of the discussion about Texas's future. Over the course of early nineteenth century, Anglo and Mexican relations had changed significantly as more Anglos moved into Texas and Mexicans increasingly found themselves outnumbered. Yet through the 1820s and into the 1830s, Mexicans continued to maintain their hold on political and economic power, while popular beliefs about the different cultures in the region began to develop. Anglos often drew a distinction between the Tejano elite and the Tejanos who made up the bulk of Tejano society, often emphasizing the Tejano elite's Spanish-ness and whiteness while emphasizing the mixed-race backgrounds of other Tejanos. Wealthy Tejanos at times worked as power brokers and cultural intermediaries for the white Americans moving into their country. Mexicans also maintained their own class and racial distinctions within their society, which Anglos sought to take advantage of as they competed for land and political power. Many of the racist ideas about Mexicans were accelerated by the Texas Revolution and the way it was understood by those within and outside of the young republic. When newer settlers who followed the earlier waves saw Mexicans, they thought of the Mexican army and Antonio López de Santa Anna. Indeed, Anglo Texans who had fought alongside their Mexican counterparts during the war had also begun to conflate the Mexican army and Santa Anna with Mexican people living in Texas, turning them all, in effect, into criminals.[9]

Despite popular support, Texas annexation efforts suffered from bad timing. Within the United States, annexationists met with a tepid reception from President Martin Van Buren and opposition from the growing antislavery movement in the United States. These forces understood that the prospect of bringing yet another territory into the United States that was bound to be a slave state might stir up more of the animosity between the free and slave states, undermining the Missouri Compromise of 1820. On July 6, 1837, the acting secretary of state sought to present Memucan Hunt, one of Texas's first ministers to the United States along with William Wharton, to President Van Buren. Hunt's mission was to get the United States to annex Texas. However, Van Buren refused to meet with him. Hunt then sent a letter on the issue of annexation to the secretary of state, John

Forsyth. In the letter Hunt recounted the Texan uprising as well as the creation of the republic. He compared Texas's history with that of Mexico, emphasizing the Mexican instability that reached its zenith with Antonio López de Santa Anna.[10]

Through his conduct in the war with Texas, Santa Anna came to represent much that was wrong with Mexico in the minds of white Texans like Hunt. The minister described Santa Ann's presidency as a "reign of misrule and career of blood," and noted that in 1837 he remained at his hacienda, Mango de Clavo, "the tiger in his lair, ready to go forth seeking whom he may devour." In the story that Hunt sought to tell of Texas and its readiness for annexation, he emphasized white Americans' role in the settlement of Texas. According to Hunt, "until the settlement of [Stephen F.] Austin's first colony in 1821, Texas, for the most part, was an unexplored wilderness." As had happened with other frontiers that came before it, those imagining Texas conceived of it as a place waiting for white Americans. Hunt claimed that "up to the year 1821, Texian civilization was only to be found within the narrow precincts of their respective jurisdictions."[11]

Memucan Hunt positioned Texas as the key to American dominance of the Gulf of Mexico. At the same time, Hunt felt the need to justify the exodus from the United States to Texas. "True, in emigrating to Texas the enterprising colonist had expatriated himself," Hunt wrote, "and foregone the well-tried institutions of his mother-land, but the institutions he now lived under were modeled upon those he had reluctantly abandoned." Hunt emphasized the shared Anglo American "blood" that white Texans and white Americans shared, noting that "[Texas'] gallant sons were born upon your soils, and . . . they ask if the single star of Texas is not worthy to be added to the brilliant cluster on their mother flag." To further encourage support for annexation, Hunt spoke about the various advantages in trade and industry that Texas statehood would bring to the United States. Texas provided an additional market for manufactured goods and Hunt touted the vast live oak forests of the interior (also celebrated by Texan president Sam Houston) and the potential for contributing to the production of U.S. cotton and sugar cane.[12]

In contrast, an independent Texas posed a possible threat to the United States due to its vulnerability as a new nation and the ways it would complicate the geopolitical landscape of North America. In 1837 the United States was one of several military and economic powers in the Gulf of Mexico. Great Britain still held a considerable amount of naval power in the Caribbean and Gulf, as well as economic power in terms of its increased involvement in the economies of Latin American countries.[13] Similarly, France also sought to gain a foothold in Latin America. In Mexico diplomatic relations were intensely strained by 1837 due to what the French saw as unfair trading practices, mistreatment of its citizens, and taxation of French imports. At the same time, Spain continued to hold colonial authority over Puerto Rico and Cuba, two major sites of sugar production. According to Hunt, such threats and political tensions with these rival powers could be easily mitigated through Texas annexation. He argued that "Texas is not disposed to yield to any foreign nation the privileges of her coast, involving the command of the Gulf of Mexico, nor can she concede them to the United States, unless in a treaty of Union." Hunt also drew on what others such as the second president of the Texas Republic, Mirabeau B. Lamar, would later argue: that Texas had the potential to be a formidable nation on its own. Hunt insisted that the United States and Texas were so similar that they would eventually come to blows, hinting that in the event of "Texas remaining in the attitude of an independent power, there will arise, from the very strict resemblance of the people and the institutions of the two countries, many questions of conflicting interest, the adjustment of which will be most difficult and painful." Pro-annexationists fixated on economic competition and the specter of war. In the coming years, anti-annexationists would use the same ideas to encourage the notion of independence by stating that Texas had the ability to maintain itself political, economically, and militarily without being included in the United States.

Memucan Hunt also hoped to put to rest any fears that Mexico would interfere in the negotiations over statehood, stressing the fact that the Republic of Texas's independence was recognized by several other nations, which would help prevent Mexico from intervening. The first country to recognize Texas's independence was, of course, Van Buren's own, the United States. Yet in 1836 the United States was neither able nor willing to confront the possibility of war with Mexico over Texas. While the United States was several decades older than Mexico, it could hardly afford the international headache that came with an independent Texas. Yet President Andrew Jackson's eventual recognition opened the door to the possibility of further recognition from Britain and France. Hunt assured Secretary of State John Forsyth that "[Texas] has no expectation of an invasion, much less of a reconquest, at the hands of Mexico." With the onset of centralism under Santa Anna, many states within Mexico rebelled and attempted to separate themselves from the new government that sought to restrict the rights of the Mexican states. Texas was only one of these.[14]

All the smoke and mirrors and the self-confident bombastic rhetoric lauding Anglo American "civilization" and its effect on the Texas "wilderness" belied a very different reality for Texas. Mexico still refused to recognize the treaties that Santa Anna signed when he was captured after the Battle of San Jacinto. In 1837 Texas was a risk. But was it a risk that the Van Buren administration was willing to take? The answer to this was no. The U.S. president's response to Hunt's report cited the main reason as the fact that "the United States were foremost in acknowledging the independence of Mexico, and have uniformly desired and endeavored to cultivate relations of friendship with that Power." While the possibility of war with Mexico led Van Buren to formally reject the idea of Texas annexation, the controversy over the expansion and continued growth of slavery also contributed to the president's caution. When the United States rejected Hunt's proposal, Houston withdrew the request for annexation. The reality that Texans faced after the failed 1837 negotiations was a struggle to achieve either annexation or independence amid the fact that the Republic of Texas was as fragile a nation-state as Mexico. While the republic was not wracked with the same level of government instability as its southern neighbor, it was plagued with mounting debt, conflict with Native American nations far more powerful than itself, and the looming possibility of foreign intervention or invasion.

TEXAN FEARS, FANTASIES, AND VULNERABILITIES

The main topic at the center of all these mounting issues in Texas revolved around slavery. Anglo Texans' need to protect the institution, which had quickly taken root prior to the Texas Revolution, remained the driving factor in much of the imagery surrounding annexation and the efforts to achieve it.

All the problems that Texas experienced between its independence and annexation continued to unfold when Matilda Houstoun and her husband arrived in the Gulf of Mexico in December 1842, intent on exploring various parts of the Gulf of Mexico and the Caribbean. While traveling from Texas to Havana, Matilda Houstoun observed that the central topic of discussion among her fellow travelers was slavery in Texas, and that this question concerned Galvestonians most of all, as their city was one of the main sites of sale and importation of enslaved persons. Houstoun recalled that Galvestonians had been so indignant over the presence of abolitionists in their town that they banished them from the city. "The person in question," she remembered of one such abolitionist, "was conveyed in a boat to the mainland, and there turned adrift to preach to the inhabitants of the woods and prairies." Unfortunately, Houstoun was silent as to what happened to an African American abolitionist who attempted to speak publicly about ending slavery, but, more than likely, he fared worse than the white abolitionist exiled to the woods and prairies.[15] The *Telegraph and Texas Register* bemoaned the growth of the abolitionist movement in the United States and commiserated with slaveholders in their "sister republic" all the while declaring that Texas was "immune from its effects." The paper went on to claim that this supposed immunity "operates as the most powerful motive, on the part of many, to oppose the annexation of this country to the United States." The author fantasized that Texas might then become a haven for Southern slaveholders from the mounting opposition to slavery that was developing in the northern states. Thus, anti-annexationists could use this anger and fear of the infiltration of abolitionists and increased sectional tensions to justify remaining an independent republic.[16]

Houstoun's travels through Texas also coincided with Galveston's efforts to restrict the movement of free and enslaved African Americans. The failure of the first try at annexation, the continuation of Texan independence, and fears of the antislavery movement gaining ground in the 1830s and 1840s in the United States pushed Texas communities to continue efforts to regulate both free and enslaved African Americans. The Republic of Texas's constitution ensured Anglos' right to own slaves as well as the right of immigrants to import more into the country. By 1840 the Texas legislature passed an act that forbade free African Americans from living in Texas. When notice of the act was published in the Galveston *Civilian and Gazette*, Galveston city officials attempted to establish further control over the free African Americans still living in the city. The mayor of Galveston declared that the town's African American population would now live under a strict 9 p.m. curfew.[17]

Anti-annexationists gained a significant supporter when Mirabeau Lamar captured the Texas presidency in 1838. He attempted to steer the young nation away from the plans of the annexationists like Sam Houston, whose ideas about Texas were tied to the expansion of the United States. In his inaugural address, Lamar made it plain that his vision for Texas's expansion had little to do with that of the United States. "I have never been able myself to perceive the policy of the desired connection, or discover in it any advantage either civil, political, or commercial, which could possibly result to Texas." He went on to state that however "strong be my attachment to the parent land, the land of my adoption must claim my highest allegiance and affection; her glory and happiness must be my paramount consideration, and I cannot allow myself to speak in any other than the language of freedom and frankness on all matters involving her safety, dignity and honor." Lamar took all the arguments that annexationists made for statehood and turned them on their heads. If Texas were annexed, it risked losing its most important rights, such as the "right of making either war or peace; the right of controlling the Indian tribes within her borders; the right of appropriating her public domain to purposes of education and internal improvements; of levying her own taxes; regulating her own commerce and forming her own alliances and treaties." In this nightmare scenario, Texas would be reduced to an "unfelt fraction of a giant power; or peradventure divide into territorial districts, with Governors and judges and excise men appointed from abroad to administer laws which she had no adequate voice in enacting." Lamar told his fellow Texans that Texas was the "cornucopia of the world"; with annexation, she would pour her "abundant treasures into the lap of another people . . . who are known to be opposed to her peculiar and essential interests."[18] Lamar's vision for an independent Texas was one that stretched all the way to the Pacific Ocean, encompassing lucrative trade networks in New Mexico and lands in California.

Lamar's interest in expansion to support independence had a dramatic effect on both the size of the military and relations with Native peoples and Tejanos. Lamar, along with his secretary of war, Albert Sidney Johnston, first targeted the Cherokee living in the eastern part of the republic. The initial band of Cherokee had arrived in Texas decades before the Trail of Tears, migrating into what was then Spanish-controlled territory in 1806. Their numbers steadily grew as others moved in from places like Arkansas, until there were roughly four hundred living in eastern Texas by 1830. Other Native American nations such as the Delaware, Shawnee, and Kickapoo also migrated to colonial Texas. Though some Cherokee insisted that the Spanish had granted them land, the Mexican government denied this claim. The Cherokee continued to attempt to obtain a land grant even as Anglos began to push into their territory. Sam Houston negotiated a peace treaty with some of the Cherokee. However, at the urging of then–vice president Lamar, the Texas Senate refused to ratify it and later proceeded to nullify the treaty entirely. Subsequently, the Texas Land Office proceeded to issue grants to the lands that the Cherokee claimed, but they did not have access to buying that land. The influx of white settlers increased pressure on the Cherokee to relinquish their claims.

For Lamar the threat of disloyal Mexicans and Native American challenges to the Anglo settlement could be intertwined. Indeed, for Anglos, any perceived threat inevitably became entangled with their struggle to dominate and dispel Native peoples. In 1839 Lamar wrote a letter to Cherokee leader Chief Bowl, accusing the band of Cherokee under his leadership of being involved in the Cordova Rebellion, a Tejano uprising that occurred in 1838, and of attempting to take part in another insurrection. Though some Cherokee warriors had joined the Cordova Rebellion, the majority had not and did not know that other Mexicans were attempting another rebellion. Referring to those Tejanos involved in these uprisings, he wrote, "You and your people have held repeated correspondence with our enemies; have received and cherished their emissaries among you; and have entered into belligerent compacts with them; and have given countenance to an insurrection raised in your own vicinity by Mexicans who have incorporated into our national family, and were enjoying all the benefits and privileges of citizenship." Lamar went on to warn the Cherokee that they could not exist as a sovereign nation peacefully under the flag of the Texas Republic, threatening them with expulsion if they did not swear to be peaceful and submit to Texan authority. In May 1839 Lamar wrote to the leader of the Shawnee, Linney, as well as other leaders of the tribe in Texas informing them that he indeed planned to expel the Cherokee from east Texas. Referring to the Shawnee as "brothers," Lamar wrote that the Cherokee were guilty of listening to the "forked tongue of the Mexicans, who are always Women in war, and serpents in peace; and they have foolishly plighted their faith to the faithless." While the letter demanded neutrality from the Shawnee, to which many eventually acquiesced, much of the missive was preoccupied with emphasizing to them, as Hunt and Houston once did to the United States, that the Texans had fully vanquished their old foes. Lamar referred repeatedly to the deceitfulness of Mexicans and his belief that Mexicans and Native Americans were working in concert against Anglos.[19] On July 16, 1839, Lamar ordered General Thomas Rusk to attack an encampment of Cherokee leaders. He also ordered the removal of all Cherokee from eastern Texas because they were allied with Mexican insurrectionists, which the Texans accomplished with a successful attack on the Cherokee and the murder of Chief Bowl. Afterward, most Cherokees opted to live in Indian Country rather than stay in Texas.[20]

Lamar then turned his attention to the powerful Comanche, who occupied a significant part of western Texas. He strengthened the republic's army by an additional 840 soldiers and sent it into Comanche territory as a show of force. On May 1, 1840, the Austin newspaper the *Texas Sentinel* published several reports of multiple Comanche leaders being murdered in San Antonio. Comanche leaders were there to negotiate peace with the

Texans. Texas commissioners had requested that they return any white captives, but they arrived with mostly Mexican children and one white woman who had been abused by her captors. The meeting quickly devolved into a fight in which many Comanche were murdered or captured. Initially, some American newspapers condemned the actions of the Texans, but eventually they upheld them when they received reports that claimed the Comanche leaders were not there to make a treaty of peace but to ransom white captives for guns and ammunition. The *Sentinel* declared that the "two races will never meet as friends" and swore that the "Comanche will be exterminated from the earth or the Anglo-Saxon race will cease to exist in Texas." Later that month, another Austin newspaper, the *City Gazette*, echoed the sentiments of the *Sentinel* that Texans had been unfairly characterized as callous and that the incident in San Antonio had been misconstrued in the newspapers of the United States and Europe. The author of the account in the *Gazette* hinted that shady characters were "calculated to injure this country, not only in the United States but also in Europe, to a want of real facts connected with this case."[21] Later in November the same paper published an account of a battle between Texan soldiers and the Comanche. Colonel John H. Moore returned to Austin from an expedition up the Colorado River to tell his tale in which ninety soldiers and twelve Lipan Apache scouts under his command rode three hundred miles into "Comanche country" and encountered a party of them. Moore insisted that they were members of the same group that had attacked the town of Linnville some months prior. He and his men killed one hundred and ten warriors and captured several women and children. The article noted that Moore claimed they killed the chief of the band responsible for the Linnville attack and that he wore a "silver medal presented to some Indian by Madison while President of the United States." The paper remarked that the Comanche had never been pursued so far into their own territory and that they would soon "be convinced of the unprofitableness of a war with the white people."[22]

However, the Comanche were not convinced, and in retaliation for both their dead chiefs and the invasion of their territory, conducted a massive raid under the leadership of Potsanaquahip (Buffalo Hump) in the same year. Five hundred to seven hundred warriors charged through Texas, along the Guadeloupe River straight to the Gulf of Mexico. They sacked the towns of Linnville and Victoria before turning back, at which point Texas Rangers attacked the party and killed several among them. Often used as a frontier policing force against peoples of color in Texas, the Rangers rode into Comanche territory and murdered one hundred and forty men, women, and children in retaliation. After these violent episodes many Comanche withdrew farther north into their own territory.[23] Notably, the upheaval caused by the conflict between Anglos and Native Americans under the Lamar administration demonstrated the way that Anglos saw Native Americans and Mexicans in relation to one another. Both were populations that needed to be controlled by white American force, whether in the guise of the Texas Rangers or through expansionist efforts farther west.[24] According to those like Lamar, Native American peoples such as the Comanche and the Cherokee needed to be pushed out of the way. For Lamar they were a suspect group and so were Mexicans in Texas who, like their counterparts in Mexico, were incapable of stability and prone to rebellion. Additionally, these conflicts shaped the question of annexation within Texas and whether it would even be possible for Texans to keep both threats at bay on their own.

The question of Texas's economic future was also a major factor in the debate over annexation, whether one was for statehood or against it. Texas newspapers and Texas boosters published countless articles about the republic's economic prospects and its superiority as a cotton-growing region. Adding to this possible agricultural wonderland was the possibility of growing sugar cane in large quantities along the Colorado and Brazos Rivers. The promise of Texas cotton that could compete with the sugar plantations and mills of Cuba and the cotton plantations of the Deep South proved intoxicating to many annexationists and independence supporters alike. Farmers living in Stephen F. Austin's original colony along the Brazos were among the first to cultivate sugar in Texas. True, the growth of sugar was small scale, and as Texans wrestled with the question of annexation, cotton crops along the coast faced trouble with wet weather and cotton-hungry pests. The reality of the Texas economy was that the republic was mired in debt. Since gaining its still-contested independence from Mexico, Texas had amounted a national debt in the millions due in part to Lamar's extravagant military spending. When Sam Houston took office as the republic's first president, the debt stood at $1.25 million; it would grow to over $9 million by the time of annexation. During his second administration, Houston went on to initiate programs that he hoped would stem the growth of the debt. Again, his administration attempted to broker treaties with Native Americans at the same time that it shrank the size of the military and relied more on volunteers. Finding ways to engineer a peace with Native American nations to the West was essentially a means of cutting costs for the cash-strapped republic.

Courting European nations that were in a position to buy into Texas's economic prospects was a goal for many pro- and anti-annexationist forces in Texas. Great Britain was chief among those to be courted, but not far behind was France. In 1837 Sam Houston nominated James Pinckney Henderson as minister to both England and France, and within a few years Henderson was successful in gaining recognition of Texan independence from France; England soon followed. France's interest in Texas grew after a trade treaty was signed in 1840, and there was a plan to create a French colony. In 1841 the Austin *Sentinel* published a lengthy article concerning French interests in founding colonies along the borders of Texas that could provide a buffer zone between the Texans and the Comanche. The *Sentinel* believed that France had played a more integral part in the creation of the Texas Republic than the Spanish Empire or the United States. In doing so, the author of the article redirected the history of Texas away from its true origins in Native American societies and their contact with Spanish colonizers. Instead, the writer noted that "it is not to be wondered at, that this rising state looks to France, as to her most natural protector." In this imagining Texas was not only closely connected to France through Louisiana migrants and a shared history, but lo and behold, it was of a similar shape and size as France! Beyond noting this resemblance in size and shape, the article went on list Texas's many environmental and geographic benefits: "magnificent prairies, ancient forests, inexhaustible treasures for navies, a soil of marvelous fertility, which can supply the whole world with cotton, which bears sugarcane, and which can furnish the products so natural to the most different latitudes, and all these having for their delivery the Gulf of Mexico to which access is had by the flowing of eight or nine great rivers ... such are the prodigious elements of wealth opened up in this region for improvement." And who would be capable of doing this improvement that the French newspaper was so eager to participate in? It was no longer going to be "that degenerate race of Spanish-Mexicans, but that race of first-rate colonists, those Anglo Americans, who have already made such, and so rapid conquests over the deserts." According to the *Sentinel* and in the view of many Anglo Texans, it was their race that had done what the Spanish and Mexicans could not do. They had readied Texas for further prosperity for themselves and other white peoples.[25]

The French colonization idea evolved into the Franco-Texian Bill, which Houston supported but Lamar had opposed. The bill was an example of the various ways that pro-and anti-annexationist plans for Texas eventually differed. It was also an example of the constant fighting between these political figures in Texas. The French were planning on possible colonies, but more importantly, proposed to send French troops to secure Texas's western region against the power of the Comanche who commanded that part of the young republic.[26] From this emerged the Franco-Texian bill that was introduced into the Texas Congress on January 12, 1841, by Frenchmen Jean Pierre Hippolyte Basterrèche and Pierre François de Lassaulx. *The Telegraph and Texas Register* reported that news of the bill was of great interest to the people of Texas but also worried that the bill would turn Texas into little more than a French colony. The bill proposed the settlement of some eight thousand families throughout Texas along its major waterways; in addition to the families, the French would construct forts and bring in French soldiers. The bill provided favorable terms to the French, ensuring them that French settlers would be exempt from all taxes and tariffs for a period of twenty years. They were also to enjoy a favorable trading relationship with New Mexico. The bill managed to pass the house, but its orchestrators pulled it from the Senate when they realized it had no hope of passing or being enacted, as Texan legislators feared that it might be too favorable to the French.[27]

During her travels in Texas, Matilda Houstoun observed the Texans discussing the fate of their country as if they were talking about a "matter of business" and remembered one gentleman traveling on the same ship to Cuba who believed Texas should become an English colony. Obtaining the status of a British colony was not a possibility, but the Houston administration entertained the possibility of some kind of autonomous state within Mexico or using the British to aid them in negotiating Mexican recognition of their independence. The fact that British diplomats had been sent to Galveston heightened worried annexationists in Texas and the United States. Beyond diplomatic dinners, Charles Elliot, a British diplomat who had been sent to Galveston, hoped to negotiate between the Texas Republic and Great Britain and work to make Texas a free nation. A year later, the Houston *Telegraph and Texas Register* reported that a treaty of commerce and navigation had been signed between the Texas Republic and Britain. When Texas newspapers reported interest in selling their cotton and establishing trade relations with Great Britain following the abolition of slavery in its colonies, it also caused many to worry over the security of slavery within the Gulf South.[28]

Another part of the economic aspect of the annexation debate was the relationship between the republic and the United States. For the small Texas port communities, this meant a consideration of their geographic place and their connection to New Orleans, the Gulf region's wealthiest and largest city. New Orleans provided Texan slaveholders and cotton planters with a ready supply of labor needed to make Texas land produce, and a large portion of Texas cotton wound up on the New Orleans wharves. In a context where there was no railroad transport in Texas, the ships that plied the waters between New Orleans and coastal communities such as Galveston, Houston, and Indianola moved goods and people back and forth and brought news of the outside world. During the Texas Revolution, New Orleanians contributed large sums of money to the Texans' cause. The Texas army gained men by advertising eight hundred acres of land and free passage from New Orleans for those willing to go and fight on the revolutionaries' side. The New Orleans Greys, two battalions of 120 men, were organized in 1835 for the express purpose of aiding the Texan army in their fight for independence.[29]

However, by the 1840s Galvestonians and Houstonians were not entirely happy with their place in the hierarchy of port communities along the Gulf Coast. Echoing Lamar's dreams of an independent Texas, an article in the Houston *Telegraph and Texas Register* remarked on the rise of Texas cotton markets and their interest in maintaining trade relationships with Europe even more than with the United States. The author worried that the proximity to New Orleans might actually slow the growth of Texas cotton. However, the editor hoped that the establishment of regular shipping back and forth between Galveston and England meant that regular trading was not far behind. Galveston cotton merchants hoped to someday be at the center of a large trade network that crisscrossed its way over the Gulf of Mexico and into the Atlantic Ocean. For those that remained wary of annexation, such a thing could be accomplished in a republic but could not be easily done were Texas a U.S. state.[30]

The possibility of continued independence raised a variety of other questions concerning Texas's ability to dominate the Native American populations on its borders, its prospects as an expansionist and imperialist country, and its economic vulnerability. In the aftermath of the Texas Revolution, these questions remained unanswered and evidence mounted that independence might not be the best option for Texas.

SEARCHING FOR A PATH FORWARD

The major sticking point in all these possibilities was Texas's geopolitical situation, which independence-minded Texans often touted as being in Texans' favor. Furthermore, the persistent possibility of conflict with both

Native Americans and Mexicans meant that the republic's place between multiple powers could be a significant vulnerability as well. Lamar may have engaged in violent conflicts with the Comanche in an effort to establish Texans' authority of the western frontier, but such violence provided evidence that Texans couldn't manage that frontier on their own. The other side of this geopolitical coin was the threat of a Mexico that still refused to recognize Texan independence.

However, in 1840 and 1841, Texas president Lamar was more interested in accessing the lucrative Santa Fe Trail rather than focusing on the possibility of Mexico attempting to retake the republic. Yet this dream still brought Texas into conflict with the Mexican government. The Santa Fe Trail carried much-needed trade into Mexico and connected Mexico to trade hubs as far away as St. Louis, Missouri. Texans were keen to gain access to these markets. In January the *Telegraph and Texas Register* remarked that Britain's recognition of Texas had created a "mania for trade" that would extend to Santa Fe and Chihuahua.[31] Texas might thus become a gateway to those trade networks as well as accessing them for the benefit of Texans. With Texas's debt mounting due to Lamar's interest in expanding the military, the Santa Fe market appeared to be an excellent opportunity to bring in much-needed revenue. In the Texas press the effort was billed primarily as a trade expedition, but it also included a fair amount of military personnel. While in retrospect Texans' belief that they could capture and possibly even absorb New Mexico seemed like the height of hubris, the political reality of the entire region of the Mexican north was unstable and had been since the mid-1830s. This opened up multiple possibilities in terms of expansionist fantasies, alliances, trade connections, and sustaining independence.[32]

On June 14, 1841, five companies of infantry and two of artillery accompanying merchants and teamsters and several wagons full of goods valued at $200,000 began their trek into New Mexico. The total expedition included 321 people. Among them was George Wilkins Kendall, editor and owner of the New Orleans *Daily Picayune*, who wrote about the expeditioners' encounters in New Mexico. While the main point of the expedition was to open trade routes, Kendall's primary objective was to travel to the far-off western prairies, which stemmed from a desire to visit "regions inhabited alone by the roaming Indians, as well as to partake in the wild excitement of buffalo hunting and other sports of a border and prairie life." The expeditioners expected New Mexicans to welcome them as traders and as possibly new leadership; however, this was not the case. Well aware that the Texans marched ever closer to Santa Fe, Governor Manuel Armijo sent soldiers to meet their main party, which surrendered to the New Mexicans. Now prisoners, they were marched into Mexico City where they were held for the better part of a year.

Matilda Houstoun believed that had the Texans been able to secure the Santa Fe Trail trade they would have had a distinct advantage over Americans and thus would have had little reason to continue to support annexation. However, that was not to be. The southwestern border between Texas and New Mexico was a territory they could not wrest either from the Mexicans or the Comanche. This amplified continued anxieties over foreign invasion of Texas and thrust the possibility of independence into question. It was also a foreshadowing of much of Southern expansionist efforts in Latin American territory that took place after Texas was finally annexed to the United States.[33]

Violent conflict with Mexico, the Texas Revolution especially, had contributed to the romanticization of Texan soldiers at the same time that it exposed Texas's vulnerability. The image of the Texan soldier as a rugged individual persisted in imaginings of the Texas frontier and the 1836 revolution. A poem written in 1840 concerning the ill-fated relationship between a Mexican woman and an Anglo Texan soldier fighting in the revolution illuminated the complex relationship between Mexico, the United States, and Texas during the annexation process. George B. Wallis's "Arabella" opened with a description of a spring morning on the Texas prairie. Campbell, the poem's male protagonist and Texan soldier, described the prairie in the following terms: "Like islands in the blue Aegean,/ The forest-isles arise,/ Surrounded by a sea of flowers,/ That scent and tint the skies—/ Was not—is not this Paradise—/ This charming land of ours?"[34] Amid the idealized prairie background, the author imagined the Texas rebels as blue-eyed Anglo saviors as compared to the Mexican people, whom he cast as supporters of an oppressive government. The character of Arabella was headstrong, rebellious, dramatic, and much more sexual than the "Yankee" women of Texas. She abandoned her "nation's duty" to fall in love with its foe. She exemplified the defeminization of female racial others and the simultaneous feminization of Mexican men. In the poem she wondered, "Why do Southern daughters, all,/ Love thy country's daring sons? They are noble, brave and tall; Ours are weak and treacherous ones." While Arabella initially attracted the Texan Campbell, he eventually married a blue-eyed Anglo American woman named Mary, thus emphasizing the importance of such relationships on the southern frontier and reminding its readers that Texas's natural companion was the United States. On his wedding night, Campbell had a dream in which a vulture searching for a possible meal "changed into a hideous snake, / And coiling round the bird in strangling folds, / After a mighty struggle down it brought/ The eagle to the sea, where both were lost." The marriage between the Texan soldier and the American woman signaled what might be possible with annexation. Within the context of the poem and the period, it likely represented the author's concerns about the struggle between the United States and Mexico to secure Texas.[35]

Annexationists in Texas played a careful game when it came to the geopolitical realities, emphasizing the critical issue of the republic's relationship with Mexico but not to the extent that it would discourage Americans from supporting Texas statehood.[36] Continued conflict with Mexico, as well as with Native Americans, contributed to Texans' desires for more diplomatic and military assistance from other nations.

Rumblings of a possible Mexican invasion were almost constant in Texas. The Galveston newspaper the *Texas Times* in November 2, 1840, announced that "our situation is absolutely looked upon as desperate!" The author claimed that "hourly do we hear intelligent men predicting our downfall unless some foreign power interferes on our behalf. Daily do we see letters from the interior filled with the same dire predictions." In January 1841 the New Orleans *Daily Picayune* reported that vessels from Galveston brought yet more rumors of an impending Mexican invasion.

Mexican troops under Rafael Vasquez crossed the Rio Grande on March 2, 1842, and marched toward San Antonio. Having been warned of their impending arrival, many San Antonio residents evacuated long before the Mexican army arrived, and the army occupied the area for two days before marching back across the river. Yet even this small and short-lived invasion was enough to throw the majority of Anglo Texans into an outright panic. Anglos also began to pull back from the western edge of settlement in Texas and move toward the eastern towns.[37]

The Mexican invasion of Texas in 1842 brought about a renewed energy among Galvestonians to support bolstering Texas's miniscule navy against a possible Mexican naval blockade of their port. While the invasion came over land, Texans, like others along the Gulf of Mexico also had to worry about their vulnerable coastline. The Texan navy had been established, on paper at least, on November 25, 1835, when the General Council passed a bill for the purpose of purchasing four schooners that would serve as the basis for a larger naval force. During 1835 and 1836, the General Council also issued letters of marque to privateers who would form a sort of makeshift navy as the Texas government struggled to gather the funds necessary to purchase the proper ships that would form the basis of a real navy.

The Texan navy had a minor role to play in the Texas Revolution, but its presence along the coastal communities of Texas was a reminder that Texans continually thought about the security of their coastline in addition to the western frontier and the Rio Grande. Indeed, conflicts with Mexico always had a naval aspect to them that included the desire to protect the Gulf of Mexico. During the Texas Revolution privateers also took on the responsibility of confiscating Mexican ships and protecting the coastal towns. In April 1837 the Texas naval ship the *Independence* was involved in a battle with a Mexican naval vessel as it made its way from New Orleans to Galveston, and the Mexican vessel eventually surrendered. While the Texas naval secretary Samuel Rhoads Fisher and commodore of the navy H. L. Thompson believed that taking the remaining naval ships for a cruise along the coast would inspire the sailors with more confidence, President Houston dismissed this idea, wary of allowing the two naval ships to go on cruises through the Gulf of Mexico. He preferred that the ships remain close to the coastal towns such as Galveston, believing that this strategy was the best way to defend the Texas coast from possible Mexican invaders. This strategy was not to last. On June 11, 1837, the *Invincible* and the *Brutus* took to the sea and began raiding Mexican towns along the Gulf Coast, capturing Mexican ships. They made their way back to Galveston in August. However, before the *Invincible* could enter the safety of Galveston Harbor, two Mexican ships attacked it. The *Brutus* attempted to render aid to its sister ship but was prevented from doing so by the treacherous sand bar at the mouth of Galveston Harbor. The *Invincible* met the same dangerous foe in the shape of the sand bar and sank over the course of a night.[38] The importance of the Texan navy at once linked it to the Gulf South, in which many communities concerned themselves with the presence of naval and army power in the region, primarily because of competition with European empires and Native American peoples. Though Mexico was not an empire, Texans certainly viewed that country as a tyrannical power, born of the perceived failures of the Spanish empire.

The fear that other incursions might occur lingered, and Sam Houston became convinced that the Mexican government was preparing to carry out yet another "war for the subjugation of Texas." John Reagan, then a justice of the peace in Nacogdoches, remembered that many Anglo Texans called for retaliation against their old Mexican enemies. The Texas Congress passed a bill providing for a war against Mexico and proposed a blockade of Mexico's

Gulf ports. Houston stated that all traffic going toward Mexico from other ports in the region would be stopped by the small Texas navy. According to Reagan, fears of Mexican invasion, coupled with hostilities between Texans and Native Americans, "kept the people of Texas in an almost continuous state of war up to the time of annexation to the United States." New Orleanians joined their counterparts in Texas in their growing fear of a Mexican invasion of the Texas coast. They held public meetings in the city to show support for the Texans and to organize militia groups. Eventually Houston vetoed the bill declaring war between Texas and Mexico. This, however, did not stop private citizens in Texas from organizing armed expeditions bound for Mexico intent on seeking revenge.[39] The invasion of 1842 was short lived and did little damage, but the fear of renewed Mexican efforts to regain Texas lingered in both Texas and the rest of the Gulf South. It strengthened the feeling that annexation to the United States would be the best option for the vulnerable nation.

In 1843 President Houston embarked on another effort to achieve Texas annexation to the United States by trying to encourage American interest. As before, the issue of annexing another slave territory raised a significant impediment. The *New Orleans Bulletin* warned its readers that Northerners were not likely to stand the idea of annexing Texas without ensuring American authority over the Oregon Territory and advised Southerners that it behooves the "South, and all the friends of an equal distribution of political power in the geographical divisions of the country, to present a strong, bold, solid and determined front."[40] The importance of protecting the vulnerable Gulf ports as global trading centers drove much of the debate. Meanwhile, John Tyler's administration, believing that Texas statehood would be the only thing to save his flagging presidency, also sought to renew U.S. interest in annexing Texas to the United States.

Texas's possibilities and vulnerabilities proved to be possibilities and vulnerabilities for the United States, especially the Southern states. The New Orleans *Daily Picayune* warned that if Texas was not annexed, as a separate nation its agricultural produce might displace that from the Southern states and disrupt trade throughout the Gulf of Mexico. A separate Texas was not merely an issue in terms of securing the enslaved population of the South but also in terms of its ability to maintain its cotton economy. In a few years, the *Daily Picayune* asserted, Texas would raise every bale of cotton that the English used in their factories, and within a few years, "English emigration, English capital, English commerce, English enterprise and English influence will overwhelm and swallow up everything that is American, and estrange the people of Texas from their loyalty to the United States."⁴¹ As a separate geopolitical entity, the Texas Republic posed an economic threat to the southern United States especially.

In part this was due to the Texas border and the fears that Southerners had concerning the relationship between Great Britain and Mexico. In 1844, echoing the beliefs of many Gulf South annexationists, the *Daily Picayune* maintained that annexation was absolutely necessary to do away with the "necessity of protecting a long line of frontier from smugglers; to defeat the insidious policy of England." Britain was "aiming to attack us in our slave property by erecting another Canada upon our borders." It also warned that Texans doubted their government could sustain the republic and might be tempted to form closer ties with Great Britain. "On these and other grounds the South will almost to a man sustain the policy of the President in bringing about annexation," the paper declared. Annexation was necessary for the survival of the South because "another Canada" on the South's border would prove a temptation to enslaved people as a safe haven, as Canada was proving to be.

The annexation of Texas was also necessary because it ensured continued U.S. expansion westward. In February, the *Houston Telegraph* published a rumor that the United States was about to ratify the annexation treaty. The news may have been "too good to be true," but the paper hoped it could be achieved. Texas was the key to U.S. imperial interests; as the *Daily Picayune* wrote, "the broad banner of Washington may be unfurled in glory on our Western border, and the burnished arms of American troops will be reflected from the sparkling waters of the Nueces. 'Westward! The star of empire takes its way!'" While in New Orleans, Rice Ballard, a Richmond slave trader and one of former secretary of war Albert Sidney Johnston's business associates, wrote to Johnston concerning the excitement over the prospect of annexation. "I am in hopes we shall have Texas annexed to our country," wrote Ballard. He felt "both North and South are interested to have Texas annexed to our country... we shall in this respect suffer a small diminution in the price of cotton, but we are compelled to have it annexed, or abandon our slaves if it is to be a British Colony of abolitionism."⁴² Johnston's views on annexation were somewhat changeable. Though he always thought it was important for Texas to become a state and supported the idea during the Texas Revolution, the fact that nothing came of it in 1837 made him more skeptical. When he retired from public life after the Lamar administration, he continued to support annexation even if he was no longer involved in politics or the military.⁴³ By July 1844, however, it appeared as though annexation was set to fail yet again, with the parties sharply divided over the issue and debates unlikely to conclude before the next presidential election.

Houston consistently fought for annexation, going so far as to play the British and Americans against each other in order to gain further support for statehood. Both Johnston and Houston were born in the upper South but found a home in Texas and felt a strong sense of loyalty toward it. Johnston's fealty toward Texas emerged from his family's connection to the territory and the Lower South. In his youth, Johnston encountered Americans migrating to Texas while he lived in Alexandria, Louisiana, a border town. Several of his siblings took part in the 1813 Gutierrez-Magee expedition, an early joint Mexican and American filibustering expedition that aimed to wrest colonial Texas from the Spanish at the start of the Mexican War of Independence. Johnston's eldest son recalled that his father claimed that, despite these familial connections with Anglo expansion into Texas, his real reason for going there was to help bring it into the Union. He wanted to "add another star to the American constellation."

However, he was not in Texas during the actual process of annexation. In 1844 Johnston's friend Henry Clay Davis urged him to run for president of Texas, telling him that "'Western Boys' think of you, a great many of them say if you are not a candidate, they do not intend to vote at all." In 1845 Johnston traveled to Shelbyville, Kentucky, where he married his second wife, Elizabeth. In March another acquaintance, J. S. Mayfield, wrote to him, begging Johnston to return to Texas. Mayfield reminded Johnston that he had always answered the republic's call to service. "When she needed your aid, counsel and sacrifices," wrote Mayfield, "you extended them with alacrity & now that she is about to pass an ordeal that must forever affect her destiny & happiness you must not stand back." James Love, perhaps the most outspoken of Johnston's companions, wrote to Johnston regularly, giving him updates on the proceedings of the Texas Congress. Johnston refused to entertain the idea of running for president but swore he would return if Texas needed military defense. In a letter written on March 30, 1845, he wrote that if the Texas president, then Anson Jones, refused to "call congress and take the mandatory steps to ascertain the will of the people, we will take the matter in our own hands, have a convention unseat him, and hang him if necessary to carry our purposes and all that may abide by him." Militarism and military men were important to Texans. Men like Johnston and Houston were seen as powerful voices for annexation within the Texas Republic and were expected to stand up for Texas's interests.[44]

White Southerners, meanwhile, worried that Great Britain might take advantage of the tense situation between Texas and Mexico and use Texas's precarious position to further extend their influence into the southwestern region. Mississippi senator Robert J. Walker recorded many of these fears in a letter he wrote concerning Texas's annexation in 1844. He linked them with the fears that slavery engendered in a population so utterly dependent on it. To encourage American sentiment toward Texas annexation, Walker posited its statehood as a "*re*-annexation" of Texas, claiming that the United States gave its claims to Texas up in exchange for the Florida territory. During the presidential election, Democratic candidate James K. Polk ran on a platform that promised this "re-annexation." Thus, by completing the treaty of annexation, the federal government was regaining that which originally belonged to it. Walker warned that if the United States did not act it would wind up surrendering the "Florida pass, the mouth of the Mississippi, and the command of the Mexican gulf, and finally Texas itself into the hands of England."[45] Walker incorporated the fears that Texas might dominate the region economically with the fear that antislavery feeling might open up Texas as a free nation, closing the South in at its northern and southern borders.

The Walker letter had a little something in it for everyone, beginning with his "safety-valve" theory, in which he positioned Texas as a place to send both free and enslaved African Americans. Walker presented some vague notion that enslaved and free Black people would eventually dissipate into the vastness of the West and further into Mexico and Latin America. As he wrote this, he imagined Latin America in the same way that supporters of the colonization movement imagined African Americans' relationship to the continent of Africa. He wrote, "They will disappear from time to time west of the Del Norte, and beyond the limits of the Union, among a race of their own color; will be diffused throughout this vast region, where they will not be a degraded caste, where, as to climate, and social and moral, condition, and all the hopes and comforts of life, they can occupy, among equals, a position they can never attain in any part of the Union."[46] Walker cast Latin American nations and the West as the only places on the continent of North and South America where enslaved African Americans might be freed from the system of slavery that men like him created and upheld. This conveniently left out the fact that the Texas Republic had its own system of slavery grown from the cutting made of the original plant. He also left out that Texans banned the movement of free African Americans into the Texas Republic and encouraged the expulsion of free African Americans who already lived there.

As Walker imagined Latin America through the lens of Texas, Ferdinand Roemer, a German geologist, imagined Texas through European eyes. He toured the republic amid the annexation efforts, which amounted to a failed treaty and then a hasty joint resolution between the United States and Texas. Between 1844 and 1845 he made his way through Texas as a part of a geological survey of North America. Fascinated by the German settlements, prairies, and towns, Roemer published a separate travelogue covering Texas and the Gulf of Mexico in 1847, and his writings reflect the way that Anglos often depicted Mexicans as Texas approached annexation. Roemer described the Mexicans who remained in San Antonio, one of the largest towns in Texas, as belonging to a "lower class of Mexican and their features plainly show a mixture of Castilian and Indian blood." He dismissed Tejanos as a "lazy and indolent frace." As he moved throughout Texas, Roemer used the same racist language to describe Tejano communities, characterizing San Antonio as full of "decay, and apparently at one time had seen better and more brilliant days." About the German colony of New Braunfels, on the banks of the Comal River, Roemer remarked on its pleasing appearance and its uniqueness in Texas and North America. He was thrilled to see familiar German people and customs taking root in Texas.[47] These statements emphasized the differences between the German, Mexican, and Anglo settlements. German and Anglo communities were described as growing and bustling. Apprehension over whether or not such growth could be sustained served as a major reason why annexationists reasoned statehood was necessary. The vast space of Texas could save the South from the mounting antislavery movement, foreign encroachment from British power, and being shut out of the riches of the cotton markets of Europe.[48]

Texas president Anson Jones put the joint resolution that had been developed by the U.S. Senate before the Texas Congress in June, framing it as a choice between Mexican-recognized independence, which involved Great Britain's backing, and annexation to the United States.[49] In January 1845 the *Daily Picayune* claimed "a large majority of the people of Texas are warmly in favor of annexation, and entertain strong hopes that a bill to that effect will pass before our present Congress closes its session."[50] The Texas constitutional convention drew up a state constitution, which was then approved by popular vote in October 1845. The formal transfer of authority occurred during a special ceremony in which Anson Jones lowered the republic's flag and proclaimed, "The final act in this great drama is now performed, the Republic of Texas is no more." He then transferred power to James Pinkney Henderson, Texas's first governor. The steamship

Alabama brought news of the approval of annexation to New Orleans where, according to Ferdinand Roemer, the news made a profound impression on New Orleanians.[51]

The annexation allowed the United States to stake even more of a claim on the Gulf Coast and continue the project of asserting its authority over the region. Annexation also made Texas's problems those of the United States. Conflict with Native Americans and Mexico, as well as Texas's economic uncertainty, was not entirely alleviated with annexation and neither was the South's worries over the growth of the antislavery movement in the nation and beyond it. Still, the fact that the United States had just annexed a large amount of territory was viewed as a triumph for Southern expansionists and served to drive their hunger for Latin American territory.

CONCLUSION

Throughout the late 1840s and into the 1850s, Gulf South Southerners both within and outside of Texas continued to be concerned with the state of the frontiers in Texas and Florida and the security of the region's richest port cities, Mobile and New Orleans. They continued to promote expansion into Latin America. In so doing, the fate of the frontier, westward expansion, and Southern interests became increasingly tied to the notion that Latin American space, and Latin American people, could be used in any way that Americans, slaveholders especially, saw fit. It was theirs for the taking.

Yet, the annexation of Texas virtually ensured that the United States would go to war with Mexico. In the coming war, ideas about Mexicans and Mexico constructed through the annexation process were used as yet more evidence of white American superiority over the nations of Latin America, especially Mexico. To expansionists, Texas fulfilled the promise of expansionism in the Gulf South and marked the United States' expansion into the territory of sister republics. Both of these developments were built on the region's already established history of expansionism, stretching back to the first shiploads of Spanish conquistadors and clergy. It was those initial encounters, fumbling and often disastrous as they were, that laid the groundwork for the connections between Mexico, Cuba, and the American Gulf Coast. Texas's image as a safe haven for Southerners, the growth of slavery and the cotton economy, and its position as the only Southern state on an international border replayed again and again in the minds of Southerners, though with different contexts as the region was plunged into war with Mexico and later against the Union. But all that lay in the future. In 1845 one Pablo, the author of a poem entitled "The Texan Soldier," celebrated the annexation of Texas by noting that even though the Texans' "swarthy brow has lost the hue, that marks the Anglo-Saxon race," he urged "Brother, peace! The Eagle guards thee! The Stars and Stripes shall o'er thee wave."[52]

In 1836, Manuel Rincon, governor of the Mexican state of Puebla, ordered that a decree be printed denouncing Texas independence as a "serious danger to the peace of the world" and a threat to the "sovereignty of all nations." Rincon decried annexation as the latest in a long list of offenses by Anglos against Mexico. He accused them of consistently challenging his own country's sovereignty and rights. The decree further called the Mexican nation to arms, claiming that Mexican law authorized Rincon to raise a military force capable of defending Mexico's claims to Texas. Rincon called on "all [of Mexico's] sons to the defense of national independence, threatened by the usurpation of the territory of Texas."[53] And when U.S. troops marched away to war against those sons of Mexico, they carried meticulously crafted images of effeminate and dastardly Mexican elites and distrustful Mexican laborers, like mental wanted posters depicting the nation's new enemy.[54]

CHAPTER 2

The Possibilities of Pensacola

In 1845 John Sanders, captain in the Army Corps of Engineers, published a pamphlet in which he wondered, "Is it possible that the Coast of the Gulf receiving the [Mississippi and Ohio Rivers], can be our weakest and most vulnerable frontier?"[1] With this publication, Sanders sought to raise the resources and men of the Ohio River Valley for the defense of the nation and the Gulf of Mexico. It was testament to the fact that concern for the protection of the Gulf Coast was not solely a Southern interest but also a western one that would involve men from Kentucky, Indiana, and Illinois. He cited several different issues that played out in the efforts of the army and the navy as well as local boosters to bring about improvements to local fortitifcations in West Florida. Throughout the mid-nineteenth century, as Texans talked about their vulnerable border, Floridians did the same. They talked about the vulnerability of these border regions to attack from outside maritime powers like Great Britain, all while they attempted to suppress native peoples, slave populations, and Latinx peoples from within.

Like the quest for annexation in Texas, the story of Pensacola's fortifications and the establishment of white American control over places like West Florida is one of big dreams and constant frustrations. By the time Sanders published the pamphlet, both Texas and Florida had entered the nation as two new slave states. One was a debt-ridden former republic troubled by conflicting visions of its future and in constant conflict with powerful Native American nations such as the Comanche as well as Mexico. The other was a territory that was similarly rife with competition and conflict between white Southern settlers and Native American nations such as the

Seminole and the Creek. White Floridians and Texans also both worried about the presence of powerful European nations within the Gulf of Mexico, the southwest borderlands, and the Caribbean, and Southerners outside of Texas and Florida worried about those threats too. Where Texans had feared the possibility of British interference in annexation efforts, Floridians in West Florida lived with the memory of the Battle of Pensacola, the Creek War, and the end of the War of 1812. These worries shaped their fears and fantasies related to Europe, especially Great Britain, during the antebellum era. Pensacolians used worries over the British presence in the Gulf of Mexico to advocate for an increased military presence in the region. Fears over the British and conflict with Native Americans fed into active worries over the expansion and salience of slavery in Texas and Florida.[2]

The First Seminole Indian War and the War of 1812 solidified what historian William Belko called "American Anglophobia" in the minds of antebellum Americans. Southerners were no exception, even though a significant share of the South's cotton crop made the Atlantic crossing to English factories. Decades after they had conquered the Florida territory, Americans, especially those in the Gulf South, recalled the early days of their fragile republic and its conflicts with the former mother country. Yet these most recent entanglements with Great Britain took on added significance in light of the United States' and Britain's shared interests in territorial expansion within the Gulf of Mexico.[3]

Those fears and fantasies included the idea that the Florida Straits, like the Texas borderlands, were valuable for trade and vulnerable to invasion. For those living along the Lower Mississippi Valley, parts of the West, and the Gulf Coast, the Florida Straits were the gateway to the Atlantic Ocean and its vital trade routes. Both Texas and Florida figured prominently into the process of expansion and Southerners' efforts to ensure their region's prosperity and security. For coastal communities, an increased military presence in the city of Pensacola came to symbolize the region's security as much as the annexation of Texas came to symbolize the state's path forward and a form of security for its own coastal communities. Most of the import and export trade conducted in the port cities entered and exited through the Florida Straits. As with Texas, Florida played a vital part in the imaginary of the South's future, even as whites fought Native Americans for control over the state.

City boosters, naval officers, and army engineers alike promoted Pensacola as a major bulwark for American expansion and security in the Caribbean. Fears concerning European naval powers like Great Britain and France were a significant part of this discourse, but it was formulated against the backdrop of conflict between Anglo settlers and the Native American nations trying to holding on to their territory in Alabama and Florida as the U.S. government continued to enforce Indian Removal.

The consequences of Indian Removal policies continued to affect places like Florida, Alabama, and Texas well into the 1850s and provided the foundation for much of the violence within the Gulf Coast. Wars with the Creek and Seminole played out around Pensacola and West Florida and were a significant reason for the continuation of the presence of the U.S. Army and Navy. While West Florida was not the epicenter of conflict during the Second Seminole War or the Second Creek War, both conflicts provided a reason for further improvements to the fortifications at Pensacola.[4] The Second Seminole War ended early in the 1840s, but the scars of this viscious war littered the mental and physical landscapes of Florida. Meanwhile the violence between Anglos and Creeks spread through Alabama to western Florida from 1836 to the early 1850s. At the same time that these struggles occurred, boosters and newspaper editors in Pensacola churned out articles fretting over the possibility that the United States might be humiliated on the world's stage by a naval war with a superior European naval force. For Anglos, the reality of wars with Native Americans and the possibility of war with Europeans provided an added and immediate cause for internal improvements in Pensacola.[5]

In the 1830s and 1840s, the relationship between westward expansion, securing the trade of the Deep South hinterlands, and national defense occupied the minds of Gulf Coast Southerners and was often used to explain the need for internal improvements to the region's military fortifications. Pensacola was also identified by residents of Mobile and New Orleans as vital to the overall protection of American authority and trade in the Gulf of Mexico. Over the course of the mid-nineteenth century Pensacola became increasingly dependent on the army and navy as a revenue source. Improvements to the naval yard as well as the army forts erected in Pensacola Bay held out the possibility that Pensacola might gain a ship-building industry in addition to being a military town. Pensacolians also argued that the fortifications and naval yards on the Atlantic Coast were in far better shape and that their coast was often and unwisely neglected. Throughout much of the antebellum period Southern politicians reflected these arguments and in Congress attempted to gain added funding for military fortifications on the Gulf Coast, Pensacola included. Newspaper editors from Pensacola to New Orleans frequently mentioned both Northern and Southern military fortifications on the Atlantic Coast that they felt were unfairly favored by the national government. The reason city boosters in Pensacola and the Gulf generally were so concerned about these internal improvements is that the naval vessels that were stationed in Florida were either in Pensacola Bay or Tampa Bay and needed better naval yards and places to get repairs.[6] During the U.S.-Mexican War, the naval yard at Pensacola provided minor repairs for the ships participating in the blockade. It also housed a small hospital that cared for wounded and sick soldiers. When improvements to the naval yard lagged, frustrations in Pensacola and New Orleans heightened citizens' sensitivity to the idea that the federal government was either unable or reluctant to provide adequately for the Gulf ports.[7]

This chapter examines the way that smaller communities factored into expansionism and how they sought to benefit from it. It explores the manner in which Pensacolians attempted to capitalize on the military's presence in the Gulf of Mexico as a way to assure the economic growth of their city and the complex discourse they used to advocate for it. The chapter employs Pensacola's relationship with its military fortifications throughout the 1840s amid the lingering impact of war with Native peoples as a lens through which to understand the various aspects of the imagined Southern empire that intellectuals, politicians, and editors splashed across the region's newspapers and journals and to explore how that imagined empire affected these communities. Ultimately the region of West Florida, Pensacola included, was sandwiched between several realms of conflict that shaped much of the community's character as well as the efforts at territorial expansion of which it became a part. Pensacola was not important so much for what it was as for what it had the potential to be: a major military bulwark that could, if outfitted properly, provide for the defense of the entire coastline from would-be invaders, the lingering threat of southeastern Native Americans, as well as providing a home for the naval squadrons that patrolled the Caribbean.

SEARCHING FOR A PURPOSE IN PENSACOLA

At first glance, Pensacola seems like the last place that would figure into expansionist interests and Southern imperialism in the Gulf of Mexico, but Pensacola Bay, and its place on the Gulf Coast, made it a victim of Florida's tumultuous past. Each time it changed hands—from the Spanish, to the British, and then to the Americans—the town's future came under new supervision, with new intentions and new concerns. In 1698 the Spanish built a presidio near what would become the location of Fort Barrancas, one of three forts erected in Pensacola in the early nineteenth century. The Spanish had been the first European power to recognize the community's military importance against British and French incursions. The British colonial period saw further construction of fortifications, but it was the Americans who began to shape it into a military outpost. During the War of 1812 and First Seminole War troops were still housed in barracks and other buildings that had been built by the British. The port was little more than one small wharf and most cargo had to be brought to the city via smaller ships. Like Galveston, Pensacola was a long way away from being a major port city, but in both Texas and Florida the small outposts served as sites of potential. Just as Galveston was fast becoming essential to Texas's economy, Pensacolians hoped that their community would prove to be essential to the military defense of Florida, Alabama, and the trade of the Gulf Coast communities. As a testament to this, one of Andrew Jackson's main concerns when he served as the territory's first governor was establishing a much bigger wharf, which Pensacolians accomplished by the close of the 1830s.[8]

Pensacola's population never numbered more than a few thousand throughout the antebellum era. When Florida became a U.S. territory, the town's population initially ballooned to four thousand inhabitants, as many settlers began to move into the territory. However, after Andrew Jackson left, the population began to decline, and in 1822, when a yellow fever epidemic hit the town, its population dwindled to roughly one thousand. While the Jacksons made their home in Pensacola, Rachel Jackson wrote her friend Eliza Kingsley in 1821 remarking on the community's diversity. She wrote, "The inhabitants all speak Spanish and French. Some speak four or five languages. Such a mixed multitude, you, nor any of us, ever had an idea of. There are fewer white people by far than any other, mixed with all nations under the canopy of heaven, almost in nature's darkness." A Spanish census taken in 1820, before Spain transferred the territory to the United States, reflected Jackson's comments. It found that French and Spanish Creoles dominated the town and surrounding countryside. One-third of the population was mixed race, and three individuals were identified as mestizos (mixed Native American and European) with thirty households consisting of a white man and a mixed-race or Black woman. Later the 1850 census recorded 2,164 total inhabitants. George McCall, a soldier stationed at Pensacola in the mid-1820s and later a brigadier general in the Civil War, wrote countless letters to his sister describing the Creoles of Pensacola and their cultural practices. He wrote that Creoles possessed a "distinct and provincial character; their prominent traits wearing a coloring peculiarity of their own." He referred to them as "listless" or "lazy." When Americans moved into New Orleans, they made similar comments concerning the racially mixed and white Creole residents. Referring to white Creoles as lazy or listless was a racist way of emphasizing the difference between white Americans and the European,

African, and Native American descendants they encountered in the South's borderlands.

Unlike many other ports along the Gulf of Mexico, Pensacola never became a major depot for the agricultural hinterlands of Alabama and middle Florida. When Florida became a U.S. territory Southerners flooded in, eager to take advantage of the newly acquired land. While this benefited the young territory overall, it did not, in the end, benefit Pensacola very much. The town lacked sufficient river access to the most prosperous cotton districts in middle Florida, and much of that trade was shipped out through other ports. The Apalachicola River and the city of Columbus, Georgia, served the growing cotton trade, bypassing Pensacola. Despite this fact, Americans did make their way into Pensacola, and by 1840 white Americans outnumbered the smaller mixed and Creole populations.[9]

In the 1820s when it appeared that political and economic power shifted to the middle counties, Pensacolians first looked to remedy their stagnant economy by supporting a Gulf Coast canal, which would link East and West Florida together. During the early nineteenth century, internal improvements and canals were the order of the day, and Pensacolians looked on at the work done on the Erie Canal as a possible example of revitalizing their community. This "faith in canals" offered a chance to open the West to trade with the more established East, allowing goods to travel through Florida without having to go around the entire peninsula. A canal across the Florida peninsula was not the only option that gained support within Florida and Pensacola specifically. Other proposals sought to connect Pensacola to Mobile or New Orleans. In 1827 John Lee Williams completed a survey of West Florida for planned improvements to Pensacola Bay. He described the bay as being "by far the best harbor on the Gulf of Mexico, or indeed south of the Chesapeake Bay." Still, even though the bay possessed a favorable harbor that would have serviced a canal, the plan failed, to be superceded by other schemes for economic salvation. In the antebellum period, Pensacola boosters touted railroads, but many of these ventures never got much closer to completion than the proposed canal. In 1834 the Florida, Alabama, and Georgia Railroad was incorporated but almost immediately it was plagued with problems. The corporation's prospects of getting the railroad connected to Montgomery, Alabama, were continually twarted in the Alabama state legislature by agents from Mobile eager to keep the shipping and stagecoach lines between Mobile and Pensacola as the sole connection between West Florida and the Alabama interior. By 1837 the economic panic that hit the nation also hindered the construction of the railroad. Another attempt was not made until the 1850s, though Pensacolians worked throughout the 1840s for a railroad to be established.[10]

Other economic prospects of interest to Pensacolians were eventually in some way tied to the army and navy presence in the region. The rationale for the construction of additional fortifications and the naval yard in Pensacola came from the events of that took place in the Gulf South during the War of 1812; indeed, the need to protect trade against foreign threats was paramount in the minds of those in Congress who approved the city's enhanced defenses. Their construction relied on the use of enslaved labor amid continued conflict with Native Americans in Alabama and elsewhere in Florida. Shortly after the War of 1812, the Board of Engineers and Fortifications created the Third System of Coastal Fortifications plan, a defense system that entailed a network of coastal forts as well as roads and canals to supply them, and a larger navy and a standing army. Forts Barrancas, McRee, and Pickens were all built as a part of this defense system from the 1820s to the 1830s, with the barracks at Barrancas eventually being dubbed the Gulf Coast's defense headquarters. The board recommended Pensacola Bay because it possessed "positions admirably adopted to the repairing, building and launching of vessels of any size, for docks and dock yards in healthful positions and as being perfectly defensible." The construction of these forts set Pensacola down a road that led to the city taking on the role as a military center for West Florida and potentially for the entire Gulf of Mexico.[11]

Along with the fortifications plan, piracy also drove the concentration of naval forces in the Gulf of Mexico and West Florida. From 1815 to 1825 pirates and privateers attacked an estimated three thousand ships. In 1825 Congress made the first appropriation for the construction of a naval yard at Pensacola and authorized improvements to the fortifications that already existed there.[12] Pensacola became a military town, with developing small industries in brick and pine lumber, utilizing the tall thin pines that littered the countryside around the town.[13] The brick-making industry developed through the army's need for materials to build the new forts along the mouth of the harbor. Materials had originally come from Mobile, but in the 1830s the army began purchasing local bricks.

To produce bricks and build the forts, Pensacola companies and the U.S. Army rented enslaved African Americans from slaveholders in the area. Indeed, most of the army's enslaved laborers were concentrated in Florida doing a variety of different work such as participating in the construction of Pensacola's forts. The navy also used enslaved labor and many enslaved African Americans worked aboard naval vessels. Historian Thomas Hulse noted that the development of the coastal defense system that Pensacola was a part of also facilitated the development of a slave rental system by the army and navy that became an essential part of Pensacola's economy. The enslaved labored to build fortifications, which helped to grow the local economy and led to the further expansion of slavery within west Florida. Congressional appropriations that paid for construction also became key to Pensacola's economy and Pensacolians came to depend on both construction and appropriations for their community's well-being.[14]

IN BETWEEN WARS REAL AND IMAGINED

The outbreak of the Second Seminole Indian War in Florida and the Second Creek War in Alabama coincided with Pensacolians' advocacy for increased coastal defenses. Due to West Florida's position sandwiched between these two regions of conflict, the buildup of both the army fortifications and the naval yard reflected the conflicts that took place all around Pensacola as well as imagined wars, those that were feared but had not yet happened, that Pensacolians and army and navy officers drew on to encourage further investment in defenses there. The real wars against Native Americans determined who came to these forts and the naval yard as well as their experiences of them, and the imagined wars with European powers to come drove the efforts to gain support for continued construction in Pensacola.

Similar tensions existed in West Florida and Alabama to those between the Comanche and Cherokee and white and Mexican settlers in Texas. The Second Seminole Indian War, which began in 1835, was the largest and most costly Anglo American–Native American conflict. It was extremely destructive and brutally violent, a war the likes of which white Southerners would not experience again until the Civil War. Shortly after the Second Seminole War began, tensions between the army, local militias, white settlers, and the Creeks boiled over into war when the latter were pressured to leave. White settlers encroached on Creek lands in Georgia and Alabama throughout the 1820s and 1830s. In spring 1836 bands of Creeks in Georgia and central Alabama rose up, attacking white communities. The army suppressed the uprising there by 1837, forcing thousands into camps before driving them to march to Indian Territory. Resistant bands of Creeks migrated to West Florida that same year. Native Americans were not a foreign presence in Pensacola, because many visited the area to hunt and fish and trade in town. That said, white settlers in other parts of West Florida remained suspicious of these groups.

The seat of war in Florida remained in middle and east Florida, where much of the Second Seminole Indian War took place. However, army troops and militias also prepared for war against the Creeks. Some forty thousand soldiers and volunteers served in the army throughout the Second Seminole War. In Pensacola the navy organized a force that would also go to war against the Seminole people. Within West Florida local communities also organized militia units to defend themselves against Native American threats. Those living within the Florida panhandle feared that Creeks might ally with Seminoles in the war. These fears did not materialize, but white settlers committed attacks against the Creeks who were resisting removal in West Florida. Creeks retaliated, further driving the cycle of violence. However, by 1838 the violence in the panhandle between white settlers and Creeks had subsided, though it did not end completely. The end of the larger war against the Seminoles came on August 14, 1842, when Brigadier General William Jenkins Worth, the commander of U.S. forces, declared the end of the conflict after many of the Seminole had either acquiesced or were forced to relocate to the West and only a few hundred Seminoles remained.

Though the Second Seminole War came to a close in 1842, much of northern Florida remained heavily militarized. Shortly after the end of the war, Congress passed the Armed Occupation Act, designed to rid the region of Native Americans by encouraging white American settlement. It required that settlers "improve" the purchased land and defend themselves against Native incursion. By 1843 Worth estimated that there were only about three hundred Seminoles left in Florida. Yet the impact of their presence continued to be felt throughout the territory. Along the Gulf Coast a small band of Native Americans attacked shipwrecked white Southerners and an enslaved woman, killing the woman and one of the men in January 1844. Most of the others scattered and escaped. One gentleman, Henry A. Nunes, a Pensacolian, guided troops from Pensacola to patrol up and down the coast in search of the Native Americans who had committed the attack. The Seminoles managed to escape, but the troops then went back and destroyed their community before returning to Pensacola. White settlers focused much of their fears on the wooded areas beyond Pensacola, knowing both Native Americans and runaway slaves might be moving through them. Creek refugees remained living along the coast, and the army at Pensacola sent out several expeditions in 1843 and 1844 searching for them.[15]

By the time Edward Clifford Anderson was stationed aboard the coastal steamer U.S.S. *General Taylor* in 1844, he was a well-traveled naval officer, having served aboard several other vessels in the North Atlantic and the Mediterranean. The *General Taylor* was a far cry from the massive U.S.S. *Constitution* and *Lexington* that Anderson had served on previously. It was a small ship that had been used to transport troops and supplies during the

Second Seminole War and was now charged with patrolling the Florida coastline, monitoring the actions of the remaining Seminole people and guarding against livestock theft. As the ship sailed through Florida's rivers toward the western coast, Anderson moved through a landscape filled with the ghosts of war. The physical markings and memories of the Second Seminole War littered the territory in which he found himself. At Fort Picolata Anderson wrote about a hotel where soldiers were stationed during the war and noted that he was shown the place where a man was killed and scalped by Native Americans. He later noted that he and his crewmates "saw at the landing notches that had been cut in the trees by the Indians during the war for the purpose of resting their rifles in," and that they had waited for army troops though none came. Though the war was over, Anderson observed General Worth drilling troops, a reminder of this recent violent past.

Several instances in Anderson's diary where he recorded his initial journey to Pensacola were framed by the connection between U.S. expansion and the displacement of Native American peoples. His journal contained a collection of memories and ideas connected to both previous conflicts between whites and Seminoles. In January, from the *General Taylor*, Anderson observed the readiness of the Worth's troops. He was impressed by the state of the American troops but claimed that from the accounts he had heard they were an "insubordinate set of scoundrels" who could not compare to the British troops in terms of their appearance. When Anderson later toured Fort Marion in St. Augustine, he recounted the details of the escape of the Seminole leader, Coacoochee, in which he outsmarted his captors by making a rope out of blankets and "kept the whole neighborhood in constant alarm & committed more cruelties than any chief of his nation." Later, Coacoochee became the best known of the war chiefs after Osceola's death. Sailors and soldiers alike claimed to respect Coacoochee for his brazen escape, and Anderson spoke of him in a similar fashion, calling him the "finest specimen of Indian."[16]

As the *General Taylor* sailed farther down the Atlantic Coast toward the Straits of Florida, Anderson again discussed the world around him and the markers of the war that had just taken place. He related an incident in which he and his companions disturbed Indian burial grounds by digging through them looking for souvenirs. Anderson took a skull as his personal prize. "I lay awake in my berth nearly the whole night thinking of deaths heads & dead Indians," he wrote. Anderson spent the rest of the night listening to mice and roaches crawling in and out of the skull, tormented by his choice to desecrate the graves of Native Americans. As historian Cameron Strang has described, the desecration of burials and bodies was an important part of the destructiveness of the Second Seminole War. American soldiers destroyed Seminole burial grounds and dug up bodies, especially the skulls, to claim that the Seminole people had no right to the land for which they fought. Through his participation in these destructions, Anderson demonstrated that like many wars before and after it, the Second Seminole War did not end neatly: its violence bled into the following years.[17]

Anderson's understanding of the "Florida War" and the larger resistance of the Seminoles, like that of many Anglo Americans, was grounded in the decades' long process of forced removal that began before his time in the navy. He stated that "this effective weapon the sword, in the hands of our national government has often been employed to chastise the poor Indians. Sometimes with dreadful vengeance I fear and should not their protection avail to draw it from the scabbard?" His feelings toward the process of forced Native American removal, one of the foundational occurrences in the larger process of American imperialism and expansion, appear ambivalent and situational.

At times the perspectives of men like Edward Anderson reflected the broader racist notions about Native Americans and other peoples of color. Anderson, like so many soldiers who fought in the Second Seminole War or any of the previous conflicts that Americans fought to conquer the Gulf South, worked in service of imperialism. However, at other times men like Anderson were able to criticize and even call that imperialism into question. Additionally, Anderson's record of his time patrolling the Florida coast demonstrates that even after the Second Seminole War, the nation's ability to control places like Florida and Texas continued to be frustrated by the peoples they claimed to have conquered. By 1845 the American flag may have flown over both Florida and Texas, two parts of the Gulf South's borderlands, but at the ground level, the authority that flag represented was still contested by Native peoples as well as Mexicans and enslaved African Americans.[18]

In many ways Anderson's journey and his journal exemplified the multifaceted ways that Americans in the nineteenth century engaged with the construction of expansionist fantasies. Anderson described the Pensacola navy yard in 1844: "The enclosure has been very much beautified of late years & has a range of buildings for the accommodation of the officers & their families—on Friday the 3rd the Poinsett went to sea with a bearer of dispatches for Mexico." Throughout the 1840s Pensacolians and others who saw the potential for a major military bulwark at this location supported improvements to both the fortifications in the bay as well as to the naval yard, namely the construction of the dry dock. Sailors like Anderson viewed places like Pensacola and the rest of the Florida coast as an isolated outpost because of the lingering effects of the Second Seminole Indian War; it was true that when it came to the need for repairs, naval ships had to travel great distances for such things. Along the entire length of the U.S. Gulf Coast there was no place to repair the larger merchant or navy ships, and Southerners in the region worried incessantly about the lack of a proper naval yard. Expansionists in the Gulf South argued for increased military presence to ensure that the United States established its authority on the coast in addition to military efforts to assert federal authority over the remaining Native American populations of the interior of Florida. To do so, the Gulf South needed improved army fortifications, naval yards, and a strong navy. These things formed a central part of the region's imagining of its place within American expansion and empire. It was about settlers, but it was also about military force.

Throughout the 1830s and 1840s, proponents of Gulf Coast defenses supported an increase in the number of ships as well as improvements to the coast's fortifications. New Orleans had a small dry dock, and there were army barracks just beyond the city. However, its location on the Mississippi River was not ideal for the Gulf ships, especially the navy's larger ships, when they were in need of repair. In order for Pensacola to become a successful starting point for U.S. expansion into Mexico and the Caribbean, it required the expansion of the naval yard located five miles away, specifically the construction of dry docks and a seawall. These became the focus of a lot of newspaper ink during this period. Dry docks were used for constructing and repairing ships, and a dry dock at Pensacola could provide a facility for ship repairs so that navy ships would not have to travel to dry docks as far away as Charleston, Portsmouth, or Norfolk. The dock would be made available for use by merchant ships in the region as well, and Pensacolians hoped it would lead the way to the development of a shipbuilding industry in the Gulf South. In 1840 the congressional naval appropriations committee introduced legislation into the Senate to which John C. Calhoun added an amendment for a dock at Pensacola. He considered the need to protect commerce in the Gulf by providing funding for an improved naval station to be vital to the South's prosperity, and Pensacola remained the most obvious choice. A number of other Southern senators supported Calhoun and the committee, maintaining, as one did, "that the whole south and west were deeply interested in the work," because commerce from both regions would need to be protected by a naval force in the event of war in the Gulf. The bill was eventually defeated, but the essential elements of the argument in favor of improvements to the navy yard at Pensacola had been made. The specter of an imagined war and protection of commerce formed an essential part of the discourse over increased military presence in the Gulf of Mexico. The reality was, however, that up until the end of the Second Seminole War and the Second Creek War, naval forces in Florida were primarily used to patrol the coastline looking for threats from Native Americans.[19]

As already discussed, in the 1840s Pensacolians, naval officers, and engineers at the naval yard began urging the federal government to complete repairs, bolster fortifications, and build a dry dock at Pensacola. Foreign naval superiority provided both the drive for increased naval defenses and the language to support it. John Sanders's proposition to use the men and resources of the West to defend the southern coast recalled this perpetual fear when he wrote that the "configuration of the coast, the character of the intervening region, it's [sic] spareness of population, the excess of the black race, and the proximity of the Bermudas, Bahamas, and Jamaica, presenting such prospects of success, will always tempt an active and powerful enemy like England to the enterprise." Expansionists often conceived of the Gulf of Mexico as the United States' own Mediterranean. Sanders certainly viewed it this way. He described the Gulf as "our Mediterranean. Its islands are but the selvage of our continent; and there the nation which aspires to the dominion of the seas will attempt to establish her Maltas and Gibraltars." Europe's dominance of the Mediterranean provided a potent symbol for the Gulf South—an image of what their region might become in terms of trade and military dominance. The *Pensacola Gazette* published a letter from Commodore Charles Stewart originally written in 1836. Stewart wrote extensively that Pensacola was the ideal place from which to establish the nation's command over the coast and the Caribbean. He wrote that Pensacola Bay was to the Gulf of Mexico what Toulon was to the Mediterranean for the French. Specifically, France had fashioned Toulon into its primary military port on the Mediterranean. By 1820 it had become the staging ground for France's invasion of North Africa when the fleet set sail from the port to Algiers. Stewart was hoping that a place like Pensacola, with its deepwater bay and naval yard, might do the same thing for the United States.[20]

When newspapers discussed the importance of defending the coastline, they often compared the United States' position in the Gulf to French defenses in the Mediterranean. This comparison encapsulated both the nation's drive to be like the European countries that dominated the Mediterranean and the fear of being dominated by those same European powers. In addition, the Mediterranean was a heavily contested space. France, Spain, and Italy all had to fight naval wars to achieve dominance in the area. Thus, the comparison alluded to American concerns about their ability to establish and maintain control over the Gulf of Mexico.

The Gulf's importance as a linkage between the South and West grew in 1845, when the United States annexed Texas and its ports. As John Sanders reflected on the significance of Texas statehood, he recalled it signaled the need for a stronger military presence in the region in order to achieve a position for the United States "fully equal to cope with England for the mastery of the Gulf of Mexico, if not, indeed, for that of the high seas." In the minds of expansionists, Britain was both a possible threat to the nation's prosperity and the standard by which it should be measured. For Southern expansionists, Britain's reputation as a consummate naval and military power coexisted with the threat it posed as an abolitionist empire.[21]

The threat and nightmare of "the enemy" attacking a defenseless Gulf Coast continued to animate the editorials published on the subject of the defenses at Pensacola in the years before the outbreak of the Mexican War. In 1843 Congress appropriated $40,000 to upgrade Pensacola's yard, including repairs to the hospital buildings as well as provisions for the dry dock, which was ultimately not enough to satisfy those looking to upgrade the site's defenses.[22] But by August 1843, New Orleans newspapers leveled charges of the misappropriation of funds against those in charge of the improvements at Pensacola. The paper claimed that much of the funds appropriated for improvement to the naval yard had been squandered by the "extravagance or criminal heedlessness of the [presidential] administration." Subsequently, Secretary of the Navy David Henshaw withheld the appropriated funds from being used at Pensacola. Feeling cheated by the federal government, the *Daily Picayune* proclaimed that New York City was "strong enough in herself and her dense population," and that the city was "made to bristle with guns and to resound with notes of preparation against threatened war." Meanwhile forts in Louisiana, at Mobile Point, and Pensacola lacked the same level of arms and ammunition and were "thus left exposed, in the sudden advent of war, to fall into the enemy's hands," who they warned, would turn their own defenses against them. Even though war did not appear eminent, the invocation of conflict, and how it might affect the great emporiums of the Gulf—New Orleans and Mobile—perpetuated the desire for stronger fortifications in the region and especially at Pensacola.[23]

Pensacolians and Gulf South Southerners interested in naval improvements often felt embittered by what they saw as an unfair distribution of federal funds. They saw the Northern ports having the ability to make repairs, while the South, in their view, was left undersupported and therefore open to invasion. During a House debate in 1844 over a bill to allow the president to direct the transfer of money for the navy, Florida representative David Levy Yulee argued for passage of the bill based on the fact that the secretary of the navy had, as just mentioned, taken money away from proposed improvements to Pensacola and used it for other navy yards. Tensions concerning the appropriation of money spoke to the rising tensions between the North and South but also to fears that the Gulf of Mexico might be left defenseless and left out of the grander nationalist and imperialist project of expansion then under way in the United States.

Several years out from the destructiveness of conflicts with Native Americans in Florida, fears about British dominance in the Caribbean continued to play an important role in the growing debate over defenses in the Gulf and in West Florida. In response to the appropriations bill, the *Pensacola Gazette* reported in August that "the late threatening aspects of our relations with England, one would think, should have opened the eyes of Government to the fact of the extremely defenceless state of our commerce in the Gulf."[24] Frances Webster informed her husband Lucien—then stationed at Fort Pickens near Pensacola—of the reaction of New Yorkers to the Oregon conflict, meaning the contested boundary in the Oregon Territory between United States and Britain. "All the talk now is of war with England," wrote Frances, "on account of Oregon."[25] The British Abolition Acts of 1807 and 1833 and the gradual emancipation of slaves within British-held colonies near the Gulf of Mexico added a new dimension to American Anglophobia, especially among the slave states.

In another complication, even though relations with Mexico and the United States quickly deteriorated after the annexation of Texas, both nations possessed a fear of Great Britain. In the years preceding the war, Britain had loaned a considerable sum of money to Mexico, enforcing a favorable trade policy for itself. By 1845 the *Daily Picayune* reported that Veracruz looked with "some trepidation" at the impending arrival of the British fleet for another blockade. Great Britain had attempted to mediate a truce between the Republic of Texas and the Republic of Mexico in an attempt to resolve the border dispute that had festered between the two prior to annexation. They attempted to do the same between the United States and Mexico in an effort to stave off what many within the United States felt was an inevitable war. Within the Gulf of Mexico and the Caribbean, the British were also threatening other slave-based societies such as Cuba and Brazil. In addition, the French and British blockaded several countries along the Gulf and Atlantic Coast of South America during the antebellum period. Indeed, in the eyes of the *Pensacola Gazette*, France pursued a "grasping policy," in which it was "looking for the moment when she may seize on Cuba." In the 1840s France joined Britain in its opposition to the U.S. belligerence against Mexico. The *Baltimore Sun* and *Pensacola Gazette* reported that the French fleet was also en route to the Gulf to protect its interests there.[26] The fraught relations of Latin American nations with European powers provided a warning sign for Southern expansionists.[27]

In addition to fears over Great Britain, competition between the Gulf and the north Atlantic Coast played a significant role in fueling Gulf South desires for further improvements to the region's fortifications. "Concentrated within a length of 500 miles of the most densely populated part of the coast," the *Pensacola Gazette* argued, "are six Navy Yards, three of which, being admitted in practice to be totally superfluous, might very well be dispensed with, leaving the Boston, the Brooklyn and the Norfolk stations as they are, or even adding to their present facilities." By comparison the twenty-five hundred miles of coast from Cape Charles to the mouth of Sabine River in Texas possessed only one naval yard. As a result of this disparity, vessels within the Gulf of Mexico had to sail some two thousand miles in order to be properly refitted in the event of an accident or repair. Newspapers used examples of ships forced to sail to a Northern port for simple repairs, such as the revenue schooner *Decatur* that had to leave the Gulf to "get so slight a repair as *caulking her sides*." The Gulf was a place of "baffling winds" and "furious gales" as well as reefs and shallow shores, all of which were the mortal enemies of sailors. Ships moved gingerly through the Florida Straits, while their "probable enemy, from some one of his secure Depots" stood ready to pounce "upon the unprotected merchantman." The *Pensacola Gazette* combined frustration over the government's focus on the Northern ports with the belief that the Gulf cities were under imminent threat.[28]

The reality of military service along the Florida Gulf Coast was that it was at times harsh and could be dull. Unlike Edward Clifford Anderson, Fitch Waterman Taylor regarded Florida with mixed emotions, and the charm of the navy yard in Pensacola wore thin. Like many sailors who wound up stationed at Pensacola, he observed that it was still an "out-of-the-way place." He felt a "deep desolateness hanging about it, as if it were more of a foreign than a home station." Yet, he believed it was "a most important station in view of the national interests" both in peacetime and wartime, especially with the outbreak of the U.S.-Mexican War.[29] Both Anderson's and Taylor's reactions to the Florida Coast and the Gulf of Mexico were reminders that the Gulf Coast may have been American soil but was still at times regarded as foreign.

In early June 1846 Taylor was back in Pensacola waiting for his ship to be outfitted for war. Taylor found the town much as he had left it, describing it as a series of "monotonous rectangular streets." Along the streets were one- and two-story wooden houses with "light piazzas—some prettily embowered in green foliage and luxuriant shrubs and flowers." Despite the sprinkling of picturesque cottages, many of the houses were dilapidated or "patched up and comfortless, as the hot sun was reflected back from the arid sand of the streets." He described flowering myrtle and althea as tall as forest trees and fig trees "richly laden with their luscious fruits." The foliage and the orange trees provided shade against the intense sun of a Florida summer.[30] By 1846 the town had grown, but there were still elements of the old Spanish presidio in the town square. Boarding houses, restaurants, and oyster houses now dotted the streets. Construction and improvement of fortifications was slow to get started, yet the squadron that patrolled the Gulf of Mexico and the Caribbean already made use of the navy yard there.[31]

The Gulf Coast's connection to Latin America stemmed in part from its place on the border between South America, the Caribbean, and the United States, and while the United States may have obtained authority over the coast at the beginning of the nineteenth century, gaining control over the diverse communities and populations of the entire Gulf of Mexico, and exerting that authority, continued to frustrate Southern expansionists and army and navy forces.

In January 1846 the *Daily Picayune* announced that the improvements at Pensacola would finally begin with the construction of a seawall around the naval yard. Pensacola's population swelled with the influx of sailors, workmen, and soldiers at Fort Pickens.[32] The navy contracted James P. Kirkwood, a civil engineer living in Pensacola, to oversee the construction, and the paper hoped that war with Mexico would speed up the work "so necessary for strengthening the position of Pensacola" and give to the navy a "port on the Gulf absolutely indispensable for maintaining permanent ascendancy there."[33] Despite the commencement of construction and improvement in Pensacola, the long-awaited floating dry dock remained stalled. Impatient with the slow progress on the project, the *Daily Picayune* reminded its readers that Congress had instructed the secretary of the navy to begin construction two years prior. The dry dock would now cost over $1 million to construct, with $200,000 appropriated that same year. The *Pensacola Gazette* quoted the *New Orleans Bulletin*'s complaint that "year after year, it has been the subject of resolutions in Congress." The successive secretaries of the navy had favored improved defenses on the Gulf for several years, but according to the *Gazette*, they had "accomplished literally little or nothing," while the dock at New York progressed rapidly. The paper declared that it was time to speak out against what its editors viewed as injustices against the South and Southwest. The *Gazette* also pleaded with congressmen from the western states to pay more attention to the subject of the naval yard at Pensacola. The senators and representatives of the West, they believed, were sympathetic to the necessity of speedy construction, and those in Pensacola hoped that they would make more of an effort to move the project further along.[34]

Captain William K. Latimer, who had previously served on the Gulf Coast, returned to Pensacola in 1846 to take command of the navy yard, where he would serve for the remainder of the U.S.-Mexican War. The *Pensacola Gazette* claimed, with growing frustration, "for twenty years past, there has been comparatively, no necessity for a Dry Dock *any where but here*; and yet, under one pretext or another, it has been entirely neglected." Floridians lamented that now "every ship of the blockading squadron, which needs repairs, must go a thousand miles out of way to procure them." This new war with Mexico provided further fodder for the slew of editorials that the newspaper published drumming up support for the dry dock.[35]

Several civil engineers proposed plans for the dry dock at Pensacola, and newspapers debated the merits of the two most likely models, either a floating dock or a stone dock. The *Charleston Mercury* speculated that the sandy bottom of the bay in Pensacola would be unable to support the weight of a heavy stone dock and the construction would take far too long. The paper expressed fear that the efficiency of the navy squadron currently stationed in the Gulf would be compromised if the Pensacola improvements were not completed as quickly as possible.[36] By June 1847 the proposition for docks at Philadelphia, Pensacola, and Portsmouth had been approved. The secretary of the navy authorized $350,000 to be allocated for the purpose of completing the Pensacola dock. However, the allocated funds would not be sufficient to finish the work, and completion would be delayed yet again.[37]

By September, with no builders and not enough money, the *Pensacola Gazette* could do nothing but forlornly remark, "Well, it is our luck—Pensacola luck, and there is nothing like it in the annals of misfortune, except the luck of the poor fellow who could throw nothing but deuce ace, until he was so exasperated that he swallowed the dice—the readers know the story." The paper's editors suspected that the delays were the result of a "contrivance of the north" to maintain their hold on the shipbuilding industry by making it impossible to repair warships or ships of any kind in the Gulf of Mexico.[38] The continued delays on the project, and the way that the *Gazette* consistently focused on the naval advantages of Northern cities and ports, wove the thread of sectionalism through the many other fears, fantasies, and plans that Gulf South expansionists concocted in the 1840s.[39]

CONCLUSION

The declaration of war with Mexico must have seemed prophetic. Gulf South newspapers had long talked of war, but the war that came was not the one they expected. In many ways these wars as well as the continued conflict between Mexico and Texas formed a basis for further militarized expansion. When the naval war that Pensacolians and many others warned of came, it was against a weaker naval force—that of Mexico, not Great Britain.[40]

With the outbreak of war those in Pensacola set their minds to thinking about how the city might fit into the new conflict and what it might do for the community's prospects as a part of the nation's continued dreams of conquest in the Gulf of Mexico. At the outset, a member of one of the city's most prominent families, the Innerarity family, sent a letter to the editor of the *Pensacola Gazette* advising that "Mr. Editor, I would respectfully suggest to the authorities at Washington that if an attack is intended to be made on Tampico by troops in combination with the fleet, that Pensacola is well adapted . . . for being the rendezvous of the men required for the expedition."[41] If New Orleans was to be a major depot for soldiers and arms in the coming war, then it was hoped that Pensacola would be the home base of the Gulf Squadron and also play a part in the conflict.

Throughout the 1840s Pensacolians existed on the edges of multiple conflicts both real and imagined. The real wars with the Creek and Seminole peoples increased the presence of both the army and the navy in the region, and the imagined naval wars with Great Britain helped give voice to the argument that Pensacola should be fortified even further and the navy made stronger. Yet the frustration of Gulf South Southerners over the sluggish developments of the Pensacola naval yard exposed the raw nerve of North-South relations as well as continued anxiety over the presence of European powers within the Gulf of Mexico. The ways in which Pensacolians looked at the English and French meddling into the politics and economies of Latin American nations came to resemble the ways they began to see their relationship to the North. Advocates of the Gulf Coast hoped that they would be able to protect and expand the nation's authority over the region.

In Pensacola, construction on the dry dock picked up toward the end of the war. Afterward, the army no longer regularly used Fort McRee and Fort Pickens. In 1853 the dry dock was finally completed, expanding the ability of the naval yard to repair ships. That same year, the *Montgomery Journal* published several letters from a young man identified as Harry. On a trip to the Gulf of Mexico he stopped at Pensacola and wrote about the general state of the city. During his stay in Florida, he and several friends were treated to a tour of the naval yard. After a ride around the bay and a tour of the forts he remarked that "the first object that attracted my attention was the Dry Dock, which cost upwards of one millions of dollars."[42] With many of the improvements to the naval yard complete, Pensacolians looked forward to new possibilities for their town and its place within the nation's expansionist goals.

CHAPTER 3

Making Meaning of the U.S.-Mexican War

When Mexican troops clashed with U.S. patrol in the disputed Texas territory between the Rio Grande and the Nueces River on April 25, 1846, Antonio López de Santa Anna was far away and living in exile in Cerro, Cuba, a town three miles from Havana. Two months prior to the outbreak of war, a correspondent for the New Orleans *Daily Picayune* traveled to Cerro, where he found the former Mexican president had "constructed an amphitheater in his yard, where all the gamblers of the city resort for the purpose of cock-fighting." While he was engaging in all of this cockfighting and gambling, Santa Anna reportedly sent emissaries back and forth between Cuba and Mexico, desperate for news of the annexation issue and Mexico's reaction. Such a report in the *Daily Picayune* signaled that perhaps Santa Anna did not intend to merely sit things out and play host to American gamblers and wealthy Cubans.[1]

Throughout the decades leading up to the U.S.-Mexican War, the multiple conflicts between Anglos, Mexicans, and Native Americans, such as the Comanche and the Seminole, shaped the way that people talked about and thought about annexation, the military, and expansion. The conflicts covered in the previous chapters reshaped many of the frontier communities of the Gulf South at the same time that the United States fought to establish its authority over this unruly coast. Those conflicts and the way that Anglos employed racist visions of Mexican people and Native Americans became essential parts of U.S. propaganda in the war with Mexico. The annexation of Texas marked a transition in the way that the United States obtained territory. The U.S.-Mexican War marked the first time that the United States went to war with another independent American nation, a sister republic. However, for Anglos in Texas, this war was only another war with the same old enemy, Mexico.

Anglo Texans were not alone in their denigration of Mexican people. By this point, Americans generally held the view that Mexico was a flawed society plagued by Southern slaveholders' ultimate taboo—miscegenation. This was linked to American views of Mexico's governmental instability and viability as a nation and used to emphasize the United States' contrasting stability and progress. However, these visions and nation-state fantasies obscured many antebellum realities. As Peter Guardino asserts in his work on the U.S.-Mexican War, Mexicans did feel fealty towards the Mexican nation, and the United States itself was wracked with growing social and political divisions. Such divisions had also shaped the lengthy process of annexation in Texas and frustrated Pensacolians in West Florida when it came to improvements to military fortifications.[2]

During this period, the reality that Mexican Texans once fought alongside their Anglo counterparts became overshadowed in the minds of Americans by the notion that they were two fundamentally different peoples and races. These ideas grew both from the broader American understanding of race as well as from the encounters between Anglos and Mexicans in the Gulf South. Several key images and racist ideas shaped Anglo American expectations and visions of war in Mexico. These ideas highlight the importance of race as a construct that Southerners deployed against Latin American peoples in addition to Native Americans and African Americans. For example, despite the fact that Santa Anna had been soundly defeated in 1836 and exiled from Mexico at the outset of the U.S.-Mexican War, he was still a vexing presence in the minds of Americans. Much of their racist ideas about Mexican people were projected onto him, and he became a symbol of everything that was wrong with Mexico. The U.S. march into Mexico was largely a result of these views as well as the American belief that their expansionist visions were ordained by God. The war furthered those views as afterward the United States turned its attention to the Mexican Cession and Cuba. Accordingly, this chapter delves into the story of how preconceived racist perspectives and racist victories over Mexicans and Native Americans reinforced expansionist visions as white Americans, Southerners among them, marched through Mexico. Southerners' deeply embedded racist assumptions combined with federal military power in Texas and the Gulf South led to war and Mexican defeat, which only helped to validate the wider American expansionist vision and bolster fantasies of Southern empire.[3]

For Texans, the evolving memory of the Texas Revolution framed their expectations of the new war with Mexico and bolstered their confidence that the United States would win in the end. These ideas about Anglos' dominance over Mexicans formed part of Southerners' overall preconceived notions of Mexico and of Southerners' ability to conquer Latin American territory either as a part of the wider efforts of the nation or on their own as a slave empire in the Western Hemisphere. Santa Anna's conduct during the Texas Revolution, especially his refusal to take prisoners after the Battle of the Alamo and his order to execute prisoners of war that resulted in the Goliad Massacre, assured that he would be forever vilified in Texas. He became emblematic of many of the racist stereotypes that white Americans, Texans especially, had developed since the Texas Revolution in 1836. The possibility that it could all go wrong and that it might have except for the wiliness of figures like Sam Houston was wrapped up in Santa Anna's presence. He was ultimately viewed as an agent of chaos in this story of Anglo superiority and Mexican inferiority.

The expansionist fantasies and nightmares that made Texas's annexation seem necessary collided with debates over whether or not Mexico was a viable nation to create a potent mixture of land grabbing and war propaganda. Such propaganda positioned the United States as the only nation that could do republicanism the right way. Pro-war propagandists positioned the country as the only one that stood ready to inherit the vast territory of Texas, the Southwest, and California and make them prosper.[4] At the center of this expansionist vision as always, was race and for Southerners, the expansion of slavery. The United States was now actively competing with a fellow republican nation that had a complex racial makeup and no chattel slavery. This new opponent required slight changes in strategy.[5]

While white Southerners such as John C. Calhoun eventually opposed annexing territory south of the Rio Grande, many who supported expansion in the Gulf South, and Texas especially, supported the "all Mexico" idea. They believed that the South's cotton agriculture and its slave-based society could extend to the Pacific Ocean and displace the "mongrelized" populations of Mexico. The U.S.-Mexican War was the latest in a long line of border skirmishes and transgressions crisscrossing the region. For Texans especially, the war was a deeply local event as much as it was a national one. Within Texas the war's significance revolved around Texan efforts to become a state, despite the fact that President James K. Polk was also interested in annexing California. Further complicating matters, although many within the Gulf South supported the war, it unsettled the region in unanticipated ways.

Soldiers and sailors brought with them experiences from previous conflicts and their notions of racial superiority as they rampaged across the Mexican landscape and through Mexican communities. The construction of propaganda, the blockade of Mexico's Gulf ports, and the movement of troops through the Gulf South's communities brought the war to the Gulf South's doorstep in ways inland communities elsewhere in the South did not experience. Once the war was over, Southerners felt they had fought for the territory ceded by Mexico. The experiences of soldiers and sailors and their views of Mexicans evolved out of the process of invasion and warfare, which further entrenched whites' racist views of Mexicans within the U.S.-Mexico borderlands and the Gulf South.[6]

RACE, LAND LUST, AND THE GULF SOUTH

The Texas-Mexico border remained the main point of contention in 1846 for many living in Gulf communities, but the fate of California was also on the minds of Americans as the possibility of war loomed on the horizon. James D. B. De Bow published a pamphlet concerning the "Oregon question," which he later republished in the *De Bow's Review* in January 1846, that touched on the California question as well. De Bow argued that under Mexico, California "must ever be of trifling importance," and if citizens in the state attempted independence, then it would have "little prospect beyond a nerveless imbecility." According to De Bow's thinking, California and much of Mexico's northern territory had little to no future if left under Mexican control. The region ultimately needed a guiding hand in the form of American settlement. De Bow's views were far from unique. Mexico's political instability and the difficulty it had in asserting control over the northern states were often viewed as reasons that California, like Texas, would be better off under the banner of the United States.[7]

Racist American perspectives shaped the way that the United States government under an expansionist president interacted with Mexico over Texas annexation and the nation's larger territorial goals. President Polk commenced his efforts to obtain territory in the West in November of 1845, when he appointed John Slidell, a former representative of Louisiana, as minister to Mexico. Born in New York, Slidell relocated to Louisiana after he wounded another man in a contest over the affections of a young woman. Slidell quickly took to his new Southern surroundings and began to practice law in New Orleans. By 1845 Slidell had gained a reputation as a strong states-rights Democrat who was very much invested in territorial expansion. Polk instructed Slidell to use a firm hand with the Mexicans, with the main goal of getting as much territory out of Mexican hands as possible and maintaining the Texas southern border at the Rio Grande. Polk requested that Slidell make it known to the Mexican government that the United States was willing to pay $5 million in exchange for Texas and New

Mexico. The offer rose to $25 million if the Mexicans threw in California. If the Mexicans refused to negotiate a deal, then President Polk planned to pursue the issue of U.S. claims against Mexico, which amounted to some $3 million.[8]

Though he spoke Spanish, Slidell thought very little of Mexicans and had no real sympathy for Mexico's economic trials or political instability. In many ways, this shaped Slidell's aborted negotiations. Before arriving in Mexico, he scribbled in a letter that he had no "very exalted idea of the caliber of the Mexican intellect." It took weeks for Slidell to make it to Veracruz. He was waylaid in New Orleans while the American consul at Veracruz attempted to ascertain whether Slidell would even be received. Slidell refused to honor the Mexican government's wishes in terms of how the American diplomat should proceed. After arriving in Veracruz, Slidell quickly made his way to Mexico City despite the fact that no one in the Mexican government authorized him to do so, and he was actually instructed to wait in Veracruz. Knowing that the U.S. diplomat was there to strike a deal for annexing California, and in the midst of governmental upheaval, Mexican officials were in no mood to entertain Slidell's interest in wheeling and dealing.[9]

Polk's 1845 message to Congress laid out the reasoning he would later use to declare war. Among the grievances against Mexico was the state of Texas' border security and its decade's long contest with Mexico over the exact demarcation of that boundary. Polk omitted from the text any mention of his interests in California and the Southwest because annexing any of that territory was perceived as illegitimate by Britain and France, to which Mexico had given tracts of land as payment for their debts. Instead, Polk focused on Texas and a series of violations on the part of Mexicans against Americans. He described Texas annexation as a "bloodless achievement," stating that "the sword has had no part in the victory." But it wasn't bloodless, and the sword played a significant part in the story of Texas annexation, as it had in the settlement of Florida. Polk also recalled the history of armed conflict between Texas and Mexico, but he separated the annexation part of this history, omitted the violence that took place in Texas that pushed Mexicans and Native Americans out of the territory, and helped to pave the way for annexation in the first place. Despite this supposedly peaceful transition, Texas, Polk argued, "had declared her independence, and maintained it by her arms for more than nine years."[10]

Polk then invoked several aspects of expansionism. He emphasized the need to maintain the principles of the Monroe Doctrine and insisted "jealousy among the different sovereigns of Europe, lest any one of them might become too powerful for the rest, has caused them anxiously to desire the establishment of what they term the balance of power. It cannot be permitted to have any application on the North American continent, and especially to the United States." Polk maintained that it was imperative that the United States and all nations in the Americas "ever maintain the principle, that the people of this continent alone have the right to decide their own destiny." "This will be a question," he warned, "for them and us to determine, without any foreign interposition," referencing Great Britain's attempt to play mediator between the Republic of Texas and Mexico. According to this line of thinking, the nation's ability to grow was not only under threat from the physical presence of such nations but also threatened by European foreign policies and political philosophies.[11]

The Gulf South and military power remained important to the process of expansion that Polk outlined, and he emphasized the need for an increased standing navy to patrol the Gulf of Mexico. He noted the importance of maintaining a small standing army, stating the nation's "reliance for protection and defense on the land must be mainly on our citizen soldiers." However, an army was incapable of protecting coastlines, harbors, or oceans. A larger navy for the protection of the commerce that exited the Mississippi River had to be achieved at all costs.[12] Recalling both the process of annexation and efforts by Pensacolians to garner funding for improvements to the naval yard, Polk's annual message emphasized both the threats of European intervention and the right of the United States to take ownership of the territory of North America, as the Monroe Doctrine assured both a hostility toward European colonizers and the right of U.S. conquest.[13]

Meanwhile, Slidell admitted defeat in his diplomatic negotiations with Mexico and proceeded back to the United States. His failure to obtain California coupled with the contested status of Texas set the wheels in motion for a show of military power in the Texas borderlands. With the diplomatic mission in ruins, Polk ordered Secretary of War William Marcy to send General Zachary Taylor's troops to the contested strip of land between the Nueces River and Rio Grande. Secretary of the Navy George Bancroft ordered the squadron under Commodore, David Conner that patrolled the Gulf of Mexico, the Caribbean, and the Atlantic to stay on high alert. Both the army and the navy now mobilized demonstrations of force.[14]

Expansionists in the Gulf South fixated on the notion of naval superiority in the Gulf of Mexico and increased army presence in places like Florida and Texas, often warning that some foreign power might sneak into the Gulf ports if they were not well protected. Polk's fears about the transgression of Texas's borders extended into the Gulf of Mexico when he ordered naval squadrons to patrol and blockade Mexican ports in the Gulf and then the Pacific Coast. Polk stated that the "result has been that Mexico has made no aggressive movement, and our military and naval commanders have executed their orders with such discretion that the peace of the two Republics has not been disturbed." One of the reasons that Polk urged for a larger standing navy was to protect the American presence in the Gulf of Mexico and to guard against the fear that if the Mississippi River "below New Orleans," was occupied by a hostile force that might "stagnate, the whole export trade of the Mississippi and affect the value of the agricultural products of the entire valley of that mighty river and its tributaries." Such fears played a central role in the expansionism that shaped the Gulf South throughout the Mexican War and beyond it.

On May 14, 1846, Commodore Conner declared a blockade of the Mexican Gulf ports, including Matamoros, Tampico, Alvarado, and Veracruz. U.S. naval power in the Gulf increased in the months between the annexation of Texas and the outbreak of the war with Mexico. Like Zachary Taylor's troops, who occupied and "monitored" the contested Texas-Mexico border region, the Gulf Squadron also took measures to militarize the maritime borderland of the Gulf of Mexico. Echoing Polk's sentiments, the *Daily Picayune* reported they went out "armed to the teeth, for the protection of our Commerce in the Gulf, and blockading the ports of Mexico." The *American Flag*, published in Matamoros, noted in November that the American Squadron exercised a "rigid surveillance along the coast" and was ordering off all Yucatanese vessels that attempted to make port in the communities between Tabasco and the Rio Grande. To prevent naval ships from entering the river, Mexican forces ran long chain cables across the Rio Grande that sunk several naval vessels.[15]

Taylor chose Corpus Christi as the site of his base camp, and by spring a significant portion of the U.S. Army was housed there. The camp offered Corpus Christi a chance to increase its trade with the army, and community founders like Henry Kinney believed that the army's presence so close to their small village would bolster its importance on the Gulf Coast. Before the army arrived, Corpus Christi was little more than a cluster of thirty houses and a few saloons. By the time Taylor relocated his camp to the northern bank of the Rio Grande in 1846, there were roughly four thousand men stationed there. Texans were quickly attracted to the camp and all manner of entertainment and services for the soldiers were erected near it, including drinking establishments and theaters.[16] Taylor's army also occupied a site across from the Mexican town of Matamoros. Mexican forces outnumbering Taylor's army took up residence outside Matamoros. Americans feared that Polk had sent an undermanned force into the disputed territory and that the camp would be obliterated and the border "stolen" once again by the much stronger Mexican force.[17]

As previously stated, for many months in 1846, the two forces had circled around each other within the disputed territory. Just weeks before, on April 25, 1846, the two forces had finally found each other and doomed any possible hope for the establishment of "friendly relation." Mexican soldiers attacked a detachment of U.S. cavalry that had been sent out to spy on Mexican troop movements, killing sixteen men. This, combined with Slidell's diplomatic failures, presented enough causes for Polk's war. After learning of the skirmish, Congress declared war. Polk claimed that the Mexican army had been preparing a massive invasion of Texas and that this was the reason to send Taylor's troops further into the territory, which Polk famously referred to as "American soil." Meanwhile, in the time between the initial order to occupy South Texas and the skirmish, the resolutions between Texas and the United States had been formalized, making Texas a state. According to Polk's thinking, Mexico invaded the United States rather than protected its interests in a region in dispute.[18]

While the navy patrolled the Gulf, the army prepared for war. In the 1840s the U.S. Army was a small force. Before the U.S.-Mexican War it numbered only fifty-five hundred men and officers who were stationed throughout the territories and newly created states. After May 13, 1846, when the United States declared war on Mexico, Congress authorized Polk to raise fifty thousand volunteers for twelve months, calling on men from across the nation to volunteer for service in Mexico. The government first called up troops from the states closest to Mexico. Throughout the South, elite men in cities and towns created volunteer regiments.[19]

Newspapers, magazines, and journals chronicled the army and the navy's efforts to occupy the Rio Grande and the Mexican Gulf Coast. The doings of Taylor's army quickly became daily news throughout the nation. For many of Taylor's soldiers it was the first time that they had come into contact with Mexican people. Yet as historian Robert Johannsen observed, it was not the first time that Americans engaged in the practice of essentializing and producing racist depictions of Mexican culture. Romanticized literature concerning the conquest of Mexico had gained popularity in the 1820s after Mexico won its independence; it had also become entangled with the contest between Mexico and Texas in 1840s.[20] Soldiers' and correspondents' descriptions of their interactions with Mexicans who also lived near the Corpus Christi camp alluded to the way that their experiences in the Texas borderlands further shaped the way Americans came to see Mexican people, as well as the way they would interact with Mexicans during the war. While encamped at Corpus Christi one *Daily Picayune* correspondent described the Mexicans who entered the camp to trade as a "rag-tail and bob-tail, thievish, cut-throat set of cowards they must be, according to some of the specimens I have seen; but they are all unsurpassed in horsemanship." Then he proclaimed, "No wonder an organized government cannot exist among the Mexicans!" The correspondent's descriptions of the Mexican traders as animal-like criminals and cutthroats were all different aspects of an emerging image of Mexican people similar to those of Native Americans and African Americans. White Americans portrayed Native Americans and African Americans as more animalistic, brutish, lazy, and untrustworthy. In the antebellum era this animalistic brutishness justified white Americans' belief that they should take land from Native Americans and continue to enslave African Americans. This racism also justified the incredible violence that white Americans used to take Native land and enslave black people.[21]

The memory of Spanish conquest of the Aztecs helped fuel 1840s racism toward Mexicans and provided an imagery and language for white American expectations of victory. William Prescott's *History of the Conquest of Mexico* was published in 1843, just in time for annexation and war. The book became quite popular with President Polk and members of his administration as well as many soldiers and sailors. Historian Jenny Franchot notes that Prescott used the story of the conquest as a metaphor for a racially pure Protestantism against a racially mixed and thus inferior Catholicism. Indeed, the prevalence of Catholicism within Mexico came to be seen as one of the many reasons the country was destined to lose the war.[22]

Supporters of the war, North and South, imagined themselves as inheritors of Spain's authority over Mexico, and many newspapermen and soldiers used the story of *La Conquista* to heighten expectations of speedy success. Overlooking Mexico's hard-fought independence, the Louisiana lawyer and political scholar Gustavus Schmidt reasoned that the Conquest of Mexico by Spain had been the most significant moment in the nation's history, calling it a "brilliant and extraordinary event," in his essay on Mexican society published in 1846 in the *De Bow's Review*. Like Prescott, Schmidt recounted a history of Mexico within which the Mexican War could be placed. Schmidt admired the ancient civilizations that lived in Mexico prior to Hernán Cortés's arrival. According to Schmidt, the Aztecs with their magnificent palaces and taste for war turned to the "bitter fruits which the descendants of the race . . . do now reap, and which will long obstruct their efforts to establish a stable and rational government," meaning that nineteenth-century Mexicans suffered from this perceived decadence, which preordained that they would never be able to create a stable government.²³ Schmidt ultimately attempted to portray Mexico sympathetically. However, the same imagery of Mexicans as a conquered mixed-race people lacking in the hallmarks of civilization persisted in his work and in other writings published in the South. The Galveston *Civilian and Gazette* remarked on the number of articles concerning the history of Mexico published in papers throughout the United States. An article reprinted from a St. Louis paper retold the story of Cortés's conquest and asked, "How long will our army be marching to the same place?" The *Pensacola Gazette* reported that the Paris journals all sided with the United States and predicted an "early conquest."²⁴ Placing the nation's war with Mexico within this larger context of Spain's conquest of Mexico helped to further legitimize it.

Newspaper editors did much of the work of legitimizing the war. They discussed the developments but also sold it to a public clamoring for stories of heroism against a new foreign enemy that had been painted as an enemy of democracy. In towns along the Rio Grande publishers churned out newspapers for civilians and soldiers alike. For example, editors Isaac Neville Fleeson and William G. Dryden published the *Republic of the Rio Grande and Friend of the People*. Dryden arrived in Texas in 1840 and became involved in the short-lived Santa Fe Expedition. Living on the banks of the Rio Grande, Dryden soon became identified with the federalists in Mexico, which led him to found the bilingual paper. The paper gained its name from a short-lived uprising in 1840 in which federalist leaders in Mexico's northern states of Tamualipas, Nuevo Leon, and Coahuila attempted to claim independence from the Santa Anna-run central government of Mexico, as the Texans had done in 1836. At the outset of the war Isaac Fleeson reorganized the newspaper into the *American Flag* with John R. Palmer. The *American Flag* ran throughout the war. Like their newspapers, Fleeson and Dryden were swallowed up in the war effort, and their lives became entangled in the process of territorial expansion. Fleeson was born in Mississippi but found himself in Texas where he began his newspaper career. Fleeson ran off with the Mobile Greys to the Texas frontier during the Texas Revolution and began working in local newspapers in the early 1840s. His first encounter with the U.S. Army and its mission of occupation in Corpus Christi occurred when he created a newspaper to advocate for the army's presence in the region.²⁵

Fleeson's life and newspaper demonstrated the various ways that people and ideas wove different stages of expansion together. He published a poem by Theodore Eckerson in 1846 in the *American Flag*. Eckerson was a veteran of the Seminole Indian Wars and now a soldier in Taylor's army in

Mexico. The poem, "The 'Lone Star,'" was a statement to both the nation and the new state of Texas that it was no longer alone in its struggle against Mexico; it also recalled the struggle that Texans faced in the long process of annexation. Eckerson wrote, "no longer alone art thou/the struggle no longer thine/but safely inaugered now/in a glorious wreath to shine!" Texas's struggle had been subsumed within the larger struggle of the nation's expansionist interests in Latin America. Eckerson encouraged Texans to strike out at Mexico, proclaiming "your conquest is Mexico: / your motto still 'onward' be—'Remember the Alamo.'" Eckerson linked several important aspects of expansion together to form a broader picture of Americans conquering Mexico through the process of settling and annexing Texas.[26]

Expansion and war were both bloody businesses, and the bloody business of the U.S.-Mexican War as it was waged in northern Mexico included a cast of characters who had fought other wars of expansion. The Texas Rangers who went to war with Taylor's army and fought in the first two battles, Palo Alto and Resaca de la Palma, already had a reputation. The Rangers formed during the Texas Republic as a mobile force employed in Texas to target Native American nations who raided settlements as well as policing Tejano communities. Their fame remained somewhat localized prior to the outbreak of war, but during the first two battles they gained national attention as Taylor's "eyes and ears," a reconnaissance force for the army of invasion. Dryden wrote about them in *Republic of the Rio Grande* as a band of rugged frontiersmen exemplifying all that Texas and Texans had to offer the nation during its war with Mexico. The paper described their military prowess by recalling that "Cos, Santa Ana, Woll and Basques, can attest how musically their rifles ring, and how deadly is their aim; and the Comanches, who have so often proved their skill in stealing horses and blinding their trail, can boast of few instances in which the right of property was left twenty-four hours undisputed." The article used those names to reference the Texas Revolution as well as the Rangers' pursuit of Comanche raiders. The Rangers were celebrated as being perfectly at home in the Rio Grande and needing little more than "his little bag of salt, to season the dry venison." He was "accustomed to rely upon himself, full of resources, and ready for an emergency when it arises, as if he had foreseen and deliberately prepared for it, he roams over the plains as fearlessly as its own wild denizen." They were the frontier ideal, combining individualistic ruggedness and the soldiering, and thus, would make perfect scouts for the army as it invaded northern Mexico.[27]

The history of Texas and Mexico through the 1830s and 1840s had evolved in both local memory and as part of the regional and national fantasy of expansion and the war. A letter supposedly written by a mother to her son who was with Taylor's army in Mexico exemplified this. It was printed in the *Republic from the Rio Grande* in June 1846. She wrote, "The bones of my first born, for aught I know, are yet unburied on the plains of Goliad, and grief for his loss, broke his father's heart." She insisted that "there is good Spanish blood in parts of Mexico, and Spaniards are not cowards as the Peninsula war will testify," bringing together war in Europe with war in the United States and the southwest borderlands. Alexander Lander, in his history of the Galveston Riflemen, wrote that he thought that the seeds of the war were planted with the first shots of the Texas Revolution, and "at last worn out with the unceasing aggression of the inhumane enemy, the people—the sons of free and independent ancestry—began to look upon the old mother states from whence they came." For these Texans, the movement of the U.S. Army under General Taylor across the Rio Grande and into the northern states of Mexico was a culmination of their efforts throughout the 1830s and 1840s. According to Lander, Taylor was on their frontier "hourly expecting to have the trouble of chastising this same treacherous foe, for their outrages."[28]

For those living in the Gulf of Mexico watching these different wars take shape, the U.S.-Mexican War was inevitable. For them the conflict was not only over a boundary disagreement between nations; rather—just as with past conflicts with Mexicans and Native Americans—it was between "widely different races on the continent," as the people of Texas cried out for another "San Jacinto style" victory over their Mexican opponents.[29] San Jacinto, the final battle of the Texas Revolution, held a special significance for those who had lived through it and those who had migrated to Texas Republic. The Anglo Americans already living in Texas, especially those who had fought against the Mexican army during the Texas Revolution possessed deeply ingrained ideas about Mexico as a land of "barbarism, superstition, ignorance, and social disorder."[30]

Mexicans had their own ideas about Anglo Americans and their persistent expansionism. Prior to the annexation of Texas, Mexico threatened to declare war if the United States made Texas a state. As stated in chapter 1, Mexicans were suspicious of American expansion and Manifest Destiny. They were also well aware of American racist depictions of their society. As Paul Guardino notes, Mexican intellectuals and visitors to the United States interpreted their northern neighbor's desire for ever-more land as avarice, and greed that infected the nation and individual Americans. While Americans tended to treat Mexicans as a single race, most Mexicans did not view themselves that way even if they did interpret the war with the United States as one between two races. Theirs was a society with multiple races, albeit one governed by the inheritors of Spanish blood and culture. Mexicans too had their racial categorizations and notions of superiority and inferiority, believing that their society was superior to that of the United States because, while the lighter-skinned Spanish descendants were in charge, Mexican society had incorporated Native Americans and mestizos in a proper social hierarchy. Ironically, Mexicans viewed American society as too racially heterogenous, due to the influx of immigrants from other nations. Mexican propagandists predicted that Americans wanted to enslave Mexicans and the writer and politician Carlos María de Bustamante reported rumors that Mexicans were being sold as slaves in the slave markets in New Orleans. Throughout the war Mexican people did not adhere to or agree with the image of themselves that American soldiers brought with them.[31]

THE ARRIVAL OF SANTA ANNA

On August 16, 1846, Antonio López de Santa Anna slipped through the U.S. blockade in the Gulf of Mexico and set foot on his home soil. Fitch Waterman Taylor bemoaned the event, writing, "Say ye no more to this gallant force... if a steamer with a Mexican General on board, with hostile intentions against the American government can be allowed to pass through the blockade uninterrupted and unquestioned." Santa Anna's presence altered the course of the war and for many Americans served as further evidence that Mexico was a weakened nation with weak people. While in exile, Santa Anna categorized the conflict between the two republics as the United States swooping down on its "sister and neighbor, Mexico, already torn by civil wars." For his part, Raphael Semmes, captain of the U.S.S. *Somers* during the war, described Santa Anna as having been "the archdemon of discord in Mexico, for more than a quarter of a century."[32]

Americans held multiple, sometimes even seemingly contradictory, images of Mexicans that were ultimately shaped by their ideas of class status. While working-class and impoverished Mexicans were often treated as an unruly and mixed-race dangerous lot, wealthier Mexicans were often portrayed differently. As a part of the larger history of American expansion in the Gulf of Mexico throughout the 1830s and 1840s, Santa Anna's image as a sinister, antirepublican, aristocratic, and temperamental figure helped to define Mexico in the minds of expansionists and in the American public consciousness as a nation that was the complete opposite of the United States. Santa Anna was called the "Napoleon of the West," despite having never successfully conquered any territory in North or South America. In Mexico, he was simultaneously reviled as a villain and adored as a hero by different portions of society and at different times in the decades after Mexican independence. Santa Anna's changeable nature and tyrannical governance exemplified the evolving vision of Mexico as a nation populated by treacherous, vain, capricious, and immoral people. In a time of mythmaking, he provided the perfect foe for Anglo Americans who saw themselves in contrast as valiant, stalwart, and moral.[33] Since the close of the Texas Revolution, Santa Anna came to exemplify all the negative aspects that Anglo Americans saw in Mexico.

Anglos incorporated Mexicans' changeable views of Santa Anna into their reasoning as to why Mexico should not be allowed to control their northwestern territory that existed under its flag.[34] Santa Anna's defeat at the hands of the rebel Texan army in 1836 and his subsequent humiliation after being taken prisoner formed the basis of Texas's foundational mythology.[35] As already discussed, Santa Ana went into exile in 1845. U.S. expansionists and war supporters continued to use Santa Anna as a part of the Texas Revolution's connection to the present war. They used his command of the army and usurpation of the presidency during the U.S-Mexican War as evidence of the guilt of the Mexican republic and further evidence that Mexican society as a whole was deeply flawed and unworthy of the thousands of square miles of land under its authority. That said, Santa Anna was clever enough to convince the United States that he would be able to negotiate a quick end to the war. As a result, James Polk allowed Santa Anna to pass the blockade and enter Mexico. The passage was the occasion for the aformentioned lament of Fitch Taylor, a sailor above one of the blockading ships: "say ye no more to this gallant force, for the blockade of the Mexican ports; and worst of all, for the strict blockade of the harbor of Veracruz, if a steamer with a Mexican General on board, with hostile intentions against the American government can be allowed to pass through the blockade uninterrupted and unquestioned."[36]

While Americans tended to paint Santa Anna as little more than a gambler and a nefarious murderer, he appealed to many in the Mexican officer corps due to his experience leading soldiers into battle and conducting war within the Mexican landscape. Throughout the 1830s and 1840s Santa Anna worked to stay involved in Mexican politics and contributed to governmental instability through his constant shifts in political loyalties. He began his career as a federalist, helping to defeat Mexico's first monarch, Agustín Iturbide, and bring about the rise of representative government. As a result, Mexicans' relationship with Santa Anna was far more complex than many Anglo outsiders fully recognized or were perhaps willing to admit. *The American Flag* related the events of Santa Anna's arrival into Veracruz on

September 12, 1846: "Santa Anna's arrival was celebrated in that city with great pomp. A public dinner was given him, which was attended by all the foreign consuls, city authorities, a carriage was in readiness to conduct his Excellency to the hall of festivity, but he preferred walking the distance, notwithstanding the irritable state of his leg. What condescension!"[37] The *Daily Picayune* initially believed Santa Ana's return to be a hoax but then concluded that the audacity of returning to Mexico from forced exile was so characteristic of the former Mexican president that it must have been true. "He is a monster of duplicity, and his affected reluctance to assume the reins of power at once and openly, may be a subterfuge by which to escape from the fulfillment of pledges which he has given," the newspaper declared. The editors suspected "that this reluctance *is* affected, is false and hallow . . . the only question with us is, who is to be made the victim of his duplicity?"[38]

Ultimately, both sides became victims to his duplicity, as Santa Anna played the two sides against each other. To the Mexicans and President Valentín Gómez Farías, he promised that he would fight the Americans but also promised not to usurp power and name himself president as was his compulsion. To the Americans, Santa Anna suggested that he might be able to broker a peace between the United States and Mexico and avoid further bloodshed. More importantly, he promised that once he entered the country, he would broker the sale of the territories that Slidell had attempted to purchase before the start of the war. Such overtures were the main reason that the Gulf Squadron blockade permitted him into the country. Yet, he quickly broke his promises to the Mexican government that the constitution reestablished as a federalist system, replacing the more centralist system that the country adopted in the 1830s, for which Santa Anna had, in part, been responsible. Santa Anna's arrival and entrance into the field presaged the U.S. invasion of Veracruz on March 28, 1847. That invasion launched a whole new phase of the war, as forces under Winfield Scott marched into the heart of Mexico.[39]

THE EFFECTS OF THE BLOCKADE

While the United States focused on the glorious battles fought by the army as it marched through northern Mexico, the navy went about blockading Mexican ports. Both the army and the navy were integral to American expansionism, and both were essential in supporting the nation's interst in dominating the Gulf of Mexico throughout the early nineteenth century. The army sought to extend the United States' dominion into the southwest borderlands and the navy was supposed to do the same on the sea.[40]

The unrelenting effort to support expansion at times affected the Gulf South communities in ways they could not predict, and the onset of the naval blockade and the march to war in Mexico were examples of this phenomenon. The coast experienced a reordering as the navy's main task shifted away from patrolling the coastline in places like Florida and the Caribbean toward stopping trade into Mexico's Gulf and Pacific ports. The region's ships, whether naval ships or civilian vessels, would also be used to move men to the front lines in Mexico. The navy commissioned several ships to transport several companies to Veracruz, Matamoros, and Corpus Christi. By May 1846 thousands of young men throughout the United States answered the call and flooded into New Orleans and Mobile. Hotels in New Orleans filled to capacity and men camped in the ouskirts of the city. The *Daily Picayune* announced that the steamship *New York* had taken four companies from the barracks located a few miles south of New Orleans and yet more steamers busily brought down young men from the towns and parishes in Louisiana.[41] While the newspapers and journals celebrated the war and the soldiers going to fight it, the constant influx of unknown young men and soldiers resulted in a riot when volunteers stormed the streets of New Orleans. There was also a riot aboard one of the steamships on the Rio Grande that was waiting to take several companies of volunteers to Camargo in Mexico. Several companies of Georgians erupted into a riot on board; when another company from Illinois boarded the ship to quell the unrest, thirty men were wounded and several were executed for instigating it.[42]

Though many within Gulf Coast communities supported the war, its conduct caused disruptions to the things they were trying to protect. In 1846 Judah P. Benjamin wrote an article in the *De Bow's Review* in which he called into question whether Gulf Coast merchants were abiding by international law. He wrote, "Already have questions occurred, growing out of this new state of things ... already have vessels, fitted out in New Orleans, been turned away from Mexican ports, without being permitted to land their cargoes; and already have controversies arisen in relation to the effect produced by this interruption of their voyages in the respective rights, duties, and obligations of freighters, ship-owners, and insurers." He then proceeded to outline all the reasons why a blockade is just during war and why New Orleans merchants should not be surprised at being turned away.[43]

Raphael Semmes's account of the blockade reflected the experience of many aboard naval ships during the war. Semmes supported the United States' efforts to expand into Latin American territory and denigrated the

Mexican people as unfit to rule over such a large territory. Yet he was critical of the U.S. strategy during the war and felt the navy was underutilized. He described the government's strategies as follows: "It was evidently its policy—indeed the only policy—to carry on the war wholly on land, leaving the navy to act the subordinate, but not less onerous part of harassing and annoying the enemy on his sea-board . . . and of aiding our forces, in the duties of transport, convoy, making descents, etc." Born in Charles County, Maryland, Semmes grew up on his uncle's tales of his nineteen transatlantic crossings and numerous other naval exploits. Semmes joined the navy as a midshipman in 1826. In 1837 he was called into duty and served aboard the U.S.S. *Constitution* during the Seminole Indian War. He married shortly after and eventually settled in Pensacola, purchasing a piece of property called Prospect Hill across the Perdido River near the naval yard. He eventually moved his family to Mobile in the hopes of providing his children with better education; however, his duties kept him primarily based in the Pensacola naval yard.

Before the war, the Gulf Squadron—of which Semmes was a part—primarily patrolled throughout the Gulf and the West Indies. From 1840 to 1845 Semmes served on several ships, doing survey work in and around the Gulf. One of the Gulf Squadron's patrol routes required them to sail from Pensacola to the Mississippi and then out to Cape Antonio along the north side of Cuba, before passing between Cuba and St. Domingo and returning to Pensacola. Their patrol routes into the Caribbean and throughout the Gulf of Mexico signaled the importance of the Caribbean to the United States. Semmes and his shipmates found themselves sailing this same route when they received news that the war had commenced in earnest. The brig to which Semmes was assigned was temporarily ordered from the Gulf and sent on a cruise of five weeks to the West Indies and the island of St. Domingo. At the time of their departure Semmes claimed that the naval officers "partook of the incredulity of our brethren of the army, in regard to the probability of a war with Mexico." Because the declaration of war did not occur immediately after the initial short firefight, Semmes and his men left the Texas coast not knowing the war had actually started. While at Puerto Plata, Santo Domingo, the ship finally received U.S. newspapers and news of their new mission, the blockade of Mexico.[44]

When news did reach the sailors, they poured over every detail of the army's movements, and Semmes "felt the more proud of our brethren of the army, from the circumstances of having received the intelligence of their exploits in a foreign land." Despite its crew wanting to set sail for Mexico, Semmes's ship remained in Santo Domingo. After sailing to Port au Prince, the ship finally made its way back to Pensacola, sailing into the bay on July 1, 1846, four months after the start of the war. Only after having received fresh water and provisions did the ship finally set off for Veracruz to join the rest of the Gulf Squadron and participate in the blockade of Mexican Gulf ports.[45]

The experience of the blockade, especially in the early days, was filled with monotony. Between the declaration of the blockade and the capture of Veracruz, Semmes believed "no duties could have been more irksome than those which devolved upon the navy." During this period they were largely confined to their ships and "engaged in the most arduous and active cruising." The blockade stopped almost all merchant traffic coming out of Mexican ports throughout the duration of the war. For Semmes, who was stationed on the flagship of the squadron, the experience of war aboard a ship that never went anywhere was far more exhausting than service aboard a blockading ship that was, at the very least, moving. "We looked forth from our ship, as from a prison," recalled Semmes.[46] Unlike the army, the navy had no enemy to actively fight as the Mexican navy was almost nonexistent. From the perspectives of those like Semmes, serving in the navy made it difficult for them to display their bravery to their satisfaction. On the *Somers*, Semmes experienced some of the most exciting events of the blockade, though these had nothing to do with battle and everything to do with the unpredictable weather of the Gulf of Mexico. The ship nearly sank in a terrible storm. Many of the men jumped overboard and a British ship later fished them out. In another incident, at a funeral for an American sailor, the fact that the Spanish and French did not lower their flags to half mast as was the custom angered Fitch Waterman Taylor. He blamed this lack of manners on Catholicism, which he deemed a "false system," and those that worshipped it degenerate.[47]

Despite the blockade, European ships remained a constant presence along the Mexican Gulf Coast. The British, French, and Spanish ships that clustered around the blockaded Mexican ports created some tensions among the various ships sailing up and down the Mexican coast. In June, the *Barbados Globe* reported that one of Britain's ships was en route to Veracruz, acting on a report that the U.S. Navy prevented the English sloop *Rose* from entering the Mexican port. The rumor in town was "that this vessel has brought orders to the commander of the Endymion, to proceed at once to Vera Cruz, there to join the Vindictive and other ships of war, in consequence of her Majesty's sloop *Rose* having been prevented by an American squadron from entering one of the Mexican ports." In response the *Daily Picayune* claimed that "we do not believe a word said about the refusal to allow the Rose to enter a Mexican port. At last accounts, we think, she was lying at Vera Cruz."[48] Trade continued even with the blockade.

However, trade stopped and panic struck as other rumors flooded Veracruz, pointing toward invasion. Semmes claimed that the Gulf Squadron remained too weak to undertake a full attack on Veracruz during the siege of the city. He thought they expected "us to lay waste to the whole of the enemy's coast, by fire and sword." San Juan de Ulua, a large and imposing stone fortress, guarded the opening of the bay of Veracruz. As a result, the city was one of the only Mexican port cities on the entire coast capable of defending itself against an American attack. Being one of the most prosperous cities with one of the largest ports as well as sitting near roads leading directly to the heart of the Mexican interior made it the most obvious point of entrance for the Americans.[49]

THE WAR ON LAND

While the Gulf Squadron conducted its blockade, the U.S. Army under General Zachary Taylor descended down through northern Mexico in the spring and summer of 1846. For many of the volunteers, their march into Mexico was the first time they saw firsthand how a foreign people lived. As in most experiences with the unfamiliar, soldiers who wrote home to their loved ones used their prior experiences and perceptions of Native Americans and African Americans to describe what it was they were doing and seeing. In so doing, they did privately what newspapers and journals did publicly, constructing racist images while waging war against Mexico.

While Albert Sidney Johnston and his family's experiences with war were not entirely representative of every U.S. soldier in Mexico, they shed light on the ways in which individuals encountered both the fantasies and realities of territorial expansion. His correspondence also sheds light on the process of mobilization in the region and provides the perspective of white men who had waged violence against racial others for the majority of their lives. Retired from military service and attempting to live life as a planter near Galveston prior to the outbreak of the U.S.-Mexican War, Johnston read the news of war along with everyone else. Though he saved an extra that was published by the *Galveston Gazette* on the day that the United States declared war on Mexico, in March 1846 his own part in the war remained uncertain.

As Johnston pondered over his choices, the Texas state legislature raised the state's military quota. Governor James Pinckney Henderson wrote to Johnston, urging him to join the Texan regiments at Port Isabel, south of Galveston, as they prepared to join Taylor's army. Taylor also wrote to Johnston urging him to join the army at Point Isabel. Henderson even pushed a mutual friend to urge Johnston to command the regiment. Johnston was made colonel of the First Regiment of Foot Riflemen of Texas, as he had hoped he would be, and was "ready and anxious to take the field."[50] Charles G. Bryant, a former Texas soldier and merchant, reasoned that Johnston could "fill up the foot Brigade, it can be done in ten or fifteen days at the farthest." Bryant even offered to raise his own company for Johnston. His letter signaled the extent to which New Orleans and the Gulf South had become the staging ground for the war and also reflected the eagerness of men in the Gulf Coast to serve in the war.[51]

The impressions of U.S. soldiers and civilians that came amid Taylor's invasion of northern Mexico were, as many other racist impressions of Mexico, linked to previous wars against Native peoples and Mexicans in places like Texas. After having crossed the Rio Grande in July 1846, Johnston's previous military experience against Mexicans, the Comanche in Texas, and Black Hawk and his band in Illinois framed much of his impressions about the arid northern country of Mexico when his regiment marched through it on its way to Camargo. To Johnston's mind the southwest was a region that Mexico did not "pretend to defend against the Indians." As the regiment embarked on a six-day journey up the Rio Grande, he recorded his impressions of the people and their surroundings in a letter to George Hancock in August. "There is a much greater portion of the land on the river under cultivation than I had supposed," Johnston wrote, "and the population greatly more numerous—the inhabitants of the Rio Grande resembling in color the Indians of the U. States & not much superior to some of them in civilization."[52] The comparison of Native Americans in the United States to Mexicans living in Mexico, some of them more than likely also Native American living along the Rio Grande, exposed the manner in which the public discourse about race shaped the soldiers' frame of mind as they entered Mexico, together with personal experience and national events. Traversing the landscape of northern Mexico, Johnston described the thatched roofs of the houses along the banks, and men and women's dress. Despite the heat, Johnston noted "there is no want of modesty in their dress or absence of it rather." The sense of surprise over the amount of cultivation found along the Mexican border stemmed in part from the popular view that the Nueces Strip, of which the Rio Grande was a part, was largely barren. Yet the rest of the Rio Grande Valley was quite fertile, under cultivation, and populated by a variety of peoples, including both Mexicans and Native Americans.[53]

Johnston's volunteer riflemen suffered from the onslaught of disease that made the U.S.-Mexican War so deadly. Due to sickness and the nearing end of their enlistment, Johnston's regiment voted to disband just before the Battle of Monterrey in August. After losing his regiment, Johnston joined volunteers under General William Orlando Butler as inspector general, extending his stay in Mexico and allowing him to complete his term of service.[54]

In August 1846 General John A. Quitman joined Zachary Taylor's army while they were in Camargo. In the early months of his service, John A. Quitman echoed many of Johnston's views of Mexican society in the northern states along the Rio Grande. Quitman was a Southern transplant. He was originally born in Pennsylvania but eventually moved to Mississippi, where he established a law practice and was elected to the Mississippi state legislature. He had been a long-time supporter of nullification, Texas annexation, and territorial expansion into Mexico. During the Texas Revolution, he mailed Sam Houston a knife with a note encouraging him to fight for Texas freedom, before leading a regiment called the "Natchez Fencibles" to Texas to participate in the war there.[55] He wrote an acquaintance living in Texas and promised that Southerners would "never permit an Indian and Negro colony to be planted on the frontier." Quitman's use of the phrase "Indian and Negro colony" fed off the idea that Mexican people were racially mixed between Native American and African Americans, a notion that was steeped in the Southern society's ideas about race and race mixing. The phrase also hinted at the reality that the Rio Grande border did harbor formerly enslaved African Americans and native peoples such as the Comanche and Apache. It was a boundary between a slave state and antislavery nation.[56] To a person such as Quitman, such a thing was absolutely intolerable and justified his assessment of Mexicans as inferior and incapable of being a nation among others in the world. He wrote to his wife and children often, discussing both troop movements and his views of the Mexicans who lived on ranchos in the region. In a letter to his children, Henry, Louisa, and Antonia, Quitman described how the Mexicans in Camargo "delighted" in the sight of Americans. The elite families moved back toward the interior, fearing the ravages of war. He described Mexican people he saw to his children as a very "lazy race" and filthy, despite bathing regularly.[57]

Quitman's regiment proceeded into the Battle of Monterrey with Taylor, just as Albert Sidney Johnston's men packed up and headed home. He participated in the opening movements of the battle and wrote about them to his wife almost before it was over. Eliza Quitman was not at all thrilled with his decision to sign up for service in Mexico. Exchanging letters with him regularly, she expressed worry on more than one occasion. She also articulated a sense of ambivalence toward the war and did not share her husband's views of Mexican people. In the aftermath of the battle of Monterrey, Eliza wrote, "It appears to me that peace is now farther off than ever, and that there are many bloody and desperate battles yet to be fought. I am not one of those who hold the Mexicans in contempt. I think they have been greatly underrated."[58] Eliza's fears about the war and thoughts about Mexicans suggested that soldiers' families did not always feel the violent racism found in the pages of New Orleans newspapers or their family members' writings. While she did not demonstrate outright opposition to the war, her worries represented those of many Americans who feared the war might last longer than expected. After the battle of Monterrey, Quitman and his troops undertook a march to Tampico. An artillery officer, Francis Collins remarked on their arrival after a grueling march. While in Tampico Quitman practiced his Spanish and dined with members of Tampico's wealthy class. He noted the wide gap between the lives of those at the top of Tampico society and those at the bottom, blaiming the lack of a middle class on their lack of institutions like those in the United States. Quitman's brigade would then move on to Veracruz to take part in Winfield Scott's landing and the march toward Mexico City.[59]

When soldiers marched out of Veracruz and through the Valley of Mexico, what they saw was very much shaped by the propaganda that celebrated the war as a second conquest in which Americans might remake the verdant landscape of Mexico. A year after Johnston returned to Galveston, his brother-in-law, William Preston, decided to enlist. Johnston wrote to his friend Hancock of his worry for Will's health and the impact that the climate might have on him. By 1847, many Americans had tired of the war despite the newspapers' intensive military coverage. The army had already won several battles, and the war was coming to a close. "I have from the beginning regarded it as a contest," Johnston remarked, "which many years would not terminate & the present position of things fully justifies my anticipations." For this reason, he hoped that Will's regiment would not be involved in combat.[60]

William Preston's time in Mexico came much later in the war, but he viewed his experiences through a similar lens as his brother-in-law and John Quitman. He kept a diary throughout 1847 and 1848 during his time serving as Lieutenant Colonel of the Fourth Kentucky Volunteers. Whereas Johnston crossed the Rio Grande, Preston sailed from New Orleans on November 11, 1847, where his regiment only stayed a night before heading downriver and reaching the Gulf of Mexico. For Preston, who was from Kentucky, the trip to Veracruz was the first time that he had ever seen the Gulf. Like many soldiers who had come from other parts of the South, he found the trip through New Orleans was just as surprising and intriguing as the experience of a foreign country. Of the Gulf, Preston wrote, "when they are at rest & only agitatedly slight winds, the sapphire sky, the light, fleecy, clouds drifting before the winds, the clear waves and delightful breeze, create a pleasant languor, which renders you careless of everything save the scene around you." When his regiment landed at Veracruz it found a conquered city. Preston remarked on the dilapidated state of the harbor, which he wrote "scarcely deserves the name, it is dangerous in the extreme." He noted the remnants of the siege and battle surrounding them as they camped on a plain between the city and the sea where General Winfield Scott's troops had marched ten months earlier. Preston recorded the scene as follows: "The trenches are still there & the fragments of the shells and round shot scattered over the plain still show the range and direction of the Mexican batteries."[61]

As his unit marched their way through the Mexican countryside, it took a similar route to that of the Cortés expedition. Preston spent more time observing the landscape and animals than had Johnston a year earlier. For Preston, the experience of Mexico was wholly foreign. He had little on which to base his experience. After over a week of marching, Preston recorded in his diary that "Small birds similar to the oriole of gaudy plumage, & myriads of flowering shrub presented to the eye of one from the temperate zone a landscape as novel as it was beautiful."[62] On the road from Veracruz to Mexico City, Preston's regiment passed Santa Anna's hacienda. He described in detail the house, which posed a great curiosity to the men of the Fourth Kentucky. He noted the imposing quality of Mango de Clavo, which was more like a fortress than a "country house," and remarked on a discussion between himself and another officer over the agricultural capacity of the land, stating, "I differ from Mr. Thompson, who thinks it would produce cotton & sugar profitably as the land can have no means of irrigation being to elevated and remote from the mountain & the alternations of wet & dry seasons being the marked to permit its being tilled very advantageously."[63] Whatever their differences, they both viewed Santa Anna's home as well as the rest of Mexico as a place the United States could exploit and from which it could extract future wealth.

The soldiers who entered Mexico through Taylor's northern campaign experienced a very different world from that experienced by the soldiers during Winfield Scott's campaign to Mexico city that commenced in 1847. The northwestern Mexico campaign was framed more by the Texas-Mexico disputes of the past and the Native American–Anglo disputes of the present. Later, soldiers who entered through Veracruz and central Mexico arrived during the final acts of the war. By mid-December, the army held the center of Mexico. The capital city itself, William Preston felt, was without equal in the entirety of the Americas, and from his ship anchored on the coast, Fitch Taylor imagined what the army must have experienced. As it marched into Mexico City, Taylor wrote, "even the unlettered could not but feel the influence of the distant prospect; and the well-read had a rush of historic associations pouring into their thoughts, while they recalled the story of the past, as they had, with the interest of romance, traced the march of the braze but bloody Cortez." As the war came to a close, ideas of la Conquista again flooded the minds of those that participated in it. In the imagination of white American men like Fitch Taylor and the many soldiers who marched through Mexico to the capital city, they were taking the road that Cortés had once taken when he conquered the Aztec empire; now they had done the same thing: they had conquered a different race related to the Aztecs, they had conquered the Mexicans. John Quitman, like the conquerors before him would go on to oversee the occupation of Mexico City at the end of the war.[64]

Whereas Albert Sidney Johnston had regarded the Mexican population as largely impoverished, and Raphael Semmes had seen a distasteful mix of races, William Preston shared Fitch Taylor's romanticized views. He described the scene in Mexico City as one in which "its mixed & picturesque population combine to render it an object of more interest to the traveler than any other place upon the American Continent." On Christmas Day, Preston recorded that the treaty between the United States and Mexico had passed the Mexican Lower House. There was much excitement in the city. The next twenty-four hours, Preston wrote, would "decide the greatest event in the relations of the United States & Mexico, whether the latter is to retain her nationality or become a province, nous verrons." Mexico did not become a province, but the United States did take half of its territory and left men like Preston, Johnston, and Quitman wondering what else they might take if they extended their war-marking farther south.

CONCLUSION

Past experiences with Native Americans and Mexicans in the Gulf region informed the justifications for the war that took the armies to the center of the Mexican Republic. The decades-long conflict over Texas as well as the conflicts in places like Florida with Native American peoples provided a context within which to situate the new war. American newspapers and even American generals vilified Mexican officers throughout the war.[65] From the perspective of those living in the Gulf of Mexico, the nation's victory over Mexico brought a decade-long border struggle to a close. In 1848, when the war ended, Anglos believed they had triumphed over what many perceived as their constant enemies and that Latin America and the western territories would be theirs. The end of the war began a whole new chapter, and it was only a matter of time before other expansionist projects appeared. Vilification of Mexico and Mexican people began, in part, with the Texas Revolution. The racism directed at Mexicans that came out of the propaganda of the U.S.-Mexican War formed the backdrop against which white Americans judged and imagined other Latin American nations after the war. Racism directed toward Mexicans became part of the way that white slaveholders and other white Southerners viewed Latin American peoples. They viewed Latin America the way William Preston viewed Mango de Clavo, as theirs to exploit. During the increasingly turbulent antebellum era they created yet more heroic visions of conquest and salvation to bolster their efforts in other parts of Latin America even as their fellow Americans began to challenge their expansionist visions.

The move to annex Cuba in the 1850s happened against the backdrop of the Mexican War and the racist justifications used to support it. Riding high on the victory in Mexico and following the model of Texas settlement, expansionists looked to make Cuba a slave state. While U.S. diplomats may have negotiated for the sale of Cuba in the 1850s, American efforts to filibuster in Cuba drew the attention of the public and illuminated the many ways that Gulf South communities saw themselves as a part of this continued violent conquest of Latin America. Filibustering was far more than a curiosity to those living there; the phenomenon revealed the ways that white Americans came to envision the island against the backdrop of the Mexican War and the manner in which depictions of Creoles played a role in fantasies of Cuban statehood. The stories of would-be conquest in Cuba and the U.S.-Mexican War were deeply entwined, as were the visions of Mexicans and Cubans that Americans constructed. Now that the Mexicans had been conquered, filibusters would try to set Cubans free.

CHAPTER 4

Annexing the Gem of the Antilles

In 1854 the bells of St. Louis Cathedral rang out for the fallen hero of the late filibuster expeditions to Cuba, Narciso López. There was no grave or tomb at which to lay a wreath: López's body had been buried where he had been executed, in Havana. Mourners gathered to listen to some of the leading men of the Cuban annexation movement mourn the deaths of the filibusters, López in particular. Later they published a pamphlet to commemorate the event. The expeditions to Cuba ended in 1851, but for several years afterward in the communities of the Gulf South such as New Orleans, Galveston, and Mobile former supporters of the expeditions and those that still supported the idea of Cuban annexation remembered López as a fighter for Cuban independence, American expansion, and Southern imperialism.[1]

This chapter focuses on the antebellum Cuban annexation movement that peaked in the mid-1850s. When the United States obtained nearly half of Mexico's territory, it galvanized a movement for the annexation of Cuba at the same time that Americans in the North and South eyed the prospect of settlement in the West. Throughout the 1850s efforts to obtain Cuba ranged from attempts to purchase the island to violently overthrow the Spanish colonial authority. The filibusters and their attempts to take Cuba by force captured the most attention within the Gulf South communities. Indeed, the expeditions proved riveting to Americans both North and South, as they watched their brethren under the command of a Venezuelan, Narciso López, set sail for Cuba in 1850 and 1851.

In the mid-nineteenth century "filibusters" was the term for men who sought to take over the territory of other nations through military force, often without any governmental sanction. The alternate meaning of the word was "pirate," and that is exactly how the Spanish viewed Narciso López. While filibustering in Cuba and other Latin American countries captured the American public's attention in the early 1850s, several filibuster-style invasions under the banner of U.S. expansion occurred during the early nineteenth century. For example, George Mathews, a former brevet brigadier general in the Continental Army and then governor of Georgia, conducted a clandestine mission to incite insurrection in East Florida in 1810, making the Patriot War one of the more spectacular filibustering efforts. James Madison, who initiated the venture by tapping Mathews, then living in the Mississippi Territory, to head up the effort to gain East Florida, quickly disavowed the entire affair. Several years later, a U.S. Army lieutenant, Augustus Magee, led an invasion of three hundred men into East Texas before falling ill and dying. The Texas Revolution in 1836, which was peopled with Americans recently arrived and eager to participate in a war against Mexico, could also be classified as a filibuster-led war. These initial forays did lead to increased settlement and eventually paved the way for the expansion of U.S. authority over the Gulf South. By the 1820s white American dominance of the region was well under way. By the middle of the nineteenth century, the United States was one of the major powers in the Gulf of Mexico; yet the residents of communities along the coast still employed fears, dreams, and racialized imagery to keep the fires of expansion burning and advocate for increased military protection.[2]

This chapter concentrates on the renewed push for Cuban annexation that developed immediately after the U.S.-Mexican War and explores the impact of the movement on New Orleans as well as examining the fantasies and imagery used to support it. Indeed, antebellum discussions of Cubans and the U.S.-Mexican War as well as the continued racialization of Mexican peoples reflected some of the older ideas that had emerged among white Southerners as they moved into the Louisiana territory and came into contact with and competed against the European and African descendants of the region's first wave of colonization. In the 1850s filibusters and their supporters utilized the victories of the U.S.-Mexican War and the country's relationship with Mexico to frame expectations of the expeditions and legitimize them. Additionally, the way that newspapers and filibusters depicted Cuban Creoles echoed the ways that Anglo Americans had discussed the Spanish and French Creoles in Louisiana, demonstrating some of the nuanced yet highly racialized ways that Anglos discussed and viewed people in the Caribbean and Mexico. Specifically, Anglo Americans constructed images of Cuban Creoles as a people in need of American rescue. Veterans of the U.S.-Mexican War and young men eager to become involved in the next stage of conquest participated in the expeditions to Cuba at a time when the national quest for new lands and the Southern ideas of empire began to diverge.

Southern whites often emphasized the whiteness of Cuban slaveholders and did not discuss the racial complexity of the island's actual population. That said, the racial and ethnic makeup of Cuba's population underwent many changes during the nineteenth century. By the 1850s Cuba and Spain still participated in the African slave trade, though Britain was trying to put an end to this continued traffic. Many elite white Cubans began calling for white European settlement to offset the large Black population. As in Mexico, the other end of the socioeconomic spectrum in Cuba comprised a large racially and ethnically mixed population. While Cuban and Mexican societies exhibited a similar makeup, the presence of chattel slavery made Cuba appealing for expansionists in ways that the Mexican interior was not. It was within this context that the whiter portion of Cuban society tended to be cast as a threatened group in need of saving.

Through the filibuster expeditions, Gulf South communities continued to play an essential role in expansionist efforts. New Orleans, being the wealthiest and largest city in the region, took center stage in the Cuban filibustering drama of the 1850s, as the city played host to Cuban exiles and filibusters. The city also connected the expansionist politics of filibustering with the complicated politics of Spanish colonial rule in Cuba. Furthermore, the Cuban annexation movement connected white Southern fantasies about empire in Latin America with fears concerning the growing threat of antislavery sentiments beyond the South's borders.

IMAGINING NEW ORLEANS CREOLES AND CUBANS

When city boosters talked about New Orleans and its relationship with Cuba, their thoughts turned inevitably to the island's geographic possibilities as a protective gate for the trade flowing in and out of the great Southern city. By the middle of the nineteenth century New Orleans had developed into the third largest port in the United States and the largest city in the South. The cotton boom of the early nineteenth century transformed the city into a frenetic metropolis and its population doubled in sized as white settlers, enslaved and free Africans, and European and Latin American immigrants filled its walls until it swelled to over one hundred and fifty thousand residents by the 1850s.[3]

Interest in annexing Cuba was tied to the need to protect New Orleans and its trade in the Mississippi River and the Gulf of Mexico. Shortly after Narciso López's 1851 expedition, Alexander Jones, a journalist and strong advocate of Cuban annexation, published a book on Cuba detailing its current state and the efforts of the filibusters to free the island from Spain's grasp. Jones began by estimating that roughly $114 million in annual exports—the majority leaving from New Orleans—made its way through the Gulf of Mexico. Trade to and from the Mississippi Valley and California, he estimated, was $200 million. The majority of New Orleans's trade was, of course, in cotton exports and the growing sugar trade as well as enslaved people. Throughout the 1840s, the annual export in cotton hovered at around one million bales annually, garnering earnings for the city totaling over $20 million. Sugar exports increased throughout the same period, reaching over 100,000 hogshead barrels by 1845, bringing $9 million into the city's coffers. New Orleans merchants also did a brisk business in everything from buffalo robes to dried apples. Coffee was the primary import from Cuba and Brazil, with Rio de Janeiro outpacing Havana.

Jones feared that this trade would be in serious jeopardy "in the event of war with a strong maritime power." "Should the enemy occupy Havana on one side, and Yucatan on the other," he reasoned, "he could do much towards destroying the trade of New Orleans." Annexing Cuba would solve these problems and put an end to the threats to New Orleans's commerce. These connections as well as the city's merchant class and its wealth and size made it a hotbed of expansionism and Cuban annexation support. Aside from protecting the New Orleans trade, Jones, like many supporters, reasoned that annexation was vital and inevitable due to the close economic ties between the United States and Cuba, as Cuban imports came primarily from the United States and its exported goods wound up in the same market.[4]

In the mid-nineteenth century, many Cuban exiles made their homes in either New York or New Orleans. Many exiles came from the planter class of the island. In the U.S. press, the term "creole" was reserved for this class, as was the term "white," such as when Jones referred to the disaffection of the "creole or native white population" toward its colonial government. Narciso López was considered to be among this class, though unlike many of them he was not a native of the island. There were those among the exiled population who began to wonder if Cuba might fare better under U.S. authority.[5] Meanwhile, among Americans, ideas about Cuban Creoles reflected some of the same ways that Southern whites imagined and depicted the Creoles in Louisiana. However, there was little of the same long-standing tension between the Louisiana Creoles and Southern whites as seen in New Orleans, where Southern whites dominated during the antebellum era. Sympathy for Cuban Creoles often overshadowed any tension between Americans and Cubans that might lay in the future if Cuba were to become a state. The sympathy with which Southern whites often viewed and imagined Cuban Creoles was also quite different from the way they often imagined Mexicans, rich or poor. Few Southern whites had ever considered Mexicans' welfare in the debate over Texas annexation.

Throughout the years of the filibuster expeditions, Southern whites cast Cuba as a society similar to their own, with a white master class, enslaved workers of African descent, and very little in between. While this was not entirely unique to Cuba, it was a departure from depictions of Mexican society, which was often cast as unstable due, in part, to its lack of African American slavery and use of debt peonage. However, as in the Gulf South ports race on the island was a complex construct with many people falling in between the Black/white binary. In reality, many Creoles were mixed race, but in both Cuba and in the United States, their whiteness was often emphasized during the mid-nineteenth century. Southern whites, whether expanding into the Gulf South states or when imagining Cuba, attempted to erase this long history of racial mixing, and white Creoles, at times, participated in this erasure. At the same time, with the continued influx of white Southern settlers throughout the early nineteenth century, French and Spanish Creoles too quickly found themselves marginalized within Louisiana. Fixating on white Creole elites allowed white Southerners to find commonalities between themselves and slave-owning Cubans. In the antebellum era, journalists and Cuban annexationists used the idea of imperiled white Creoles in Cuba to craft both their dreams of success and their nightmares of failure.[6]

While many white Southerners thought that territorial expansion could sustain the South's economy and society, for many Cubans the issue of U.S. expansion and imperialism raised troubling possibilities and questions. Cubans both on and on off the island were far from being of one mind about annexation. Cuban exiles, including a revolutionary junta operating in both New York City and New Orleans, vigorously lobbied for intervention and generally supported filibustering. There were, however, many others within Cuba as well as in the exile community who believed American annexation would not bring total independence. Still other Cubans interested in independence thought that encouraging American appetite for territory in Latin American might help them in their cause, and that even if this meant becoming a state rather than an independent country at least they would be a part of nation based on republican ideals. Others viewed U.S. interest in Cuba as an immediate threat, an exchange of one colonial power for another.[7]

When Cubans and the idea of Cuban annexation arrived in New Orleans, they entered a city already defined by divisions along racial and ethnic identities, including ideas about Creole identities created by white Southerners. At this time in New Orleans, Creole referred to those of white European descent but also to those of mixed-race descent who could trace their roots back to the French and Spanish colonial eras. For white Creoles, the label was a way of differentiating themselves from the white Southerners who were moving into Louisiana, and white Southerners also began using this term to refer to them as well. Local Creoles were a part of the very organization of the city and its neighborhoods, known as faubourgs. Anglo Americans moving into the Louisiana territory after the turn of the nineteenth century largely viewed Creoles as remnants of the last empire. These new arrivals typically lived outside of the "old city," which later became known as the French Quarter. Constructing the image of Creoles as a dying race was not solely a New Orleans–based project. In 1845 Benjamin Moore Norman, the owner of a bookbinding and printing office and travel writer, published *New Orleans and Its Environs*, and he wrote similarly of New Orleans Creoles. Norman defined Creoles as "all who are born here ... without reference to the birth place of their parents." In comparing the Old City where the majority of Creoles lived and with the newer neighborhoods where white Americans lived, Norman noted that the areas of the city in which the two cultures existed reflected their differences. He described the French Quarter as composed of brick buildings with a few "ancient and dilapidated structures" at its heart. Meanwhile the "modern" structures of the Faubourg St. Mary, where many Americans had settled, was described as comprising houses three to four stories high with lots of embellishment.[8]

Woven into Norman's descriptions of the city were ideas about the descendants of the European settlers who lived in New Orleans, little unfavorable jabs that pointed toward the white Southerners' rightful ascendance over their Creole counterparts. For example, Norman claimed that the Frenchmen rarely ventured into the American part of the city, but that, when they did venture "three squares beyond their favorite cabaret," they were incredulous at the amount of construction happening in St. Mary. Emphasizing the gleaming structures and granite fronts, Norman, like many interested in emphasizing the importance of Americans to the growth of the city, focused on the progress of the second municipality.

In 1836 the Louisiana state legislature repealed the town charter of New Orleans and created three separate municipalities each, with its own separate government, in an effort to prevent continued ill feeling between Creoles and Americans living in the city. The first municipality was the city proper, or future French Quarter, the second was the Faubourg St. Mary, where most Americans settled, and the third was the Faubourg St. Marigny, which housed a mixture of immigrants, free Black people, and French and Spanish Creoles. Throughout his observations, Norman referred to the Creoles and their buildings as either "ancient" or "foreign," out of date and out of place in this vast commercial emporium of an American city. Yet what Norman was really observing was a decade's worth of American efforts to assert their control over the city from within their own municipality. Still, while recognizing the Spanish and French as the original inhabitants of the city, Norman widened his definition of Creoles to include all those residents who were descended from other European nationals.[9]

The changing cityscape represented the decades-long tug of war between Creoles and Americans, one that Americans ultimately won but not without qualifications. In the view of Southern whites, New Orleans, and the Gulf South more broadly, was indebted to the "vast improvements which, as if by magic" rose up to the "astonishment and confusion of those of the ancient regime, who live in a kind of seclusion within the limits of the *city proper*."[10] The "American Sector," which lay just beyond the boundaries of the French Quarter, stood in sharp contrast to the narrow streets and European-style eighteenth century buildings. In 1851 the *San Antonio Ledger* related a story about New Orleans's old Creole mansions. As the paper's correspondent described, these new buildings replaced the "swaying cane field, the white cottages of the negroes and the picturesque mansion of the old Creole planter, made up the features of the landscape." The paper lamented that the Creoles were reminders of "many pleasant episodes of early life in the 'Sunny South.'"[11]

Pierre Soulé moved to this divided and chaotic city at the same time that the landscape around the Creole community was changing and Americans were positioning themselves as the wizards of progress. Before he settled in Louisiana, his life had all the hallmarks of an adventure novel. Originally born in a small village in the French Pyrenees, Soulé experienced both exile and imprisonment for opposing the government and supporting revolutionary activities. He was imprisoned several times during his youth. The first arrest was for conducting anti-Bourbon activities. Soulé was pardoned in 1818 but was again arrested during his time as a law student for publishing revolutionary articles in Paris. In 1825 he escaped and traveled from Great Britain to Haiti and finally settled into a new life as a lawyer in New Orleans.[12]

Benjamin Norman asserted that the Creole community was insular and referred to its members as "remarkably exclusive in their intercourse with others, and with strangers, enter into business arrangements with extreme caution." Yet Soulé wound his way into the community and early on in his political career became a mouthpiece for them. When he arrived in New Orleans, he spoke very little English, which was quickly becoming the most commonly used language in the city. Soulé learned it as quickly as he could, becoming a master of oratory in both languages which, as one later biographer put it, gave him incredible influence with the French and Spanish Creoles community.[13] As Americans encroached further on Creole property and power within the city, Soulé was "one of the first to see this danger, and at the head of his co-citizens of French origin, he disputed the ground piece by piece with the Anglo-Americans."[14]

Soulé came to support expansionist policies during his first term as U.S. senator in 1847, when he sat in the Senate for a brief six months as a Democrat. His adopted Creole identity afforded him entrance into yet another form of identity, that of Southerner and his support of the South caused outrage among non-Southerners in the Senate. By 1850 Soulé was in the midst of his second Senate term during the height of the filibustering mania in New Orleans, which coincided with the political fights over the extension of slavery into newly gained territory. "The impudence of a foreigner who comes to the United States and tells the people of one section of our country that they should not tolerate the residence among them of the countrymen of another section is beyond all endurance," complained the *Trenton State Gazette*. "Mr. Soulé deserves to be hissed out of the republic."[15] Soulé balanced several different identities simultaneously and "understood & accepted willingly the future fusion of the population of La. and of the Anglo-American race." He worked to form a bridge between the Creole community and the Southern whites in their midst.[16]

The French and Spanish Creole community underwent a variety of changes during the antebellum era. While Creoles in Louisiana generally sought to establish an identity that defined them against the increasing power of white Southerners, white Creoles in New Orleans may have owned plantations and built their power on slavery but white Southerners believed they were able to make slavery pay in a way that the Creoles could not. During the height of the excitement over the Cuban expeditions, Cuban Creoles were seen as yet another slaveholding class that could be incorporated into the South like the Louisiana Creoles of the past. However, white Southerners felt they should be the ones to usher in that inclusion and guide it. The presence of exiles in the immigrant neighborhoods of New Orleans provided an immediate example for white Southerners of Cuban Creoles who required American assistance.

While many of the nation's Southern proslavery politicians long supported efforts to obtain Cuba, they were wading into the middle of a long history of Cuba as a Spanish colony. By 1850 Cuba's racial and class structures were becoming more like those found in the Southern U.S. due to the increased sugar production on the island. Since the 1780s Cuba's slave and free Black population had increased to nearly half the island's population. Cubans moving to New Orleans in the mid-nineteenth century contributed to the image of "Creole" people and culture in the city and also entered into an alliance of sorts with white Southerners intent on annexing Cuba as a state.[17]

The Cuban community in New Orleans grew over the nineteenth century and included cigar shops, coffee shops, and newspapers. Additionally, by 1850s the Spanish consulate was established at New Orleans with its own news organ, *La Union*. Into this burgeoning immigrant community came those exiles escaping the Spanish colonial authorities on the island. The exiles living in New Orleans provided yet another point of connection between New Orleans and Cuba that stoked the fires of Southern interest and justification for Cuban annexation.

It was within this world that a court case concerning a Cuban exile named Juan F. Rey, the Spanish consul, and abduction exploded into the public discourse of New Orleans and the entire Gulf Coast community. Though not directly tied to expansionism or Cuban annexation, the court case illuminated the various ways that Cubans fit into the world of New Orleans and the manner in which New Orleanians imagined U.S. and Cuban relations. Rey served as a jailer in Havana for five months before March 1849, when he aided two inmates who had allegedly taken part in a rebellion plot. On March 31, 1849, he and one of the other inmates sailed to New Orleans, where they took shelter in various boarding houses throughout the city. Rey hid among other Cubans in a cigar shop and took on the name Juan Garcia Rey. Several months after his arrival in the city Carlos de España, the Spanish consul, learned of his whereabouts, arrested him, and shipped him back to Havana on an American ship called the *Mary Ellen*. Hearing of the arrest, possible assault, and abduction of Rey, Mayor Abdiel Crossman promptly wrote de España, requesting more information. España responded with two letters. The first was a cordial note that invited Crossman to his home for a private discussion about the matter. The second, sent a day later, was a lengthy letter accusing the mayor of putting de España's career in jeopardy and insulting his honor by implying his involvement in the arrest of Rey. Eventually, España was arrested on charges of abduction.[18]

In the days surrounding the abduction and the subsequent trial of Carlos de España several different stories floated around in newspapers throughout the United States. This stemmed in part from the conflicting story that Rey gave in Havana and in New Orleans. Initially, as the details of the case mounted, there was much debate over whether or not Rey left the city of his own free will. When the American ship that transported him back to Cuba arrived in Havana, port authorities placed the ship under quarantine. In an interview with Lewis Campbell, the American consul in Havana, Rey stated that he was in Cuba of his own free will. However, after Campbell left the ship, Rey immediately wrote him and disclosed that España's men had forced him onto the ship. He then asked for protection under the United States and to return to New Orleans. Rey explained in his letter that he had lied due to the fact that captain of the ship was present in the room. It was after this that Rey was handed over to the American consul by the Count de Alcoy, the captain-general in Havana, and returned to New Orleans pending a judicial investigation of España by the circuit court. In an affidavit Rey declared that España's men forcibly abducted him under forged orders from the recorder of the Second Municipality and asked to be taken back to the United States. As a result of España's acquittal and Rey's published story, the city's newspapermen treated the trial as another example of Spain denigrating American authority.[19]

Annexationists used the case as yet another example of the threat of Spain's colonial presence so close to U.S. borders, and of its burdensome rule over the island. In a letter written to the editors of the *Texas State Gazette*, one anonymous reader reasoned that Rey escaping to New Orleans as a refugee was no different than all of the refugees who had supposedly fled to the Republic of Texas from the United States before its annexation. Reviewing the recent history of diplomatic relations and Spain's actions in Cuba, the *New York Daily Times*' New Orleans correspondent recalled the efforts of Cuban Creoles on the island to "throw off the shackles of Spain." The *Times* correspondent accused the U.S. government of allowing Spanish spies to infiltrate the Crescent City's Cuban exile community, which, according to the correspondent, was what led to the abduction of Juan Francisco Rey.[20] The *Daily True Delta* called the outcome of the trial an "insult to the community." It also lambasted the choice of men for the jury, arguing that several were close friends of España. The paper declared that the selection of the jury to try the issue between España and the United States only proved that the trial was a travesty of justice and "the composition of the jury is evidence of it; the tone of the papers defending the Spaniard, and laboring to defeat the enforcement of the laws against him establish it."[21]

New Orleanians questioned the jurors' ties to Havana industry and trade just as much as their ties to España himself. Newspapers claimed there was nothing wrong in these connections, but the choice of men with such ties did smack of conspiracy. The irony here was that scarcely half a year later, pro-annexationist news organs would support a militarized expedition to Cuba and ties with Havana would be celebrated in the city.

The España/Rey case occurred during the planning of the López expedition, and both Rey and López existed within the larger power struggle between Cuban nationalism and Spanish colonial rule as well as the shifting space of Creoles within New Orleans. The American newspapers were also involved in this power struggle and used it to foster further support for Cuban annexation. For example, the New Orleans *Daily Delta* opposed the jury's decision in the Carlos de España case. In reference to the Spanish consul's apparent triumph over American sovereignty, the paper wrote, "Is it come to this, that an American Secretary of State has dared to tamper with the administration of our laws, and in order to conciliate a power, contemptible for its imbecility to the whole of Europe, has covered the national escutcheon with dishonor, and bowed the heads of the people in shame?"[22] In addition to challenging the sovereignty of the United Sates, the *Delta* also believed that the federal government had also overstepped its boundaries by interfering with what it felt was a city matter, not a federal issue. To many annexationists, the sovereignty of the United States had been defied, its borders weakened by this action in New Orleans.

Newspapers in New Orleans used the case as an example both of Spain's trampling over American sovereignty and of their cruelty because of the way they treated Rey. The España case occurred in the midst of what many in the city had come to see as a series of instances in which the Spanish government, often depicted as an inherently effeminate and weak body, had triumphed over the United States, a nation of strong Anglo-Saxon citizens, men especially. These events helped shape the U.S. depiction of Cubans and the Spanish during the Cuban annexation movement. The bitterness exhibited by the press hinted at the expectation that Spaniards were supposed to lose and Americans win. The value of Cuba as an additional slave state made Rey's story more appealing to those interested in Cuban annexation.[23]

THE EXPEDITIONS AND THEIR RECEPTION IN NEW ORLEANS

Narciso López's bitter feelings toward the Spanish colonial government emerged long before he entertained the idea of a filibustering expedition to Cuba. They stemmed in large part from his inability to rise through the ranks of the army and maintain a government appointment in Cuba. Narciso López spent his entire adult life drifting throughout South America and the United States looking for a purpose and for a decent payday. The son of a wealthy merchant, he was born and grew up in Caracas, Venezuela. During Venezuela's battle for independence, López experienced his first brush with revolution. Yet he ended his time in Venezuela by fighting on the side of the Spanish against Simon Bolivar's faction. López eventually found his way to Cuba, where he soon turned against Spain. He attempted to find his place in Cuban society through various business ventures, and each failure soured his attitude toward Spain's management of Cuba. He joined the annexationists and began planning for Cuba's independence. His charisma allowed him to connect with those around him, which made it easy for him to gain followers. After an early bid to launch an armed uprising in Cuba in 1847, López narrowly escaped arrest by migrating to the United States and settling among the Cuban immigrant community in New York City, where he began working with a junta dedicated to Cuban annexation.[24] Complicating matters, many of the early attempts at Cuban independence occurred within Cuba and depended on the Cuban planters' support. In order to gain their allegiance, those interested in an independent Cuba often had to assure Cuban planters that slavery would not be abolished.[25]

Supporters of the filibuster scheme painted the Cuban Creoles as tragic figures. Southerners who had led the charge toward economic growth in the Deep South would swoop in and save Cuba from its overbearing master, the way they had swept through Texas, banishing Mexico back beyond the Rio Grande. During the U.S.-Mexican War both soldiers and the print media often depicted lower-class Mexicans as oppressed and degraded as a direct result of the excesses of the upper class, though the mixed-race aspect of this population made them undesirable candidates for incorporation into American society. Cubans were a different story or, rather, expansionists interested in annexing Cuba crafted a different story that was more like the one they had crafted about Creoles in Louisiana. In conceiving of Cuba as tragic and oppressed by Spanish colonial authorities, they wrote themselves as the heroes of the story even as Northern antislavery opposition increasingly cast them as the villains of American history.

One thing that New Orleanians often omitted from their imaginings of Cuban annexation was the fate of Cuba's slaves. Yet the specter of slave rebellion continued to be a potent symbol for those interested in obtaining Cuba as a possible new slave state. López played on these fears, feeding Southerners a vision of Cuba as an "unarmed, and menaced by Spain's perpetual threat of converting into a worse than San Domingo, the richest and loveliest of Islands beneath the sun." To call up Haiti was to trigger a powerful collective memory that slaveholding classes throughout the Americas understood. In North America, Louisianans had a special connection to the Haitian Revolution. Louisiana's German Coast Uprising in 1811 was a direct descendant of that uprising.[26]

López moved his base of operations to New Orleans and began attracting men interested in taking part and joining the volunteer army. Francis Calvin Morgan Boggess was one of these men. He was a white overseer from Alabama who arrived in the city and enlisted with a Louisiana regiment. Boggess, like many of the men who were attracted to the expeditions, had participated in other armed conflicts in the region or felt they missed out on the war and were eager to stake their claim of martial prowess. Boggess was a perfect example of these types of men. He descended from a military tradition; his father fought in the Second Seminole War and his grandfather at the Battle of New Orleans. Enlisting with an Alabama company in the final months of the U.S.-Mexican War, Boggess only saw skirmish with guerrilla fighters in which the company lost two men. That was the extent of his military experience.[27]

In describing the types of men López aimed to recruit, Boggess stated that the expeditions were to be made up entirely of U.S.-Mexican War veterans. He believed that thousands of unemployed and discharged soldiers would willingly engage in the expeditions despite the danger, and while Boggess himself was not unemployed he certainly did fall in the category of men looking to continue these types of forays into Latin American territory.[28]

Throughout, López encouraged the commitment of his soldiers by promising them success and that they would remain in charge of the expedition and their potential Cuban Creole accomplices. According to Boggess, López assured the filibusters that the men involved "were to be put in charge of the Cubans," once the revolution began in Cuba. López played on both the filibusters' expectation of wealth and their understandings of race. He framed Cuban society as one similar to their own, with Cuban Creoles at the top. The project of winning Cuban independence would be led by Anglo Americans, and a new state would be brought into the nation by Southern white men, as had Texas and Florida. The expeditions promised to repeat previous drives for Latin American spaces. The New Orleans *Daily Picayune* announced that it received letters from Cuba's wealthy merchants claiming that many Cubans favored independence and annexation to the United States. Thus, American observers assumed that the oppressed Cuban natives were prepared to rise up in rebellion as soon as the filibusters landed.[29]

In memoirs, former filibusters discussed the fact that war veterans made up some of their ranks, and those who were unable to go to war hoped to repeat the valor and glory celebrated by the United States and heaped onto its soldiers. López invoked both in his address to the filibusters, and newspapers noted the presence of veterans in New Orleans. While the images of Creoles as prostrate victims became a central aspect of the heroic rhetoric of the armed expeditions, another important thread was the way in which the U.S.-Mexican War bolstered enthusiasm for continued expansion into Latin America. In 1850, while planning the first expedition to Cuba, López targeted not only Anglo Southerners interested in expansion but more specifically veterans. He promised the privates of his makeshift army a pay similar to that of soldiers in the U.S. Army. Filibusters were often called "adventurers," and this was very much a conscious choice as they sought to pattern themselves after the soldiers who had just fought in the U.S.-Mexican War. Throughout both expeditions supporters and filibusters would evoke the battles of the U.S.-Mexican War in propaganda like a spell or a prayer, hoping to capture the magic of that war and transfer it to their own.[30]

Throughout the months leading up to the expedition, Narciso López circulated through the Gulf South states seeking support. Sitting in the front parlor of the Governor's Mansion in Jackson, Mississippi, he offered command of the entire filibuster army to U.S.-Mexican War veteran and governor of Mississippi John Quitman. Quitman was a long-time supporter of Cuban independence and possible annexation. López even hinted at the possibility that Quitman might rule over a new Cuban republic if the expeditions were a success. Later, Quitman wrote to Mansfield Lovell, Quitman's former aide-de-camp, "Your old commander is invited to become the Liberator of a beautiful and rich island in the Gulf." Quitman went so far as to wonder if his old comrades might join him in a military expedition to Cuba, where he would become prime minister. As Quitman confessed to Lovell, in his mind he often reverted "to the free air of the camp," for he was by nature a soldier. In some ways López was telling powerful people what they wanted to hear in order to gain the support his expedition needed, and Quitman was as enchanted by the prospect of taking a central role in this new stage of Southern expansion as he was with reclaiming the thrill of the battlefield.[31]

Other white Americans formulated expectations in the same way that filibusters did, through the lens of the U.S.-Mexican War. Quitman had formed his opinions of Latin America and expansion during the war, where he observed the people along the Rio Grande as he marched through the villages and towns of northern Mexico. This was Quitman's first taste of the possibilities of expansion, as he began to take real notice of what lay beyond the warm water of the Gulf Coast. Quitman eventually restrained these fantasies of ruling Cuba himself. He chose to remain in Mississippi, though he supposedly aided López in preparing his expedition. That it was done in secrecy makes it difficult to gauge the level of Quitman's involvement in these preparations, but he did put López in touch with his friend, John Henderson, then working in New Orleans as a lawyer. Additionally, Quitman's sister Louisa wrote to him in March 1850 indicating her anxieties over the possible expedition. She refused to lend any credit to the statements made against her brother, but they continued to make her uneasy. She was fearful that his political opponents would use the accusations against him and other Southerners. Still, through Quitman and Henderson López was able to make contact with others in the city who were able to help him outfit his growing army.[32]

Quitman's reminiscences of camp life during the U.S.-Mexican War mirrored the ideas López used to frame the expedition. In May 1850 López addressed his fellow filibusterers with a proclamation outlining their mission. Referring to them as the men of the "field of Palo Alto and Churubusco," he assured those who were not veterans of the war that they were the "brethren and worthy peers of the men of those immortal victories." López went on to predict that the Cubans would rise up once they saw a "legion of choice spirits amply powerful to deal Buena-Vista fashion with any force" that the Spanish government could muster against them. Echoing both López and Boggess's references to U.S.-Mexican War veterans, the New Orleans *True Delta* surmised that three-fourths of the filibusters who set sail with López "served with distinction in Mexico."[33] Linking the filibusters with the soldiers of the U.S.-Mexican War gave the expeditions an air of legitimacy they otherwise would not have. The expedition to Cuba was not sanctioned by the United States federal government and was in violation of American neutrality laws; its participants were vilified by the Spanish as little better than villainous pirates.

In addition to conferring legitimacy, the linkages between filibusters and U.S.-Mexican war soldiers also recalled the success of the war. López went so far as to promise participants laurels and victory in Cuba, and beyond that, perhaps most importantly, he presented the filibusters with a vision in which they would "establish permanent and happy homes on the bountiful soil of the Island." American victory meant the migration of Anglo American settlers to the island. Cuban Creoles would ultimately play a very small part in their own liberation and in the projected annexation process.[34]

The 1850 invasion was over almost as soon as it began. The architects of the expedition—López, John Henderson, and Ambrosio Gonzales—had split their forces so as to continue to keep the enterprise secret. Ships filled with filibusters left from various parts of the Gulf and were to rendezvous on Mujeres Island, just off the coast of the Yucatan. Once there the filibusters grew anxious, and Boggess reported incidents of mutiny, one of which he directly participated in. Boggess and several other filibusters threatened the commanding officers of the expedition when they were not allowed to eat at the same table. The mutinies and the filibusters' conduct betrayed the notion that they were following in the footsteps of U.S.-Mexican War soldiers. Many of the filibusters were paid to be there and expected to be treated in ways that soldiers often did not. Soldiers who invaded Mexico adhered to the military structure that filibusters were not obliged to follow. In essence, many of them were playing soldier but were not prepared to live the military life. Thus, even though as Cuban annexationists and filibusters attempted to claim the lineage of the Mexican conflict, the realities of the expeditions and their structure made that legitimacy difficult to maintain. Still, despite the difficulties for the first few days of the voyage, the filibusters eventually landed at Cardenas on May 19, 1850. López went ashore with three regiments from Louisiana, Kentucky, and Mississippi. As they marched toward the city's center, they encountered Spanish troops and a skirmish quickly ensued.[35]

The Filibustero, an anonymous author of a memoir concerning these events, recalled López's plan to leave Cardenas in the hands of the Cuban Creoles once the filibusters had taken control of it. Yet the Creoles at Cardenas did not rise up to support the filibusters. The latter were a paltry force compared to the size of the Spanish army; to support them would have been disastrous. According to the Filibustero, López hardly knew what to think of their lack of enthusiasm. Unable to reconcile their unwillingness with the "promises and statements of the Cubans," López persisted in his conviction that Cubans in other parts of the island remained ready to support the expedition and its attempts at sparking a revolution. López pressed forward to Matanazas, a town further north along the coast. According to the anonymous author of the *Life of General Narciso López*, the Creoles had come to believe that the filibusters were interested in creating a revolution for the sole sake of pillaging the island's communities. The *Life*'s author emphasized that López and his men told Creoles at Cardenas, "We will not waste any more time, nor take another step until we see something on the part of the Creoles besides promises."[36] In his own reminiscences, Boggess recalled that the filibusters had been led to believe that "all the soldiers and citizens of Cardenas were represented as friendly to their cause." By the end of the first day it was obvious that this was not the case and that the island possessed a large standing army in comparison to the five hundred filibusters. Rather than risk complete annihilation, many of the expedition members made their way back to the ship that had brought them there even as López still considered making a stand against the Spanish troops. No Cuban reinforcements materialized, and even López made his escape.[37]

In the aftermath of the expedition, supporters, detractors, and participants shaped the narrative of the failure to their own ends. *El Diario de la Marina*, a Cuban newspaper, rejoiced at news of the Spanish victory, calling the invading filibusters "piratas" and "malvados." The *Diario* published personal accounts from Cardenas, detailing the events of those few days, the behavior of the army, and the rosters of the battalions that had overrun López's ragtag force. Others on the island proclaimed, "Gloria a la Nacion Espanol," making it clear that Cuba remained part of Spain and that the glory of victory went to the Spanish empire. "The Spaniards of both hemispheres that have been born here or lived here," the editorial proclaimed, "are not willing to wait to show that they have neither lost the energy of their fathers nor the noble blood of their ancestors."[38] In New Orleans, the *Daily Picayune* feared for the fate of the filibusters and worried that the Spanish might hunt down the "dispirited Creoles" who had supported the filibusters and punish them. The failure of the expedition also dampened confidence in the efficacy of American assistance. The author of the *Daily Picayune* article lamented that the skill and bravery of the men who fought against "mighty odds" during the U.S.-Mexican War imbued the filibusters with the "charm of the invincibility," which the events at Cardenas "cannot fail to weaken, if not break entirely." This framing served to reaffirm the connection in the minds of readers between the victories of the U.S.-Mexican War and the filibuster expedition despite the fact that it ended in failure.[39]

Despite all this, enthusiasm for Cuban annexation continued. Even as the filibusters went to trial for violating U.S. neutrality laws, support for similar expeditions did not wane, and Southern newspapers often defended López's actions. Southern desire for Cuba and belief in the filibusters' narratives of heroism and conquest proved too strong, too resilient to be wholly thwarted. Complicating matters, the filibusters' trial came in the midst of the controversy over the Compromise of 1850 and the fallout from the Fugitive Slave Law. While Southerners fought for their place in westward expansion and against an increasingly antislavery North, they also fought for their interests in southward expansion. John Quitman's trip to Cuba prior to the expedition, and possible involvement in its organization exposed him to charges of collusion with the radical filibusters. With the failure of the expedition and a looming trial, Quitman's political career was now in jeopardy. His wife Eliza wrote to him to celebrate July Fourth and simply asked, "What will you do about that Cuban affair?"[40]

The story quickly shifted away from López to the scandal of the Mississippi governor's arrest and trial. By February 1851 Quitman had returned to New Orleans to stand trial for contributing money to and meeting with the filibusters. His sister again wrote him, concerned about the trial and Quitman's reported connections with López and suspecting his enemies of orchestrating his arrest and trial.[41] Meanwhile, some New Orleanians celebrated Quitman and his expansionism, hosting a public dinner for him. In response to the invitation, Quitman wrote, "I am now fully satisfied that no southern statesman can ... discharge his duties to his country, without subjecting his name, his character, and his reputation to ... abuse." He responded in the same manner to his daughter, also named Louisa, stating that the "southern question" had made him a target for the federal government and the North.[42]

Eventually the charges against Quitman were dropped due to lack of evidence, but he was forced to resign as Mississippi's governor. The Houston *Democratic Telegraph and Texas Register* called the entire trial "one of the most ridiculous efforts to display the power of the Federal government that has been attempted since the days of the gag laws."[43] The Compromise of 1850 had determined the process of expansion into the West, and Southerners had come out of it with a series of victories in terms of assurances on the protection of slavery, financial benefits for Texas, and the promises of Southern expansion. The visceral reaction of the Northern states against the fugitive slave law made suspicions of Northern and federal power difficult to ignore and the trial brought those suspicions around full circle.

During the trial as during the expedition, the U.S.-Mexican War shaped both critiques of and justifications for filibustering in Cuba. For example, James De Bow published an article in his *De Bow's Review* in which he described a growing American "military spirit." With the U.S.-Mexican War, he claimed, "the nation entered upon a new career, which was predicted of her, and to which her institutions and positions peculiarly inclined—one of *war and conquest!*" According to De Bow, the nation possessed an insatiable appetite for new territory, for a universal empire. Yet De Bow felt it important to call attention to the fact that this expedition did not bode well for the Americans currently living on Cuba, fearing that the colonial authorities might place restrictions on them and noting that the newspapers in Cuba denounced daily the "Buena Vista Yankees," recalling the last major battle of the U.S.-Mexican War.[44]

During López's trial, the *Daily Delta* published a history of the expedition as a defense for López's actions. J. C. Davis called the expedition the "most extraordinary piece of Knight-errantry on record—at least since the days of a certain Spanish gentleman dubbed 'Don Quixote.'" He insisted that the Cubans had asked the filibusters as "individuals having a right to leave home and go to Cuba, California, Hungary, Italy, or anywhere else" to sail to their assistance. Davis emphasized the centrality of López, the Cuban independence movement, and the Cuban people as a whole.[45] In response to doubts about the filibustering expeditions, supporters such as López's lawyer John Henderson stated, "I still believe in the importance, the morality, and probability of the enterprise." Henderson further believed it was one that "the South should steadfastly cherish and promote," emphasizing the region's vested interest in expansion and the annexation of Cuba. Information had been received from the island claiming that the Cubans were fully behind the expeditions, he insisted.[46]

The federal court eventually acquitted López, and he immediately began planning the next expedition, which set sail in August 1851. The court's decision did not sanction the expeditions, but acquittal did suggest to those interested in joining the filibusters that no real harm would come to them if they did so. As the ships arrived at Bahia Honda in Cuba, Gulf newspapers announced López's arrival and quickly began relating rumors of revolution on the island. Many of the revolutionaries who López had been in contact with on the island sent word to other possible hotbeds of revolutionary activity. Creoles in Cuba took independence into their own hands and on July 3, Joaquín de Agüero y Sanchez and a small band of men who had joined him rode into the town of Principe, shouting "Liberty—Death to the Spaniard!" Cubans under Agüero y Sanchez had hoped to gather significant forces to their cause. The message came back to New Orleans that Creoles at Puerto Principe would support the filibusters and had made a demonstration there on July 4, at which time a declaration of independence was read aloud to the local townspeople. This, the filibusters hoped, would inspire others across Cuba to rise up against the Spanish and join them. What the filibusters failed to understand in this moment was the extent to which they were caught up in multiple contests simultaneously—the contest between Americans and the Spanish over Cuba; the simmering conflict between Creoles on the island and the Spanish government; and the escalating tensions between the North and the South.[47]

News of the expedition came slow. It was shoddy and incomplete, making it difficult for those within the Gulf South cities, New Orleanians especially, to know exactly what was happening to the filibusters. At one point the *Pensacola Gazette* all but proclaimed López and his men victorious, claiming that a Spanish commander had offered López concessions and that Spanish soldiers daily joined López's ranks.[48] Yet in reality López's hopes of arriving in the middle of a revolution disintegrated when the planned uprisings yet again failed to materialize. During one of the final battles between Spanish troops and the filibusters, the Spanish army took fifty-one members of the filibustering expedition prisoner, including López. One of the better-known members of the expedition, William Crittenden, son of U.S. Attorney General John Crittenden, had been taken prisoner and would be executed, together with numerous members of his Kentucky regiment. With the expedition in spectacular ruins, the captured filibusters knew what awaited them—execution at the hands of their Spanish foes.

The expedition members came from all parts of the United States. Among them were Southerners and Northerners, Anglo Americans and Creoles from the Gulf South communities. They were transported to Havana's El Morro castle, where they awaited the firing squad. The filibusters were executed in groups of six to twelve. Crittenden was executed alone. López was also executed, at seven o'clock in the morning on September 1, 1851. Spanish colonial authorities meant to make an example of him, condemning him to execution by strangulation via a garrote.[49]

When the news of the expedition's outcome finally reached the United States, residents in Gulf South communities lashed out in anger. The target of New Orleanians' rage were the very neighborhoods in which Cubans and other Hispanic residents lived. Rumors spread throughout New Orleans that the Spanish consul refused to hand over the filibusters' final letters. A resident of the city reported the details of the end of the expedition and the reaction of New Orleanians to an acquaintance. The author of the letter denounced the Spanish as acting inhumanely toward men under López and Crittenden's command. Public outrage grew into outright violence and targeted destruction as mobs rioted in the streets. At two or three o'clock in the afternoon on August 21 New Orleanians gathered in the streets and marched to the offices of the Spanish newspaper, *La Union*, in Exchange Alley just below Conti Street. Angry demonstrators proceeded to storm the newspaper's printing room, destroy the presses, and throw the metal type into the street. The crowd then tore down the Spanish flag and consulate sign, carried them to Lafayette Square, and proceeded to burn them. They continued marching through the streets, arriving in the neighborhood where many Spanish and Cuban businesses were located. The crowd destroyed some forty Spanish-owned coffeehouses and cigar shops. Commenting on the extent of emotion that New Orleanians felt at the news of the executions Charles Colton Jones, a presbyterian minister and planter in Georgia, wrote his parents, noting, "no wonder the people of New Orleans should have been greatly excited at the murder of the fifty Americans." Later, in an effort to protect the local Cuban community from any kind of punishment from American or Spanish authorities and maintain favorable relations between Cuban Creoles and Anglo Southerners, the *Daily Picayune* stressed that Cubans did not take part in the riot and that no Cuban-owned businesses were harmed.[50]

The end of the expeditions and the riot in New Orleans presented Southern expansionists with a problem, a blight on the South's record of successful conquest. To keep the dream of Cuban annexation alive, Southerners now set about turning López into a martyr for their cause. Prior to the filibusters' execution, Crittenden and many of the doomed invaders wrote letters home, which were published in newspapers throughout the country. Crittenden wrote that López had decieved him, yet the idea of López as a deceiver did not survive the memory making that took shape after the end of the expedition. In 1855 a traveller named William Perkins sailed to Cuba to view the last resting place of Narciso López almost as a kind pilgramage and lamented that the country remained in Spanish hands. López entered into Southern mythology as "a pure, high-minded, noble-hearted patriot."[51] The failure of the expeditions to liberate Cuba and the executions went against the intertwined ideas of white American superiority and expansionism. Throughout the antebellum period expansionists consistently referred to the Spanish as an aging colonial power with a "skeletal" grip on Cuba; however, in reaction to the expeditions they displayed a military and political power the filibusters and diplomats like Pierre Soulé had not been prepared to encounter. López was memorialized, the Spanish were villified in order to preserve the connection between Anglo Americans and Cuban Creoles, but that connection took some blows with the outcome of the expedition. Remembering the end of the expedition, Boggess remarked bitterly that "there was not a particle of difference between the Spaniards and Cubans; the big majority have their price." While negative views of Cubans emerged out of the expeditions, this did little to diminish interest in annexing Cuba and the more popular vision of Cubansas sympathetic figures. The *San Antonio Ledger* maintained that the "Creole is a dog under the heel of a drunken and wrathful owner—a galley slave under constant goad. They ask, too, the many exiles whom tyranny has driven away to this dear soil to bestir themselves in their behalf. Alas for Cuba!"[52]

With the failure of the expeditions, expansionists changed tactics, pinning their hopes on purchasing the island through Pierre Soulé's efforts as minister to Spain, which culminated in the Ostend Manifesto. Through his involvement in both local city affairs and his senatorial duties, Soulé became interested in Cuban annexation and had been an enthusiastic supporter of the filibusters as well as Cuban exiles' efforts to gain independence.[53] Soulé's efforts eventually led him to journey to Spain in 1853 as U.S. minister, where he promoted Cuban annexation. Yet, by 1854 when American diplomats Pierre Soulé, John Mason, and James Buchanan crafted the Ostend Manifesto, the political tides changed and many Americans reacted with extreme hostility toward what they saw as yet another example of the planter class's overreaching command of national politics. All three were interested in orchestrating a treaty with Spain that would allow the United States to peaceably purchase Cuba. They met in Ostend, Belgium, in October and spent three days discussing the subject. What emerged was a document that the trio hoped would be the final push needed for the United States to finally purchase Cuba. Soulé and Buchanan were believed to have been the principal architects of the manifesto, with Soulé writing a good portion of the original and Buchanan taming his aggressive tone. The proposal came with the familiar warnings of race war and the threat that a Spanish-controlled Cuba posed to American trade flowing out of the Mississippi River. The authors evoked the threat of Black revolution, arguing that they would be committing treason and going against the generations past who fought to stave off such occurrences should the nation "permit Cuba to be Africanized and become a second St. Domingo, with all its attendant horrors to the white race." The manifesto argued that not only was it proper for the nation to annex Cuba but that such an action was also absolutely necessary for America's survival. Soulé, Buchanan, and Mason articulated a need for Cuban annexation based on the notion that to secure the South was to secure the nation. The trio's vision of Cuban annexation as a necessity for both region and nation preserved the idea that the futures of both remained entwined despite the fact that sectionalist sentiment grew ever louder between North and South. Efforts to gain Cuba now stood against the backdrop of the controversial Kansas-Nebraska Act, and American efforts to expand west started to diverge from Southern efforts to expand south.[54]

CONCLUSION

The process of memorializing the filibusters as martyrs to the cause of Cuban independence and American expansion involved the commemoration of the death of Narciso López. For several years after 1851 in New Orleans and other parts of the Gulf South, Cubans and white Southerners commemorated López's death on the anniversary of his execution and sought to keep the memory of the expeditions alive. Citizens of New Orleans held memorials for López despite the fact that his body was never returned to Louisiana. In New Orleans, the cathedral bells rang on Wednesday, September 1, 1852, much the way they had when the city first learned the news of the death of López and the other filibusters. New Orleanians were asked to go and pay tribute to General López, the "Washington of Cuba." The *Daily Picayune* again related the commemoration of López's funeral in the city in 1853.

During the 1854 commemoration the speeches were recorded in small pamphlets that could be purchased throughout the city. John S. Thrasher, one of John Quitman's associates, spoke about López and the relations between the United States and Cuba, which he viewed as being intrinsically linked as a result of López's expeditions. When Thrasher addressed the crowd, he highlighted López's tragic glory and the heroism of his executed men. However, throughout most of his speech he focused on the new relationship between the "Iberian" races that lived in Latin America and the "Anglo Saxon" race of the United States. Thrasher declared, "Here in this common tomb, and in these common glories, we have the perfect demonstration that the Iberian and the Saxon can unite." "Northern and Southern America," he continued, "would stand united before the world upon the noblest sentiment that can animate the heart of man; liberty and the elevation of the masses." Yet embedded in his call for North American and South American unity along the lines of liberty and the "elevation of the masses," which excluded those still held in bondage, was a critique of South American countries and their road toward independence. Thrasher declared that to Cuba, "the last remnant of the Spanish power in the New World, was reserved the glorious task of avoiding the errors of her elder sisters, and of initiating the true theory of their regeneration and welfare." As testament to the Cuban interests in memorializing López, Gaspar Betancourt Cisneros, a Cuban intellectual and annexation supporter, did not support slavery like many of his American brethren who favored Cuban independence or statehood. He also spoke at the commemoration ceremony. Betancourt believed that in 1854 there were "more men, more hearts, more sympathies, more resources and means ready to be sacrificed for the cause of Cuban independence than Narciso López had in 1851." Betancourt emphasized independence in his speech, and later in his life, he would support an independent Cuba rather than annexation to the United States.[55]

The year 1854 also marked the publication of the first novel concerning the final López expedition. Writing under the psuedonym H. M. Hardimann, Lucy Holcombe of Texas penned a novel that blended fact and fiction, effectively spinning both into the fabric of mythology. In 1854 she was a young woman from the planter class fascinated by the story of the filibusters and driven to write about it in a way that both memorialized the filibusters but also exposed the concerns of the planter class in the aftermath of their failure. She cast the expedition as one of a heroic army that sailed away to fight for another nation's freedom. Holcombe's novel goes to great lengths to contribute to the martyrization of López, going so far as to include the word "martyr" in the title, *The Free Flag of Cuba: or The Martyrdom of Lopez, a Tale of of the Liberating Expedition of 1851*.[56]

As Soulé, Buchanan, and Mason crafted their manifesto, the Kansas-Nebraska Act wound its way through Congress and soon led to the outbreak of violence between antislavery and proslavery supporters. In the United States the Ostend Manifesto's propositions seemed increasingly ludicrous, especially against the backdrop of fighting taking place in Kansas. In this heated environment the manifesto caused a severe backlash, as many antislavery proponents used it as yet another example of the South's intent to take complete control of the government and perpetuate slavery throughout the nation by gaining yet more territory. Political battles between North and South shaped many Southern interests in expansion, military protection, and Latin American territory as much as the threat of European abolitionism and the growth and the protection of trade. The shift in focus, toward the domestic threats to Southern expansion, also affected the way that community boosters argued for increased naval and army protection for their communities in places such as Florida and Texas. Where filibusters depended on racialized images of Creoles and Mexicans as well as on the narrative of victory from the U.S.-Mexican War, those calling for increased protection focused mostly on protecting the vital trade routes in and out of the Gulf of Mexico and securing new trade routes in the U.S.-Mexico border region. The rush to annex Cuba remained only one half of continued efforts to control the Gulf of Mexico. In Texas the 1850s brought continued struggle on the part of Anglos to assert their dominance along the new U.S.-Mexico border and Texas interior. As ever, coastal communities like Galveston worked to be a part of this story.

CHAPTER 5

Galveston and the Fight for the Texas Borderlands

A month after the signing of the Treaty of Guadalupe Hidalgo, in March 1848, Texans celebrated the anniversary of Texas independence. It was an auspicious time, a time to take stock of the last few years. Anglo Texans had much to celebrate and much to ponder. The *Houston Democratic Telegraph and Texas Register* published a lengthy commemoration of both the end of the war and the anniversary. "The twelfth anniversary has just passed by, and lo the astonishing change! The proud banner of the Union floats triumphant over the battlements of the Mexican Capital," it announced. The "proud banner of the Union" also floated above the Texas state capital, and when the treaty was ratified by the United States Senate, the Rio Grande became the state's southern border. All was as the Texans wanted it to be. The newspaper's celebration of the U.S. victory as a part of Texas independence signaled a belief that one stage of expansion had come to an end and the expansion of agriculture and trade in Texas could now proceed with vigor.[1] For Anglo Texans, territorial expansion now shifted direction away from the invasion of Mexico and back to securing the Texas hinterlands. After the war, the Gulf South faced a central question: now that the war was over, the treaty ratified, and the old villain supposedly put to rest, how was the actual process of expansion going to proceed in places like Texas and how would that affect the coastal communities?

The efforts to answer this question came amid the Cuban filibustering expeditions and their disastrous endings. Galvestonians, like many along the Gulf South, always thought in two directions, toward the Caribbean and toward the Rio Grande. During the expeditions Galvestonians supported them much as New Orleanians did. Galveston newspapers recorded and posted notices about meetings held in New Orleans by the nation's leading filibusters, and in 1850 a party of 250 men left Galveston and Corpus Christi to participate in Cuban filibustering. Peter Hansborough Bell addressed a large meeting in Galveston calling for the immediate annexation of Cuba to the United States. Later in 1851, Sam Houston traveled to New Orleans, where he addressed a large fundraising meeting of citizens and also pledged Texas's support for Cuban annexation.[2]

At the same time, American and Mexican commissioners endeavored to survey the new dividing line between the United States and Mexico. As Rachel St. John notes, this was easier said than done. At the end of the U.S.-Mexican War, Texans, Americans, and Mexicans thought that the hard work of securing the border was largely over. However, the coming decades proved that assumption to be incorrect. While the portion of the border that is defined by the Rio Grande appeared to be more settled than the western portion, efforts at settlement and upheavals within borderland communities revealed that Anglo Americans struggled to enforce their power in this part of Texas.[3]

While the end of the U.S.-Mexican War seemed like an immense victory for the nation, the Gulf South, and Texas, the reality was far more complex. Mexico may have been defeated, but through the 1850s it became evident that the war had, in reality, settled very little concerning the Texas borderlands. Anxieties over continued tensions between Anglos and Mexican Texans remained and the security of slavery appeared to still be as imperiled as it had been prior to annexation. In the aftermath of the U.S.-Mexican War, pro-expansionists sought to solidify their hold of Texas's economy and territory. They hoped to knit together the various pieces of the state—the rich cotton districts, the coastal trading centers, the western border, and the growing river trade. The port towns of the western Gulf sought to solidify their status by facilitating the growth of these connections. To do this, the Texas interior would have to be settled, and to that end, Anglos worked to assert their dominance over what they viewed as the unruly borders of their state. In their struggles to assert that mastery in the years following the U.S.-Mexican War, Galveston city boosters' use of expansionist ideas revealed much about the state of Southern society in the borderlands at the beginning of the 1850s.

Galveston became one of the main ports of entry for migrants and immigrants as well as a primary site for trade. In order to encourage further settlement in Texas, Galvestonians supported efforts to open up trade along East Texas's main rivers. Texas ports continued to encourage new steamship lines that connected them to the other Gulf cities. In addition, the coastal communities supported the continued militarization of the newly established U.S.-Mexico border and participated in the spread of slavery throughout Texas. The army and local governments not only protected settlers but also aided in policing the state's racial order during the 1850s.[4]

This chapter considers how Anglo Texans sought to control the lives of immigrants, Mexicans, Native Americans, and free and enslaved African Americans in order to finally lay claim to the Texas borderlands. As the state's white population grew, so too did its Black population, especially its enslaved Black population. Indeed, the movements of free and enslaved African Americans through Galveston and the Lower Rio Grande Valley were a constant worry for Anglos, and the reason they fought to control the lives of these various groups. The chapter also considers how these latter pushed back against those attempts at supremacy. More specifically, Anglo Texans hoped to control the political voices of European immigrants and Mexicans during the 1850s partly because they believed that both communities harbored antislavery sentiments and might potentially have the power to act on them. Following from these fears, continued violence between white settlers and Native Americans in the western counties and between Mexicans and Anglos on the Rio Grande caused many to question the federal government's ability and willingness to monitor this region. Thus, the presence of Latin American peoples, Native Americans, Mexicans, and European immigrants within the Gulf Coast took on new meaning as settlement in Texas expanded, the rift between free and slave states widened, and the slave population grew.[5]

Antebellum Galveston's connections to its neighboring port towns as well as Anglo Texans' continued efforts to control and secure their borders occurred within the context of mounting national divisions concerning the spread of slavery into the western territory. Texas might yet again provide examples of the South's expansionist success if Anglo Texans could bring their state's frontiers to heel. Gulf ports along the Texas coast might have competed with each other for the lion's share of the exports from the Texas hinterlands, but they were also part of this much larger project of settlement and worked as the gateway to the rural plantations and farms beyond. Yet, Galveston remained Texas's crown jewel and a symbol of the Texas Coast's future and the possibilities of expansion.[6]

GALVESTON IN 1850

The multiple processes of physical expansion of Anglo settlement, as well as the extension and solidification of state and municipal power, happened simultaneously and were intertwined. As settlers moved farther into west

108   Chapter Five

Texas, coastal towns began to see the value of the interior and its importance to the coast's economic viability. The coastal town of Indianola's newspaper emphasized the importance of connecting the interior and the coast, and of pushing white settlers to west Texas, which they urged "must ever be eminently a producing State." Such a region, "with a territory as large as several of the largest States in the Union, must ere long, in the progress of events furnish cargoes for more vessels than any States in the Union, and hence build up a tremendous commerce." This was the next step in the process of expansion for the Anglos living on the Texas coast.[7]

By 1840 Galveston had already emerged as Texas's main port. A visitor to the city in 1850 wrote that the "appearance of Galveston is imposing and cannot fail of striking the stranger with a favorable impression." In the antebellum era, Galveston paved the main streets with bleached white shells and imported fragrant oleanders, which eventually led to its nickname as the "Oleander City." The city's wharves lined the water's edge along the backs of the merchant buildings of the Strand, the city's main thoroughfare, and rental houses popped up on the city's streets at a record pace.[8]

By the time of the U.S.-Mexican War, Galveston looked much more permanent than it had at the start of the Texas Republic, with brick structures and bustling streets full of a myriad of different peoples. "The population of Galveston is a medley of all nations, stimulated and urged onward by the universal and indomitable spirit of Yankeeism, a spirit that is to revolutionize the world," proclaimed the *Texas Planter*. The paper promised that agricultural and cultural comforts of civilization would soon become available, tying together the city's prosperity and rapid growth with the dreams of expansion and the "indomitable spirit" of American Yankeeism. Such articles hoped to demonstrate to those living in the region that the city was well on its way to becoming as sophisticated as New Orleans or Mobile. Galvestonians boasted that the growth of their city made it the "Queen City" of Texas. Though cotton was Galveston's main export throughout the 1850s, its export of sugar also grew steadily. It possessed a foundry and a sugar mill, and the newspaper advised sugar planters to use Galveston's facilities rather than going farther afield to New Orleans or Havana. In 1850 Galveston exported 2,782 hogsheads of sugar and roughly the same in molasses. By the close of the decade these numbers reached fifteen thousand barrels of sugar and nine thousand barrels of molasses.[9]

With the growth of cotton and sugar plantations came the growth of the enslaved population of Texas, from 30,505 in 1846 to 48,145 in 1850, and Galveston also provided the main market and site of importation of the trade in people as well as the commodities that they produced. By 1850 Texas had a total population of 212,000; within a decade, that number would grow to over 604,000. According to the 1850 census, Galveston's total population stood at just under four thousand, with three hundred slaves and thirty free African Americans. Galveston's free Black population was never as substantial as those of the eastern Gulf South ports, and it did not possess the deep historical roots of the free people of color found in New Orleans or Mobile.[10]

Enslaved and free African Americans and Galveston's white working class often inhabited the same residential spaces. Because most of the town's space was given over to merchant houses, rental houses, and wharves, the city's residential space became connected through a system of alleys and back yards. During the 1840s, slaves inhabited these areas along with the city's free African Americans and working-class whites. Housing for slaves also included other outbuildings, such as carriage houses and kitchens, and these remained in the back of most lots, creating a network of pathways used primarily by servants.[11]

By the 1850s, shipping routes between Galveston and New Orleans had become firmly established, with vessels running back and forth weekly between these two cities.[12] Incoming ships transported European immigrants as well as goods and enslaved African Americans. By 1853 Galveston's neighbors touted the growing trade between small western port towns and the larger Gulf cities. In the latter half of the 1850s, Galveston received over 65 vessels from Europe and 483 from the Gulf Coast cities in one year. The *Indianola Bulletin* boasted, "A regular line of packet schooners has been established to run from Philadelphia to Galveston, Indianola and Port Lavaca . . . and hereafter two vessels per month may be expected." "We are very gratified," wrote the *Bulletin*, "to see these increasing developments of our trade, and the growing facilities springing up to enable our country to carry on its trade with the larger cities with speed, certainty and cheapness." As testament to this growing trade and increased shipping, Galveston provided other services for sailors, such as room and board and sail making.[13]

These ships transported the wealth of Texas's inland plantations, and they also brought enslaved African Americans who traveled with their owners or traveled to the Texas port cities for sale. The development of new shipping lines and the continued arrival of European immigrants became one of the primary ways that Galveston connected the settlement of Texas with the growth of the maritime economy in the Gulf South. When newspapers announced passenger lists for recently arrived ships, they also stated the number of African Americans on board. This mention was a potent reminder of the Gulf's part in the internal slave trade and forced migration of enslaved African Americans to the Southern hinterlands.

As already suggested, the movement of free and enslaved African Americans through Galveston as well as the presence of European immigrants caused Galveston's municipal government to enforce strict racial hierarchies through ordinances and city laws. European immigrants, though white, provoked anxiety among Anglos in Texas, especially slaveholding Anglos and particularly in places like Galveston where African Americans and European immigrants could interact. German immigrants were believed to harbor antislavery sentiments and were perpetually looked on with suspicion. Certainly, their community was large enough to project a significant presence in Galveston as well as some towns around San Antonio. German immigration began during the 1830s and continued through the 1840s. Yet, the reality of their attitudes toward slavery was far more complex than Anglo Texans tended to believe. Germans who had come to the state as political refugees tended to oppose slavery while other German immigrants were either indifferent or accepted its reality; some owned slaves. There is an irony here in that both Anglos and Germans were recent arrivals to Texas, but when the United States annexed Texas Anglos dominated the state's political and economic structures while the Germans continued to be looked upon as immigrants. Anglos in Galveston were able to enforce their idealized racial hierarchy with little pushback from the state's previous inhabitants, even as that pushback continued in other parts of the state.[14]

While Texas continued to attempt to remove Native Americans and peoples of Mexican descent and limit the political agency of European immigrants, Galveston's boosters began to organize their city in ways similar to older Southern cities. Throughout the antebellum period, Galveston slave owners and city officials alike worked to establish control over the movement of slaves, free Blacks, and immigrants. During the 1840s there was little in the way of regulation, but by the end of the decade, the city passed ordinances attempting to limit fraternization.[15]

During Galveston mayor John Sydnor's time in office, the city issued several ordinances that attempted to codify and dictate how free and unfree African Americans interacted in the city. In his first year in office Sydnor approved vagrancy laws, which were used to target Black people moving in and out of the city, as well the movement of teamsters, wagons transporting goods, into the city. Most teamsters during the antebellum period were of Mexican descent, which was one of the reasons that they were so heavily regulated. Sydnor passed ordinances that made it unlawful for anyone to "buy, sell, or receive from any slave or slaves any commodity of any kind of whatsoever, without the written consent of the owner or employer of said slave." Breaking this ordinance resulted in a ten-dollar fine. Secreting or hiding slaves within town limits resulted in a fifty-dollar fine. Slaves were not permitted to hire themselves out. Free persons of color were prohibited from hosting gatherings for other free persons of color or slaves. Free Blacks arriving in Galveston were required to pay a tax to the mayor upward of five hundred dollars or be sentenced to work hard labor in the city. Ordinances required free persons to keep up the appearances of their houses and be "peaceable." Other ordinances targeted all lower-class individuals, such as those found "begging, or drunk in and about the streets, or loitering in and about tippling houses, all who can show no reasonable course of business in said city, all who have no fixed place of residence." Such persons could be rounded up by Galveston police forces and brought before the mayor. The ordinance also targeted "public" prostitutes and women leading "notorious lewd or luscious" lives.[16]

Now that the land was secured through annexation and a war of conquest, the trade between the border South and the Southern interior had to be protected and increased. As early as 1838, travelers to Texas coastal towns remarked on the flood of settlers. On his way through Houston, Roemer noted "a great number of those whom I saw entering the city did not stop in it: but their passage gave it a most animated appearance."[17] While the city attempted to capitalize on the exploits of land agents and merchants, the real work of transforming the city from a backwater stop to one of the fastest growing cities on the coast was accomplished by free African Americans, poor whites, and, most importantly, by slaves. Even with the turn toward commercial expansion in the city, its newspapers still touted territorial expansion and Galveston's involvement in it as important for the city's prosperity.

ATTRACTING SETTLERS AND SELLING THE ENSLAVED

Though Galvestonians were far from the state's western border, merchants and city leaders interested in expanding its economy and position within Texas took an interest in western counties. Many efforts to construct railroads and strengthen river transportation were aimed at enhancing connections between west Texas and the Gulf ports, as well as supporting military actions in the frontier. One of the more widely supported schemes was the Galveston, Houston, and Henderson Railroad, which many believed would connect coastal and western counties. In order to make these counties safe for further economic development, Galvestonians urged further military protection of the western counties.[18]

The promise of Texas land had long attracted settlers to the region, and the state fought to maintain favorable land policies to attract even more arrivals. As a part of Mexico, Texas had been allowed to administer its own public domain. During annexation, Texas insisted on maintaining this tenet of Mexican federalism. For example, as a state, Texas continued many of the land policies it had practiced as an independent nation. In 1854 the state legislature passed the Texas Preemption Act, offering homesteaders 160-acre plots of land for 50 cents an acre, a price which was significantly lower than the U.S. government's price.[19]

To encourage settlers and aid them in their move to Texas, journals like *De Bow's Review* published articles detailing Texas's landscape, weather, and population makeup. The June 1851 issue of *De Bow's Review* contained instructions for emigrants on what to expect in Texas. The authors warned settlers about the cold north winds but attempted to show these aspects of Texas in a positive light. "These periodical winds," they advised, "doubtless tend greatly to purify the atmosphere." *De Bow's Review* listed the best times of the year to travel and which routes to take, depending on the settlers' place of origin. If a person's main destination was the Gulf Coast or the western frontier, the article recommended a sea route, as driving oxen, a wagon, family, and belongings across the entirety of Texas was a much harder prospect than disembarking at Galveston and proceeding from there. New Orleans emigrants, according to *De Bow's Review*, could purchase passage on several steamships for a "trifling expense." "The active and enterprising New Englander, the bold and hardy western hunter, the chivalrous and high-spirited southern planter meet here upon common ground, divested of all sectional influence, and lend their combined energies to the improvement of this infant but delightful and prosperous country." For *De Bow's Review*, settlement of the Texas prairie from all sections of the country had the potential to quell mounting sectional tensions.[20]

Land was fundamentally important to all settlers, but the planters intent on settling Texas also valued the slaves forced to work it. *De Bow's Review* warned those going to Texas, including European immigrants, to be cautious about purchasing land. Texas entered the United States owning its public lands and having created a land system that attempted to both attract larger numbers of settlers as well as protect the property of those living there. However, land speculators abounded, and the *Review* rated the various land titles according to their authenticity. The editors stated there were three main forms of land titles, all with varying degrees of authenticity. The Spanish colonial and Mexican titles were among the most dependable. Those titles issued under the Texas Republic and the state of Texas had varying degrees of dependability. A poorly informed settler might purchase a land title only to find that it had been a forgery. No matter which form of title an emigrant possessed, the *Review* advised that "the best way for emigrants to gain correct information is to go and examine personally for themselves."[21]

Galvestonians attempted to capitalize on land hunger in a variety of ways, but after the U.S.-Mexican War enhancing the river trade became paramount. Attempts to improve the region's river transportation system had begun before the war, gaining further support thereafter. Enhancing river access was urgent for sustaining Galveston's pride of place among Texas cities, given that Anglo American settlement was pushing further inland and away from the coast after the war. Opening up navigation to the plantations and farms far north on the Trinity River was a primary goal. Several Galveston newspapers reported on a meeting in Livingston calling for a convention of the counties surrounding the Trinity River to send men for the purpose of clearing the river of logs and removing shallow shoals to make steam transport easier. Other plans consisted of canals to be built along the Brazos River, allowing access to Galveston Bay. On February 8, 1850, the Galveston Brazos Navigation Company obtained a charter to construct a canal connecting the bay and the Brazos. Unlike the doomed canal projects in Florida, the Brazos-Galveston canal was eventually finished in 1855.[22]

While canals and river transportation brought cotton down to the coastal communities like Galveston, the city's participation in the extension of slavery also upheld its prominence in the region. In 1833 Stephen F. Austin concluded, "Texas *must* be a slave country." "Circumstances and unavoidable necessity compels it," he wrote, and "it is the wish of the people there, and it is my duty to do all I can, prudently, in favor of it."[23] As Galveston developed, the institution of slavery underwent significant changes in Texas even as it continued the process of expansion in the urban and rural parts of the western Gulf South. Slaves moved from the upper South through the internal slave trade or with their owners. Historian Sean Kelley cites several major groups migrating during the antebellum period. While his work focuses on the Brazos region of eastern Texas, these stages of migration correspond with the experience of slavery in other parts of Texas and shed some light on Galveston's place in its growth.[24]

The first stage of migration took place during the initial settlement of Texas starting in the 1820s and 1830s, when Anglos first brought their slaves with them. The second, which also involved Anglo settlers, took place during the transitional period from annexation to the outbreak of the U.S.-Mexican War; the third took place during the early 1850s when many of the enslaved were brought to Texas by slave-trading firms. Many enslaved African Americans in the eastern coastal plains of Texas also came through the developing markets in both Houston and Galveston. In addition to African American slaves from other parts of the South, slavers shipped enslaved Africans from Cuba to Texas during the early antebellum period, making them the fourth and smallest migratory group. Because of this, Galveston and Houston slave traders eventually became interested in efforts to reopen the African slave trade.[25]

The slave trade through Galveston was operated by auctioneers who dealt in land as well as slaves. Unlike other ports throughout the South, such as New Orleans and Mobile, Galveston did not initially possess a main site of sale. However, after his time in office, John Sydnor became one of the city's slave traders, primarily selling slaves out of the warehouse he used for his cotton business. The *Houston Telegraph* maintained that Sydnor's market was the largest slave market west of New Orleans, and Sydnor did the auctioning himself. Sydnor placed an ad in the *Civilian* establishing himself as an auctioneer of "merchandize, Produce, Real Estate, Negroes." Josephine Ryles, a former slave, recalled that she was sold in Galveston and that slaves were not shipped elsewhere to be sold. Another woman, Mintie Maria Miller, remembered being sold in Houston and described the market there as an "open house, like a shed."[26] These types of sales highlighted the shifting and fluid manner of slave markets beyond the more traditional sites of the Old South. Ex-slaves not only told stories of being sold in Texas but also tales of forced migration. During his travels through Texas, Fredrick Law Olmsted elicited similar stories from enslaved African Americans he encountered. While camped on the banks of the Guadalupe River, Olmsted met with an elderly Black man and woman traveling to their plantation. The husband had been in the country longer than their master. He told Olmsted, "I've been in these parts these four year" and related his life as a slave, telling Olmsted that he'd been sold many times from masters in Maryland, South Carolina, Tennessee, and Arkansas before finally being sold to a man traveling to Texas. Sydnor sold hundreds of enslaved persons during the 1840s and 1850s but was not the only slave dealer on the island.[27]

While most slaves came from the interior parts of the South, some came to Texas from Cuba through the illegal African slave trade. There has been much debate on the extent of this trade and the numbers of slaves who entered the United States via Cuba. Describing the continuation of the African slave trade in Texas, Randolph Campbell maintains that illegal cargos of enslaved Africans on Cuban ships never amounted to more than a few thousand of the state's growing number of slaves. Campbell estimates that some two thousand African slaves came through Galveston during the antebellum period.[28]

Free African Americans' lives in Texas were buffeted by the stages of expansion and annexation in ways similar to those that affected African Americans in other parts of the Gulf South. They continually had to advocate for their ability to stay in Texas as Anglos poured in and became hostile to their presence. The hostility and suspicion shown toward immigrants, free African Americans, Mexicans, and Native Americans was a consequence of white Southern domination and the extension of slavery into Texas. Before the Texas Revolution, free African Americans had migrated to Texas of their own accord. Under Spanish rule, Tejanos in New Spain lived under several laws that could provide pathways to freedom for enslaved African Americans. Once Mexico gained its independence, it deliberated the abolition of slavery, making clear slavery would not be allowed to grow unchecked, which also meant that African Americans searching for a better life for themselves and their families could settle in many of the coastal towns. The separation of Texas from Mexico was a devastating blow to them. The Texas Republic's new congress passed a law expelling free African Americans from the state. Free Black people had to obtain special dispensations from the congress or leave by January 1842. This law touched off a feverish race on the part of the state's free Black population to obtain petitions from their local communities supporting their right to remain. They first petitioned the Republic's congress; after annexation, they asked the state legislature to allow them to remain in the state.

Free Black petitions came from all over Texas, many of them explicitly detailing the good character of the free person of color. Petitioners were described as industrious, peaceable, courteous to whites, and not a "bad influence" on slaves. Likewise, their standing in the community and whether or not they had obtained property was often mentioned, as was the length of time they had been in Texas. An 1840 petition filed by fifty-six Anglo citizens in Houston requested that a freewoman named Zelia Husk and her daughter Emily be allowed to stay in the republic, as they had been residents of the country since 1835. They described her as a "good and industrious woman peaceably earning her own livelihood," who "has not the means to transport her own child beyond the limits of the Republic." The petitioners used Husk's status as both an asset to the community and as a mother in the hopes of gaining permission for her to stay in Texas. For Husk and her daughter, the result was positive, but for others the experience did not turn out as well.[29]

In Harris County, another free woman of color, Fanny McFarland, filed a petition to stay in the republic, in which she justified her continued residence in Texas by emphasizing that she, like many of the white men in power, had moved to Texas during Mexican rule. McFarland maintained that her master freed her for good service and that she lost all she had in the Mexican invasion. By mentioning the loss of her property at the hands of Mexicans in her petition, she invoked the shared experience of the Texas War of Independence as a part of her claims to citizenship. In addition to these justifications, she, like Husk, also emphasized motherhood, as well as her old age. Both women may have emphasized their status as mothers in the hopes that it would sway the congressmen hearing their petitions; motherhood might also have given them an air of respectability.[30] Sadly, the historical record remains silent about the result of her petition, but McFarland's words demonstrate at least one way that African Americans understood the white fantasy of expansion and used it toward their own ends. Though the attempted expulsion of free African Americans from Texas meant their expulsion from the Anglo fantasy of expansion, some nevertheless appropriated expansionist ideas. Free African Americans continued to live and work within the coastal cities. They did so alongside enslaved African Americans who continued to arrive on Texas's shores.

Enslaved peoples' experiences of forced migration and sale in the Southern borderlands speak to the extreme level of displacement they often experienced and how that displacement formed a central part of Anglo American expansion and Southern imperialism. This displacement also provided a record of the continuous violence of white expansionist fantasies as much as the wars of conquest Anglos fought in Texas, Florida, Mexico, and Cuba. Galveston's involvement in the perpetuation of slavery through its market and port linked it to this larger process of expansion, as did its interest in pushing settlement further into the Texas interior, past the coastal plains. The Gulf ports aided in the visions of prosperity that drew settlers to Texas, and slaveholding settlers attempted to impart those visions to their slaves as they migrated to borderlands.[31]

Slaves remembered and recounted the stories of their journeys to the Southern borderlands. Betty Farrow, born in Virginia, was forced to migrate to Texas with her master's family. She remembered the children treating their departure like a celebration, but the journey over the mountains was so perilous that it quickly drained them of any excitement. According to Farrow, another woman recalled that the women and children rode in wagons while the male slaves were chained together and walked alongside during the passage to Texas. Ex-slave Lewis Jenkins claimed he had emigrated with his owners from Green County, Alabama, as a child, fleeing family scandal. Jenkins's mother was one of the white Jenkins women, and his father a slave owned by the same family. Rather than acknowledge an interracial child born of a white woman and the subsequent scandal that would ensue, the family moved to Texas, forcing young Lewis to go along as their slave.[32]

John White, unlike Jenkins, was sold from an eastern plantation to a woman in Linden, Texas. Remembering the long and tedious journey from the East Coast, White claimed that it seemed "like we going to wear out all the horses before we gets to the place."[33] The passage to Texas was often dangerous and lengthy for Southerners, immigrants, and slaves alike, but for slaves in particular, the journey was characterized by uncertainty of their condition there upon arrival, the violence they encountered, and the forced separation from family over a long distance.

The passage of slaves to the Texas borderlands was a vital part of Anglo Southerners' continued attempts to dominate the region. Anglo Texans' agricultural production, as well as their own identity, was dependent on the slaves they brought with them. Slaves' experiences in the growing slave markets of the Gulf Coast provide a window through which one can see the evolution of Texas's slave society. For them, forced migration was both a significant part of their lives and a significant part of the process of expansion. While ideas about expansion focused on Anglo-Saxon superiority, the reality of Southern expansion continued to be grounded in the region's dependency on slave labor.

Once they arrived in Texas, enslaved African Americans described being forced into pens as protection against such dangers as mountain lions on the prairies and in the woods. Texas slave owners were known for being particularly harsh. For many enslaved Black people, the frontier was a far-off place where owners sent them as a punishment. Others told stories of harsh conditions similar to what Edward Baptist described in his work on the Florida frontier. Plantations in the Southern borderlands, Baptist reminds us, were often rudimentary organizations that demonstrated the extent to which they were little more than moneymaking enterprises driven by extreme violence and cruelty. In many ways, the actual process of expansion stripped the South bare of its imaginings and fantasies that Southern intellectuals had concocted during the antebellum period in order to portray the region's slave institution as benign. During his time in East Texas, Olmsted was struck by a "peculiarity in the tone of the relation between master and slave." He described a warlike mentality on the part of the masters regarding to their slaves. "Damn 'em, give 'em hell," was said to be a frequent expression of the "ruder planters." Out beyond the South's more settled parts such as Virginia or South Carolina, fantasies about expansion took over, but even those could not cover up the reality of slavery in the Southern borderlands. The experiences of slaves, their migration, and the stories that slaveholders told them about Texas reveal the fragile nature of Southern imperialism in the antebellum era and the brutal reality of expansion along the South's borders.[34] The continuous fear of war and border instability generated harsh measures against nonwhites as Anglos worked to enforce their dominance.

The U.S.-Mexico border, not predatory animals, formed the primary worry for slave owners in Texas. As Alice Baumgartner has demonstrated, enslaved African Americans did not view the Rio Grande as a barrier but as a possible gateway toward freedom; many of them escaped through it. In this landscape of freedom as Alice Baumgartner refers to it, African Americans sought out ways to escape enslavement as well as form communities in Mexico. She puts the number of enslaved people who escaped to Mexico in the 1850s between three and five thousand, and from the beginning of the Texas Revolution to the outbreak of the Civil War as many as three-quarters of enslaved people caught in Texas as runaways claimed their destination was Mexico. One of the main reasons that Mexico was so attractive to enslaved African Americans was that the Mexican Congress passed a law granting freedom to any enslaved person from any country who set foot on Mexican Territory in 1849. That same year, as Alice Baumgartner notes, the Seminole leader Wild Cat decided that Mexico would be a better place for his people than the Indian Territory. Black Seminoles accompanied Wild Cat's group as they traveled the hundreds of miles to negotiate with the Mexican government, which gave them land and aid in exchange for the Seminoles setting up a military colony on the border that would provide protection against raids from the Comanche and Lipan Apache as well as stop any potential Anglo American filibusters.[35]

The end of the U.S.-Mexican War did not alleviate anxiety over the border between the United States and Mexico. In fact, as the decade of the 1850s wore on, it would become evident that Anglo Texans still grappled with many of the same issues they had dealt with as a young republic, including slaves fleeing to Mexico. Slaves invested the state's boundaries with just as much meaning as their enslavers, perhaps even more. For them, the borderland meant hope and refuge. The line between free and enslaved that others saw as dividing North and South also existed in the boundary between the United States and Mexico.[36]

Newspaper advertisements for runaways frequently cited the slaves' intended destination as Mexico. The Galveston *Civilian and Gazette* published a lengthy article taken from the *Houston Telegraph*, in which it reported the observations one Anglo Texan, W. Secrest, made about the presence of runaways on the Mexican side of the Rio Grande. Secrest estimated that 270 slaves crossed the ferries at Eagle Pass and Laredo in 1850. He claimed that at least eighteen hundred runaways from Arkansas had crossed through the border towns and lived in Mexico along with five hundred formerly enslaved African Americans from Texas. The *Civilian* remarked that if the numbers ascribed were correct, "we have a worse Free Soil settlement on our immediate border than any at the North, and one which cannot be permanently tolerated." The *Galveston Weekly News*'s San Antonio correspondent related the story of an African American thief who had been arrested along with a "fine stout negro fellow, doubtless belonging to some of our planters on the coast." The correspondent anticipated that both were headed for the "negro's promised land—Mexico." The *Texas Almanac* warned settlers that the counties along the Rio Grande desperately wanted slave labor, but "many slaves escape, every year, into Mexico."[37]

Some Texas newspapers lamented the lack of protection for slavery in the Treaty of Guadalupe Hidalgo of 1848. This did not, however, stop masters from marching down to the border to retrieve their runaway "property." During the latter half of the 1850s, the Texas Rangers functioned as a border patrol and helped to enforce the boundaries that Anglo slaveholders sought to create in order to control their slave populations. Others crossed the border to capture runaways, but without much success.[38] Mexican state officials did not look kindly on armed bands of strange Anglos arriving unannounced and invading their northern frontier. On the other hand, some Mexicans worked as slave catchers, allying themselves with the east Texas planters.[39]

POLICING THE BORDERS

Although the Rio Grande was several hundred miles from cities such as Galveston and Houston, residents in the rural communities located on the Texas coastal plains and port towns worried about the different populations of free and enslaved African Americans, European immigrants, and Mexicans living along Texas's borders and supported a strong military presence to police them. In the aftermath of the U.S.-Mexican War, Anglo Texans reaffixed their attention to those Mexicans living and working within Texas as well as those living directly across the border. In fact, at times it seemed as if the war had not settled anything at all, with continued conflicts between Mexican and Anglo border towns and competition among Mexican and Anglo merchants. Tensions along the border were a potent reminder of the resistance of Mexicans against Anglo rule, suggesting that the U.S.-Mexican War did not end tidily. Much like other American wars before and after, it had ended chaotically and with much uncertainty. White Southerners fought to reinforce their superiority and maintain the fantasy of expansion into Latin America even as enslaved and free African Americans, Mexicans, and Native Americans pushed back against those dreams. For example, by the 1850s Mexicans and Germans had managed to carve out a small amount of economic and political space for themselves in the Gulf South. The German population of Texas numbered twenty thousand and the Mexican population numbered fifteen thousand. Many Mexican Texans lived in San Antonio, one of the largest towns in Texas aside from Galveston, and in smaller communities in the Rio Grande Valley. European immigrants were mostly German, but their numbers also included Czech, Polish, and French immigrants. European immigrants and Mexican Texans created newspapers and organizations and participated in local politics. In Galveston, German immigrants formed societies to help their fellow immigrants become acclimated to life in Texas.

In border communities where Anglos and Mexicans interacted and competed for land, any small altercation had the potential to turn into an armed conflict. On May 13, 1851, the *Galveston Weekly News* published several letters from Brownsville and Roma, two border communities experiencing skirmishes between Mexican troops and Anglo militiamen. There are conflicting accounts as to what led to that particular firefight. While one letter stated that Mexican troops fired on Roma merchants for exporting cowhides to Mexico, another from Brownsville claimed that Roma citizens crossing the border to attend a dance were fired upon by the Mexican guard. Either way, it ended with the "red flag hoisted on both sides of the river, and a war of extermination declared by both parties."[40]

As he commented on Anglo Texans' continued hunger for more of Mexico's northern frontier, Frederick Law Olmsted's descriptions of Texas highlighted prevalent attitudes about Mexicans. "The Mexican masses," according to Olmsted, "are vaguely considered as degenerate and degraded Spaniards; it is, at least, equally correct to think of them as improved and Christianized Indians. In their tastes and social instincts, they approximate the African." The difference between Africans and Mexicans, he further noted, was "less felt" than those he saw between northern and southern Europeans. There were "many Mexicans of mixed negro blood," and Olmsted felt that even those "in respectable social positions whose color and physiognomy would subject them, in Texas, to be sold by the sheriff as negro-estrays who cannot be allowed at large without detriment to the common wealth." For Olmsted, it seemed that "between our Southern American and the Mexican, an unconquerable antagonism of character, which will prevent any condition of order where the two come together."[41] Farther into the interior, in communities such as San Antonio where Mexican Texans continued to live, city officials attempted to curtail displays of Mexican culture such as bullfights and cock fights while also monitoring the entry of Mexican peoples from outside the community.

The *Galveston Weekly News*'s San Antonio correspondent kept readers well informed about life there and focused much attention on Mexicans within the city, often describing murders and crime involving the Mexicans who migrated in and out of the city. While riding through the countryside in the vicinity of San Antonio, Olmsted observed instances of elite Mexicans directing their slaves to work alongside Mexican laborers on their "plantations." Though Olmsted intended only to observe and record images of Texas slaveholding society, as an Anglo American, he also participated in emphasizing the distinctions between Mexican classes. Anglo Texans often conflated elite Mexicans with notions of "civilized" gentlemanly mannerisms and increased participation in slavery. Olmsted repeated this racialization process.[42]

Just as slaveholders in Galveston sought to restrict the movement of free Blacks and slaves on the island, Anglos in western Texas also tried to limit the mobility of working class and impoverished Mexicans. *El Bejareno*, one of San Antonio's two Spanish language newspapers, reported that the town of Seguin in central Texas had decided to expel all Mexican laborers from the county. Vigilantes destroyed carts belonging to Mexican teamsters and drove Mexican families from the area. *El Bejareno* commented on the irony created by this situation. The expulsion of Mexicans may have preserved the stability of Anglo mastery over the local slave populations, but it forced planters to transport their cotton crop to San Antonio, where Mexican teamsters were available to haul cotton down to Port Lavaca on the Gulf Coast.[43] Curtailing the movement of Mexicans within the state continued throughout the 1850s.

Because of anti-Mexican and anti-German attitudes, during the 1850s the Know Nothing Party enjoyed a brief surge in popularity. Texas Know Nothings addressed many of the same anti-Catholic and anti-immigrant issues as did their counterparts in the North, but their suspicions of both Mexican and German populations were also tied to the desire to keep them separate from enslaved African Americans. All of this put Gulf ports such as Galveston in an awkward position because they were entry points for immigrants moving to Texas and thus benefited from their presence. As a result, the Know Nothing party often focused on issues concerning the construction of railroads from Galveston to the western counties. The city was home to a large number of German immigrants and one of the main sites of German immigration. Spanish speakers asserted the right to remain culturally Tejano while being American citizens, just as Germans in Galveston and Houston also asserted their heritage through celebrations and associations. In the mid-1850s, the San Antonio Know Nothings sought to make it harder for Tejanos to participate in politics by discontinuing the practice of publishing government documents in Spanish and German. Meanwhile, Anglos in the Texas hinterlands also scrutinized German communities and their attitudes toward slavery. These accusations were given credibility in 1854, when, during a yearly festival, many German representatives from towns across the state stood together to criticize slavery.[44]

Throughout 1855 Sam Houston made several speeches in Texas on the subject of American nativism. His opposition to the Kansas-Nebraska Bill a year earlier had alienated him from colleagues within the Democratic Party, and his opposition to the mounting anti-unionist sentiments led him to espouse support for the Know Nothings. In Washington, Texas, a small town several miles north of Galveston, he spoke to an audience where years earlier he had witnessed the signing of the Texas Declaration of Independence. The local newspaper called the speech a "very tame and a very lame effort." Houston moderated the anti-immigrant stance of the Know Nothings by arguing that it was no more anti-immigrant than the Whig and Democratic Parties. Houston had to explain his efforts in the senate at a barbecue in Austin, Texas's capital, where he explained that he opposed the Kansas-Nebraska bill because he thought if the Indians "were dispossessed of this territory which had been so solemnly guaranteed to them, they would be thrown within the borders of my own state." Houston focused on the imperiled western border in order to legitimize his decision to oppose the Kansas bill in front of his Texan audience.[45] His fixation on protections on the frontier was not unique in Texas. By 1849 the U.S. Army had constructed seven garrisons in an attempt to keep the thousands of settlers pushing toward western Texas apart from the Comanche. The trouble was that the presence of the army in southwestern Texas only encouraged further settlement of the territory.[46] After the border had been determined, it now had to be protected, and, like those living in other parts of the Gulf, white settlers within the borderlands felt that it required both a patrolling force as well as fortifications. In 1855 Secretary of War Jefferson Davis created four regiments to patrol the Texas frontier. In a report published in the *Galveston Weekly News*, Davis recommended the establishment of new posts west of the Mississippi, and in Texas especially, where the majority of "Indian depredations" occurred. The Second Cavalry regiment was known for its officers, who were primarily from the South. Among them were several who would serve as Confederate generals during the Civil War—Albert Sidney Johnston, Edmund Kirby Smith, Robert E. Lee, and John Bell Hood. Shortly after the U.S.-Mexican War the *Houston Telegraph and Texas Register* criticized the current state of the military on the Texas borders as insufficient to protect settlers there. They stated that "while the military posts and trading houses remain close to the settlements, there will always be danger of collisions."[47] These cavalry soldiers had their work cut out for them. They were meant to guard the scattered forts and a thousand-mile frontier region from Arkansas's western border to Eagle Pass, a border town that overlooked the Rio Grande. Texans would remain critical of federal forces patrolling this western region of the Texas borderlands well into the onset of the 1860 presidential election, and beyond. The presence of the Comanche as well as the tensions surrounding the Rio Grande played important roles in how Texans viewed the federal government and its ability to protect them.

As noted earlier, since leaving the Texas cabinet, Albert Sidney Johnston had tried to make a go of being a plantation owner. In 1843 Johnston and a friend, Albert T. Burnley, purchased China Grove, a plantation just outside of Galveston. Johnston was to live there and maintain the plantation. The venture was extremely risky because the contract stipulated that they had agreed to pay off the previous owner's debts with interest over the next five years, but the plantation itself was not valued at the sum they owed the previous owner. China Grove frustrated Johnston for years and his debts mounted due to crop failures or an inability to obtain enough slaves to work the entire plantation and bring in bigger crops. In 1853 Johnston reenlisted in the army as paymaster for the army in the southwestern region of Texas. Several years later he was promoted to colonel in the Second Cavalry. Johnston's promotion was in part due to the efforts of William Preston, Johnston's brother-in-law, and while in Kentucky, his wife, and Albert Sidney Johnston's wife, Eliza, advocating for him. They wrote to President Franklin Pierce and Jefferson Davis urging them to promote Johnston.[48] When Johnston was placed with the regiment in 1855, the Texas legislature celebrated his involvement due primarily to his service in that region during the years of the republic. Eliza and several of their young children followed Albert with the Second Cavalry into West Texas. At the outset of their journey, she wrote, "Well, here am I soldiering, my gude [*sic*] man appointed Colonel of the Second Regiment of Cavalry, a new Regiment just enlisted. We are on the march with 850 men for the Texas frontier." She confided in Johnston's eldest son, William, that it was a hard and busy life for Albert, "camping night after night and riding through a rough country filled with hostile

Indians 30 to 40,000 in a charge at a time and an escort of only *4 men*, all that can be spared from these badly manned frontier posts, this offers a great temptation for whites as well as Indians." Much of the anxiety displayed by those in West Texas as well as those along the coast stemmed from the kinds of observations that Eliza recorded in her diary.

It took the Johnstons several months to reach San Antonio. During this period Eliza recorded their experiences in her journal and counted the number of miles they marched each day and the conditions of camp as well as her children's enjoyment at being on the march with the military. In August, Eliza wrote an acquaintance explaining her husband's regiment had driven the Comanche farther back into the interior of the Indian country, and though many may have celebrated the seeming peace, it could not last. The country, Eliza Johnston wrote, "is as open as the ocean. They [Native Americans] can come when they like, taking the chance of chastisement. If they choose, therefore, it need only be a question of legs."[49] Eliza's notes on the cavalry's difficulty in maintaining control of the region resembled the kinds of observations of people like Edward Clifford Anderson on the Florida frontier, and the concerns espoused by those advocating for Cuban filibustering.

In the late 1850s, frustration and hostility best described the state of relations between Native Americans, white settlers, immigrants, and federal and local governments. The federal government dictated Indian policy, but the state government controlled the public land that Native peoples often inhabited. The relationship between the federal government and Mexicans, land, and citizenship also remained murky in the decade before the Civil War. In 1858 Congress enacted a joint resolution to raise a regiment of cavalry to attempt to protect settlers in West Texas from attacks from Native Americans. However, on many occasions Texans living in west Texas lashed out at both governments for failing to protect their lands.[50]

THE STATE OF THE BORDER

In 1859 a series of border skirmishes occurred between Mexicans and Anglos, which horrified many Southerners within the Gulf of Mexico. By the election of 1860 these matters became part of the mounting debate over secession, and whether or not Texas, like its sister slave states, might be better off without the federal government, which no longer appeared capable or willing to aid them in ensuring the security of their enslaved property and the expansion of their region.[51]

During President James Buchanan's 1858 annual address, he illustrated prevailing notions concerning Mexico since the war's end. He discussed the current relationship between the United States and Mexico in two different lights, which elucidated the changing nature of expansionist fantasies concerning Latin America. First, he emphasized Mexico's tumultuous political atmosphere. Buchanan cited the number of coups, presidencies, and governments that came to power after independence, as well as the struggles for liberal reform in the 1850s, which he believed contributed to the lack of protection for both Mexican and U.S. citizens "against lawless violence." As a result, the Treaty of Guadalupe Hidalgo between the United States and Mexico amounted to little more than a dead letter. Secondly, he focused on the state of the U.S.-Mexico border. "There is another view of our relations with Mexico," Buchanan stated, which arose from the "unhappy condition of affairs along our southwestern frontier, which demands immediate action." He cited "large bands of hostile and predatory Indians ... lawless Mexicans from passing the border and committing depredation on our remote settlers"; he further accused the local governments of northern Mexican states of being helpless to stop them.[52]

Throughout the 1850s the growth of settlement, slavery, and cotton in Texas heightened anxiety over the security of the U.S.-Mexico border and the West Texas borderlands, but the added tension of sectionalism, John Brown's Raid on Harpers Ferry, and a host of local conflicts between Anglos and Mexicans posed additional questions concerning the Union for Gulf South citizens. The Galveston *Civilian and Gazette* recorded an exchange between several senators concerning the Indian appropriations, in which Illinois representative Owen Lovejoy moved to strike down an appropriation for maintaining Indian reservations in Texas and in the Oregon and Washington territories. Texas representative Guy Bryan opposed the amendment on the grounds that he feared what would happen if Native Americans in Texas were allowed to leave the reservation. "Say you will not give us that protection, and we will protect ourselves. We have done it, and can do it again," said Bryan. The *Civilian and Gazette* wrote, "It seems that life and property are not safe anywhere, and that the great mass of the responsible portion of the community look to the United States as their only hope."[53] The mention of these issues at the close of 1859 stemmed from the past years' conflicts. While both Mexican Texans and Anglo Texans worried over Native American incursions on their borders, violence between their own communities dominated the debate over Texan border defenses throughout the closing months of 1859.

In the summer of 1859, an altercation between an elite ranchero, Juan Nepomuceno Cortina, and the Brownsville marshall ended in the marshall's death and sparked a series of violent clashes that resulted in the First Cortina War. In the years since the U.S.-Mexican War, Cortina had run afoul of a group of Anglo judges and attorneys in Brownsville, whom he accused of appropriating lands from Tejanos in the county. Between September and November, Juan Cortina and an armed group of supporters numbering forty to eighty men occupied the town of Brownsville, a bordertown on the Rio Grande. They rode through the streets shouting "Viva Mexico!" and "Death to the Americans!" In a moment of cooperation, Brownsville citizens actually pleaded with Mexican officials in Matamoros for help, and they negotiated with Cortina, who agreed to evacuate the town. However, tensions remained high throughout the fall and several armed bands of men from Brownsville targeted Cortina's followers.[54]

A letter written by a Brownsville citizen to the *Daily Picayune* in October related the events through an Anglo's perspective. The writer worried that all Mexicans, even the elite and officials from Matamoros, would join Cortina. In November the paper argued that American troops should string Cortina up no matter where they found him, whether on the American side or the Mexican side of the Rio Grande. The *Daily Picayune* urged Congress to authorize the president to send in troops to occupy both sides of the river due to Mexico's "distracted condition." Eventually, the Texas Rangers and the army were called in and chased Cortina and his company, which had grown to four hundred men from the region. The Rangers defeated Cortina on December 27, 1859, and he fled across the river, hiding in Mexico.[55] Although the federal government regarded this as a victory, many Texas newspapers criticized federal troops for their inability or unwillingness to cross into Mexico to capture Cortina and his men.[56]

Events such as the Cortina War of 1859, coupled with the far off events at Harpers Ferry, led many Anglo Texans to wonder if the border might be exploited by enemies to target them and inspire slave insurrection. All of these events contributed to the complex nature of the secessionist and unioinist sentimentsin the Gulf South. As Buchanan had stated, the border region was inherently unstable. The extent to which the government worked to maintain the racial order by maintaining physical control over the region remained a central issue for the Gulf states.[57] Governor Hardin Runnels's annual message expressed these sentiments. He wrote, "Witness the recent invasion and attempted insurrection at Harper's Ferry, and which, though differing in the commission of the overt act, events have had counterparts in our state ... not less ominous." Runnels ended his message by proclaiming that "equality in the union or independence outside of it should be the motto of every Southern state."[58]

CONCLUSION

On August 4, 1860, the Galveston *Civilian and Gazette* published a letter supposedly written by Republican conspirators in one of the state's western border counties. If real, the newspaper reasoned, the conspiracy provided "a clue to the late outrages in Texas." The paper believed that these conspirators intended to destroy Southern merchants and millers and use preachers and teachers to instruct Texans on the evils of slavery. The supposed conspirators believed they had at least "one more struggle to make—that is, free Texas." After they accomplished their goal, the imagined conspirators planned to connect the Great Lakes with the Gulf of Mexico creating a corridor of free territory. Slavery would then be "surrounded by land and by water, and soon sting itself to death." The paper allegd that these conspirators proposed to have meetings at night with African Americans and "impress upon their clouded intellects the blessings of freedom, induce all to leave."[59]

Throughout the 1850s the U.S.-Mexico border and western Texas became a microcosm of what was happening in the rest of the country and the precarious position the American South was now in.[60] To Southerners living in the borderlands, the federal government did not appear to be able to effectively protect them or their economic interests, and it seemed as though that same government wanted to leave the South out of its national expansionist plans. At the close of the U.S.-Mexican War, Anglos turned their attention back to making Texas secure and prosperous. They hoped to control Mexicans, immigrants, Native Americans, and free and enslaved African Americans. While the population of Anglos rose and the production of cotton increased in the state, these different groups still resisted the extertion of Anglo political and economic power as well as white settler expansion. The unruly Texas borderlands continued to frustrate Anglos well after the U.S.-Mexican War. Elements of the events that took place in Texas in the 1850s continued to be shape how Texans viewed their state in relationship to the United States, and those same elements would play an important part in the secession crisis. The actual process of secession took shape in a variety of different ways throughout the region. Each was as dramatic as the unionist and secessionist forces that met to decide Texas's fate in 1861. Each city experienced secession in ways that were similar to those of other Southern communities. Yet those experiences were also shaped by the unique confluence of events and ideas that had given rise to the Gulf South's violent expansionist history. Yet all of that lay in future in 1859.

In the tension-filled years leading up to the secession of the Southern states, newspapers and citizens in the Gulf ports used the region's recent history of expansion to provide a context for the sectional debates mounting within the United States. While the borders of the South were always imperiled in some way, the world beyond them always seemed to hold the promise of continued expansion, but as the decade came to a close, that world held more threats than it did hopes.[61]

CHAPTER 6

Launching a New Nation

In 1850 Louisa Lovell Claiborne wrote to her brother, John Quitman, about the crisis over the future of slavery in the territories. "I hope the South will yet be able to obtain what she asks, tho' she seems fated to much battling still to gain it," wrote Louisa.¹ A decade later, John Quitman was dead and white Southerners battled still for the things they desired most. The breakup of the United States in 1861 was not necessarily the end of Southerners' imperialist fantasies about Latin America, but they bet the survival of those fantasies on the Confederate States of America and winning the Civil War. The secession crisis caused many white Southerners within the Gulf South communities to rethink the way they related to the national government and to the army and navy. This was true of white people in other parts of the South, but the communities of the Gulf Coast were used to seeing themselves as the vanguard of American expansionism and Southern imperialism. Secession brought all of that into question.

This chapter examines the ways that secessionists and unionists deployed expansionist ideas. Antebellum experiences with expansion and imperialism shaped the ideas and actions of those living within the Gulf Coast as the United States hurtled toward the secession crisis. Essentially these ideas created a filter through which they understood the outbreak of secession in 1860. During the breakup of the Union there emerged a new dream of the Confederacy that depended on Gulf Coast communities and the entire Gulf Coast as a lifeline. Thus, through the Civil War the Gulf Coast attained a crucial new position within the South.

Like all of the other conflicts that happened within the Gulf South, the secession crisis and the outbreak of Civil War came along with a cavalcade of hopes and fears that were tied to both expansionism and race. Historians have long noted that the secession crisis was framed by racism and that slavery was central to both the action and the language of secession. Yet, this process also had a transnational aspect tied to the antebellum expansionism on display in the public discourse of Gulf South communities. Fears concerning the salience of white supremacy were framed against both the threat that Abraham Lincoln's election posed to slavery and the threat it posed to the South's ability to expand into Latin America. Additionally, the racist aspects of the region's residents' past attempts to conquer both their own frontiers and the parts of the Caribbean played a crucial role in how white Southerners in the Gulf South discussed and understood secession.[2]

For nearly twenty years before the Civil War, white Southern expansionists fought hard to obtain more territory in Latin America, with the federal government playing a large role in that endeavor. During the antebellum era, those efforts came under growing criticism. By the time of the 1860 election, many white Southerners saw the federal government as more of an impediment than an aid to their goals. To those expansionists, secession seemed like a logical choice, perhaps even the only choice. However, other expansionists pushed back against this idea. Residents of Gulf Coast communities debated secession in ways similar to those in other parts of the Lower South, but they always gauged how Union or secession would affect the South's prospects at expansion and viewed their future as tied to that question. Though the Lower South seceded quickly after South Carolina, residents in each of the communities discussed in previous chapters confronted the unknowable outcome with more complexity and division than their states' speedy secessions might suggest. Additionally, expansionists were not all of one mind when it came to secession. Some of the region's most outspoken proponents of annexation, war, and territorial expansion did not support secession. Others supported it tacitly, and yet others threw themselves into the secessionist cause.[3]

After secession, the port cities of the Gulf became the Confederacy's southern coast, one of its most vulnerable yet essential regions. As a part of expansionism in the Gulf of Mexico, community boosters throughout the region had spent much of the antebellum era advocating for the presence of increased military and the construction and improvement of military installations. When the states of the Lower South seceded, some of the first contests between the United States military and Southern state and local authorities occurred in many coastal communities over the forts, naval yards, and armories for which they once advocated. When Abraham Lincoln called for a blockade of the Southern ports, blockade runners and commerce raiders became vital to the Confederate war effort. As in the case of the filibusters before them, not everyone may have approved of blockade runners' and commerce raiders' methods, but they were fascinating new figures within the Southern cultural landscape of the Civil War era. At the same time, the communities of the Gulf Coast experienced two blockades in less than twenty years from completely different vantage points. During the U.S.-Mexican War the U.S. Navy's blockade of Mexico's ports heavily involved the support of Gulf South communities. When the same navy imposed a blockade of the Southern states in 1861, these same communities experienced the trade blockages and frustrations that Mexican communities once felt. Blockade running proved to be difficult in the Gulf of Mexico, but the movement of military supplies and cotton through the port cities in support of the Confederacy occurred because of the connections formulated through the expansionism of the antebellum era.[4]

EXPANSIONISM IN SECESSIONIST TALK

Throughout the nation's short history, filibustering was an essential part of expansion. In the early nineteenth century, white Americans pushed into the territories claimed by the French and Spanish colonial governments, as well as into Mexico, through a combination of violence, diplomatic negotiation, and purchase. Additionally, as historian Amy Greenberg notes, filibustering, which was an integral part of these processes, was also tied to notions of white supremacy and manliness in the antebellum world.[5] Indeed, the Texas Revolution, the Bear Republic in California, and the U.S.-Mexican War were, in many ways, the high points of filibustering in the mid-nineteenth century. However, after the U.S.-Mexican War, the ability to seize territory through martial methods receded. Even diplomatic efforts such as those intended to purchase Cuba fared little better.

Yet Americans continued to support and participate in these expeditions. Southern expansionists continued to believe in them one after the next. After the deaths of Narciso López and his men, others picked up the mantle of filibustering, but their efforts met with no success. Though he lost faith in López's ability to manage the expedition to Cuba, John Quitman attempted to organize his own venture in 1853. Quitman and two of his associates were fined several thousand dollars in 1854 for plotting to sail to Cuba. Then, on July 4, 1854, George Bickley and several other men founded the Knights of the Golden Circle in Lexington, Kentucky. The secret organization was so named because of its founders' fixation on Havana as the center of a grand empire encircling the Gulf of Mexico, the Caribbean, and Central America. While they started in Kentucky, Bickley soon had chapters, which were called "castles," through various parts of the United States, including the Gulf South.[6]

Aside from that of López, William Walker's was the most dramatic attempt to capture Latin American territory. Walker managed to take over Nicaragua by 1856 and eventually install himself as president for a short time before surrendering to U.S. troops in 1857 and winding up in New Orleans attempting to raise another expedition to Nicaragua. As historian Walter Johnson noted, New Orleanians continued to support ventures like these, as did residents of other parts of the Deep South such the Mississippi Valley. The notion that the acquisition of additional territory would help mend the cracks in the unity of white Southern society did not die with the end of the López expeditions; nor did the idea that the best way, maybe even the only way, to get that territory was through filibustering. That said, others began to look at cracks of a different kind, namely the ones that widened almost yearly between the slaveholding states, the free states, and the federal government.[7] William Walker's takeover of Nicaragua came to a close as tensions rose between proslavery and antislavery factions in the United States.

Not all approved of continuing the filibustering. Many of the Southern critiques against the filibusters centered on the worry that bringing additional Latin American territory into the United States, and into the South especially, would add a mixed-race population and additional free African Americans to the region, endangering white Southerners' ability to maintain their position at the top of Southern society and their control over enslaved African Americans. Figures like John Calhoun had warned of such things during and just after the U.S.-Mexican War. Antebellum expansionism had been premised on the idea that one of the big advantages to obtaining additional slave states was spreading out the enslaved population of the South, which would lessen the risk of slave rebellions. In the aftermath of the U.S.-Mexican War, white Southerners continued to be frustrated by Native Americans, Mexicans, and enslaved African Americans in places like the Texas border region. With no successful filibustering expeditions on the horizon and growing antislavery opposition, these multiple threats amplified each other.[8]

Yet there were other reasons why white Southerners might not support filibustering even though they still supported acquisition of more territory. One was that the illegal nature of the filibusters' activities made expansion more difficult, which drove an additional wedge between the South and the United States at a time when that relationship was increasingly precarious. Essentially, one could be both expansionist and unionist, or conversely, expansionist, secessionist, and still against the filibusters.[9] Albert Sidney Johnston was concerned with many of these issues. In 1856, while stationed in San Francisco, he wrote to his son, remarking on the mounting opposition to Southern interests: "I notice with sorrow the progress of fanaticism in the North. What do they want? We want to share in its glorious, benevolent, civilizing mission, and its high and magnificent destiny." Johnston, who had toiled on the front lines of American expansion in Texas and Mexico, still believed that American expansion and Southern expansion were one and the same, even though others had begun to argue that Southern expansion with its emphasis on slavery was separate from American expansion. Others who had favored annexation of further territory, such as Pierre Soulé, advocated obtaining it in different ways but also saw that gaining more territory from Mexico was not necessarily warranted any longer considering the resources that could be found in the West.[10]

William Preston Johnston later related a story concerning his father, Albert, and a younger cavalry officer, in which he warned the young man against going out on a filibustering campaign. As the gentleman retold the story to William when he was compiling his biography of his father, Albert told the man the "days of Quixotism are past, and with them the chance for name and fame in all such enterprises as this." "Tell me not of philanthropy as a plea," he stated, "if you are pining for adventure . . . fanaticism will soon bring on a sectional collision between the States of the Union, in which every man will have to choose his side." Johnston's apparent dislike of filibustering stemmed, in part, from the fact that filibusters to Cuba and Nicaragua did not end with the annexation of either country to the United States. His belief that filibustering was mere piracy, which it was, also stemmed from his career in the military. Others shared these sentiments. Reporting on the challenges to Walker's diminishing prospects for success in Nicaragua in 1858, the Galveston *Civilian and Gazette* lamented that the filibusters of today were "but little, if any, better than their progenitors of two hundred years ago" recalling, like Johnston, the pirates among whom the term had originated.[11]

Running as a pro-union Democrat in the election of 1860, John Reagan, a congressional representative from Texas, issued a circular discussing the central issues facing Texas and the South. Among them was a rejection of the filibustering strategy. Reagan declared, "I am opposed to any unlawful private expeditions being fitted out in our country to rob and murder the people of neighboring nations, with whom we are at peace, either for territory or other booty, and whether in the name of liberty, or of the South, or any other name." He rejected his opponent's claims that because he denounced filibustering it meant he was against further acquisition of "southern territory." Reagan maintained that he was strongly in favor of the acquisition of Cuba "by fair and honorable means," which meant through purchase. The alternative was the government seizing Cuba forcibly. Reagan reminded his readers that if any other nations gained control of Cuba, it would endanger the South's institutions and commerce. Reagan asserted that he supported further acquisition of slave territory even beyond Cuba by similar means, which, like many Southern expansionists, he believed would "strengthen the power of the slave States, and tend to the preservation of the Union by increasing their power to resist the sectional fanaticism which exists in the free States." Reagan's platform on the subject of Cuba demonstrated that it was a critical issue for Texans, just as it was for New Orleanians. He presented voters with the view that Cuba should only be purchased by the Union and that doing so would also help maintain unity against the onslaught of sectionalism. Reagan's stance was both expansionist and unionist, as he saw the South's best chance of expanding as still being within the United States. His pro-union stance, however, did not preclude him from supporting a secessionist candidate for governor, Hardin Runnels, who was running against the staunchly unionist Sam Houston in 1859.[12]

Houston, by contrast, was an expansionist and a unionist who had, at times, supported filibustering, though he did so cautiously. In 1851 he spoke at several meetings in New Orleans in support of López and to raise funds for the filibusters. However, he also spoke critically of those who compared the Texas Revolution and the López expeditions, which, he claimed, "nothing has ever been more misapprehended on earth." He criticized the expeditions because they had gone to aid a revolution in Cuba and referred to the filibusters as "deluded" for thinking they could take Cuba from Spain.[13] Houston's objections to the Kansas-Nebraska Act took two main routes that also seemed contradictory for an expansionist. One was the idea that the popular sovereignty for western territories called for in the act actually threatened the South, because it would repeal the Missouri Compromise. In his remarks, Houston also reminded the Senate that the lands west of the Mississippi were guaranteed to the Native Americans that lived there, which would render the entire slavery question moot and thus not as divisive. Both ideas drew instant rebukes from Southerners and Midwesterners. Afterward, Houston left the Democratic Party.

Houston proposed an ill-fated protectorate for Mexico and Central American in 1858, a proposal that derived from a similar sort of benevolent racist view he had of African Americans and slavery. He eventually limited the proposal to just Mexico. In a speech amending his original proposal,

Houston explained that Texas had a vested interest in an "orderly government in Mexico." He reminded his fellow senators that Texas was as closely linked to Mexico as it was to any other state in the Union and that the state made up one thousand miles of the border between the United States and Mexico. Houston warned that Comanche raids in the border region had pushed other people out of it and that the line of "civilization" was receding. Similar to the way that proslavery intellectuals and politicians talked about their responsibility to control the African American population of the United States, Houston framed the protectorate as a duty to both Mexico and the United States' own self-interest and talked of the "grave responsibility" the United States would assume by bringing a population like that of Mexico under its control. He warned that "to suffer her to be parceled out by filibusters—each chief perhaps a despot—would be to fraternize with every desperate adventurer in our land, and to invite to our continent all the wild, vicious spirits of the other hemisphere. Nor, could we consent, without palpable dishonor, to see her placed in the leading strings of any European owner, even were their disposition manifested to so place her." Houston continually attempted to get the Senate to approve the resolution, but each time he was defeated. He was so convinced that Mexico needed a protectorate that he wrote to Ben McCulloch, who had served with him during the Texas Revolution and would later serve in the Civil War, about his plans while he was serving as governor. His ideas about how the United States should conduct itself toward Native Americans and Mexico both came from a position that these groups needed some kind of white American leadership or stewardship, but they also stemmed from his wariness over the political battles waged between North and South. His positions spoke to the multiple ways that expansionists viewed and thought about territorial interests and empire in conjunction with the growing tensions and talk of disunion.[14]

As always, local, regional, and transnational issues merged. By the time of the 1859 Texas governor's race, Houston's political prospects had taken many twists and turns. He ran against Hardin Runnels, who beat him in the 1857 election, but since then had become unpopular in the state. Houston's main points of contention with Runnels dealt with many local issues, such as Native American raids, which were always an important subject in Texas politics. Runnels supporters attacked Houston's voting record when it came to increasing the size of the army on the frontier, which Houston consistently voted against. On February 26, 1859, Houston explained why he did so. He argued that it was not the regular army that had defended Texas;

rather, Texan volunteers were the ones who had defended their own borders, so there was no reason to provide funds to army troops that were not going to do the job. The newspapers that supported him for governor claimed that regular army troops "lie secure in their forts until some opportunity occurs to distinguish themselves by cutting off a band of helpless Indians, and thus did more harm than good." This had become a common complaint by those living in Texas, one that shaped Texas politics as much as the regional and national concerns.[15]

Questions concerning the South's ability to gain access to new territory and the possibility of war generated additional questions about the expansion of slave-owning in the region. The debate over reopening the slave trade emerged alongside the secession debate and split expansionists in the region in ways similar to the idea of filibustering. When it came to the controversial topic of the African slave trade, Houston was of the mind that it was a terrible idea. As he claimed, "Re-open the African slave trade and the South will be deluged with barbarians." Houston argued that the price of domestic enslaved people would plummet, and the "barbarian" qualities of enslaved Africans imported from Cuba would then be transferred to enslaved African Americans in the United States. Houston also believed that further importation of enslaved Africans would result in a cotton glut on the market due to the increased number of laborers, thereby lowering the overall price of the crop. Even freight prices would go up due to the large number of Africans the South imported.[16] The idea of importing slaves from beyond the United States would mean nothing but ruin for the South and the nation.

While faith in filibustering grew more tenuous, secessionists such as South Carolina's Leonidas Spratt and New Orleans' James De Bow drummed up enthusiasm for reopening the African slave trade. The success of such an effort would be a truly astounding feat for the proslavery intellectuals, who began lobbying for it in the South's newspapers and journals. De Bow published many pieces in favor of reopening the slave trade in *De Bow's Review*, though he claimed to be presenting both sides of the discussion. In August 1859 De Bow informed his readers of the formation of the African Labor Supply Association, and that he had been made president of the organization. The African Labor Supply Association was founded in Vicksburg shortly after the 1859 Southern Convention, during which the attendants had voiced their support for reopening the slave trade. De Bow published an exchange between himself and William Lowndes Yancey, who inquired about what the association's plans were in case those supporting the reopening of the trade could not reverse the laws that made it illegal. The ban on the trade was unconstitutional, he argued, and the association would never do anything to violate the Constitution. De Bow insisted that Southern planters could not wait for the enslaved population of the South to increase naturally and should begin importing enslaved Africans. He also envisioned a kind of apprenticeship for Africans that could work around the ban on the slave trade. Slaveholders in Texas had actually proposed something like apprenticeship for their slaves when Mexico outlawed the practice. Like many others who supported reopening the trade, De Bow argued that it would benefit nonslaveholders in a similar way that advocating for more land was supposed to benefit them because it would give them access to landowning and slaveholding that would not disrupt the slaveholding class in the rest of the South.[17]

For people like De Bow, the prospect of reopening the slave trade also meant asserting white Southern dominance in the United States, the Gulf of Mexico, and beyond. For the reopeners, the rising tide lifted all boats and might mean increased profits for the communities of the Gulf. Reopening the trade also potentially meant establishing a legal trade in enslaved Africans between the United States and Cuba, which would draw the Southern ports and the island closer together. A small clandestine trade already existed among the Gulf ports of the South and the Caribbean. New Orleans merchants and shippers were involved in shipping enslaved Africans to Brazil and Cuba during the 1850s. Texas had a history of still accessing the trade even after it had stopped in the United States, and Louisianians illegally imported slaves from Texas, the Caribbean, and Africa throughout the early part of the part of the nineteenth century. As stated in an earlier chapter, there were several instances of slave ships making landfall on the coast of Texas during its time as a republic. A revived slave trade would bring this existing trade out into the open and expand it, benefiting or affecting the people of New Orleans and the rest of the Gulf ports. A renewed slave trade, though, also recalled the period when Texas was a wedge in the lower half of North America that provided several geopolitical possibilities for the South, Mexico, the Caribbean, and United States.[18]

Reopening the slave trade proved to be a contentious issue within the larger secession debate. As historians have noted, the question of reopening was driven by rising prices of enslaved people, worries over class conflict within white Southern society, and the ability to maintain white mastery. Some within the Gulf South, though, also attempted to redirect the slave trade question toward some of the same issues that had served Southern expansion so well in the past, like the protection of Gulf South ports. Despite approving the continued importation of slaves into the Caribbean in April 1859, the New Orleans *Daily Picayune* spoke out along these lines to counter those who advocated reopening of the slave trade. The paper suspected that most Southerners supported reopening the trade simply because Northerners found it offensive, rather than out of an actual belief that reopening the trade would bring the South any real economic or social prosperity. And these same men, wrote the *Daily Picayune*, "who seem to have become possessed with this idea as the remedy for an thousand fancied ills, are ready to declare, if the laws declaring the slave trade piracy be not repealed, the South must set up for herself."[19] For Southerners, the "importance of making the Gulf of Mexico an American sea—of acquiring if possible, by honorable means, the Island of Cuba—of exercising a predominating influence in Central America—and reconstructing the distracted Government of Mexico. These are true Southern as well as national questions." In laying out the view of the reopening question as a threat to Southern territorial expansion, the paper envisioned a future in which the South held ultimate authority over the "future highway of the world's commerce," as well as the starting point for the Pacific railroad then under debate in Congress.[20] In editorials such as these, newspapermen looked to redirect Southern passions back to the business of conquest in Latin America. However, the fantasies of the past, of making the Gulf South prosperous through gaining territory in faraway lands, now increasingly reinforced new ideas concerning a rekindled trade and maybe even an independent Southern nation.

From the position of the Gulf Coast communities, the question of reopening the slave trade also revolved around the much longer story of U.S. competition with European nations within the Gulf of Mexico and the Caribbean. Since the early nineteenth century, Great Britain's efforts to stop the slave trade meant that British ships sailed near the Gulf Coast. That presence had been a constant worry and a driving factor for the pressure that Gulf Coast Southerners put on the federal government to improve naval and army defenses in their communities. In a speech given to Galveston's Baconian Society during the graduation ceremony of the Texas Monument and Military Institute's first graduating class in 1858, Ashbel Smith, one of the city's physicians and leading citizens, spoke about the threats of sectionalism and the threat of British presence within the Gulf of Mexico. Both, in his estimation, challenged the continued expansion of the nation and Texas' place within those efforts.[21] Smith, who had lived in Texas since the revolution and its founding as a republic, gave several speeches concerning expansion throughout the 1850s. He began by discussing the seizure of American ships in the Gulf of Mexico and off the coast of Cuba. Though he was still largely against secession in 1858, his speech was essentially a critique of the North and the efforts of the British to limit Southern expansion in the Gulf of Mexico. Smith cautioned those who would put faith in the "delusive lie which England has been indiscriminately whispering through unknown channels into the ear of the South for five and twenty years." The lie that Smith referred to was the claim that if the South separated from the North then they would find an ally in Great Britain. "Friend! Protection!! Yes such protection as the wolf gave the lamb," Smith declared.[22] In the aftermath of the speech, one of those in the audience wrote a letter to the editor of the *Houston Telegraph* to tell them, "His subject was the great value of national power in connexion with our present domestic difficulties."[23]

Echoing this fear of Great Britain, in 1860 Richard Henderson, editor of the Galveston *Civilian and Gazette*, began publishing the *Crisis!*, a newspaper that celebrated and further spread the diatribes of the South's pro-secessionists. Through the *Crisis!*, Texans learned about the secessionist ideas circulating throughout the South and how the Gulf of Mexico figured into them. For residents of coastal communities, these fiery speeches drew on national events made intimate by the Gulf's location at the center of expansion. James Chestnut of South Carolina, for example, claimed that free states in the West would "bound forward with such power and prosperity as would be without parallel . . . Cuba and Brazil would be beneficiaries of the first result." Jefferson Davis's address, published in the *Crisis!*, included similar themes. Namely, he stated, "British interference finds no footing, receives no welcome among us of the South; we turn with loathing and disgust from their mock philanthropy."[24] These speeches and circulars presented a dire vision of the future for the Gulf South that was grounded in the real international tensions that existed within the region.

While secessionists and unionists were on opposite sides of the debate, they both viewed Cuba as emblematic of Southern fears amid the mounting uncertainties of the time. Both sides were concerned with maintaining the racism they had constructed to uphold and spread slavery in the antebellum era. For unionists and secessionists, Cuba and its history could provide a window into the South's future in addition to a goal in terms of annexation. In 1860 in New Orleans, T.J. Semmes, Louisiana Attorney General, stood up at a mass meeting and warned the audience that unless the United States protected slavery in the new territories, their efforts to obtain places like Cuba were doomed. He worried that a wave of northern settlers might "incite the mongrel half breeds to exclude slaves." As the nation approached the election of 1860, speeches such as Semmes's served as a reminder of the fact that great contest for territory in Mexico, Central America, and the American West always affected the Gulf South communities in unique ways.[25]

SECESSION OR UNION? THE GULF SOUTH CHOOSES

If the debates over secession caused people to rethink the ways that the South related to expansion, then the actual process of secession saw Gulf South communities' relations with the army and navy change dramatically. Faced with the reality of separation, each community went through its own processes of meetings, voting on candidates for the secession convention, and preparing for whatever might come afterward.

Public meetings continued all throughout the summer months, and politics consumed Gulf South peoples' lives much the way that talk of trade and expanding transportation up river had done only a few years prior. Galveston epitomized this trend. William Pitt Ballinger had served Albert Sidney Johnston as adjutant during the U.S.-Mexican War; by the time of the election of 1860, he had served as attorney general for Texas and was part of a law firm in Galveston. Ballinger recorded his thoughts on the series of meetings that went on almost nightly and the constant talk of the election and the possibility of disunion. During the summer of 1860, he wrote things like "wasted all morning in political discussion which amounted to nothing." He went on, noting, "same all over town." Ballinger disliked Stephen Douglas and eventually favored the Constitutional Union Party's nomination of John Bell for president. Ballinger recorded his thoughts on the calamity of the Democratic Party's nominating conventions in Charleston and Baltimore. On June 24, 1860, he commented that the "news is that the Baltimore Convention has broken up worse than Charleston—Va. Tenn. & almost all the Southern State have now seceded. Violence prevails among them—Rather a fit finale to the Democratic Party." Like many wary unionists, Ballinger did not often voice his thoughts in public but kept them private or related them to friends. In August that changed, when Ballinger spoke at a Union meeting, but later he worried over how such a public demonstration of his views might affect his growing law practice. Galvestonians were not all of one mind concerning the presidential candidates going into the election, and already unionist talk was proving risky.[26]

Secessionists invoked the fear of a blockade impeding Southern trade alongside a host of other fears, such as race war and race mixing, to drive home the idea that an independent nation was the only thing that could save the South from this fate. Gulf South communities were well aware of the power of blockades and always wary of multiracial societies. They had seen several blockades throughout the first half of the nineteenth century and had watched emancipation come to the Caribbean from front row seats. The journals and newspapers of Gulf South communities had also fed their residents and the rest of the region a steady diet of racist diatribes against the multiracial societies of Latin America. Secession answered the question of what would the slave holding states do to preserve their hold on the institution of slavery, but it also posed questions about the possibility of war, and what that might look like within the Gulf South.

In November 1860 James De Bow published an article in *De Bow's Review* titled "The South's Power of Self-Protection," in which the author wrote that "Texas, Louisiana, Alabama, Florida, Georgia, Mississippi, and South Carolina, have seaport cities, which are natural outlets to export, so necessary to millions of people, that they cannot be blockaded by the Black-Republican party without the overthrow of that party." De Bow warned that these states would "be justified . . . in taking possession of their ports, and holding them against that party . . . until they are fully assured that our government is not to be broken up or changed by that party." He urged the Republican Party, Congress, and the new president to "leave the labor question as free as the question on religion." Before South Carolina seceded, or any other state for that matter, De Bow invoked the fear of blockade, echoing the long-held fear that the sea ports would be attacked or limited in some way by those favoring the limit of slavery. The author tied that fear to the idea of disunion, of seizing control through secession and protecting the ports against federal power. According to De Bow, if the Republican Party did not actively work to protect slavery where it existed and let it expand where it didn't, then the party would "Africanize and Mexicanize the best portions of North America." In this nightmare scenario, without slavery to control African Americans, and Southern white supremacy to control Latin American people the inclusion of Mexico and Central America into the United States would mean that the "colored races of the continent will be free to roam at large over the land. By the natural course of events under such circumstances, the idleness, the robberies, the civil wars, the bloodshed and anarchy, which now reign in Mexico, will spread over the continent." For the author of the article, it was only Southern white people using slavery and racist hierarchy that could control such peoples and avoid these outcomes. As the fire eaters fanned out across the South to coax life into the secessionist movement, writers played with nightmare visions that encapsulated both the domestic events that led up to secession as well as the transnational events taking place within the Gulf South borderlands.[27]

Still, even on the Gulf Coast, where secession struck like a firestorm, there were divisions and uncertainties about the prospect of leaving the Union. Some political figures in the Gulf South who had been advocates of annexation for Texas and Cuba did not support secession. After the presidential election, Sam Houston remained a staunch unionist. Pierre Soulé, one of the architects of the Ostend Manifesto, filibuster supporter, and an outspoken political voice for expansion, also supported unionism. Both made speeches in support of the Union, but as governor, only Houston was in a position to slow the process and possibly even stop it altogether in Texas.

In the aftermath of Lincoln's election on November 6, 1860, Texans organized meetings to consider secession. William Ballinger noted that in Galveston, Lincoln's election brought a "deep sensation in our midst." He wrote in his journal that "we shall have serious danger to our govt. if not its disruption—Many of our wise & good men are in favor of immediate dissolution—Still it seems to me that much of the sentiment is the offspring of party heat & is not mature & well considered." According to Ballinger, the secessionists of South were "clamorous for disruption, but how to bring it about is the great trouble." Though Ballinger favored unionism, he involved himself in preparations for a meeting in Galveston to propose calling for the state legislature to begin proceedings to take Texas out of the Union. Publicly, he wrote a short article about who should be chosen to preside over the meeting, but in his diary wrote that "all sorts of efforts are being used to commit men to this course," which perhaps alluded to the extreme pressure felt by unionists in these communities. On November 14 he made note of the final meeting, the largest he ever witnessed in his life. The coastal town of Indianola, Texas, reported the largest meeting in the town's history as well, which began with a procession led by citizens to the courthouse where it was held. The Lone Star flag led the way, and citizens held banners emblazoned with sentiments such as "states rights," "we are with South Carolina," "Texas is Sovereign," and "none but slaves submit." Banners such as these conflated Texas sovereignty with the argument for Southern independence. They communicated very clearly where a majority of the community stood. People who were nervous about the prospect of secession or who outright opposed it faced strong opposition, and this no doubt helped to keep them quiet and unify the Lower South in favor of disunion. The memory of Texas independence was particularly potent, as were many of the events attached to it. Ballinger spent a sleepless night afterward, fearing for the future.[28]

Texans did have a third possible route during the secession crisis: beoming an independent country again. Independence-minded Texans such as Edward H. Cushing of the Houston *Telegraph* argued, "We all know the Republic of Texas can be sustained in independence, and unless we can better our condition materially, we for one, should be in favor of standing aloof. Self-protection is the first law of nature, and the great law of States." In Galveston, William Pitt Ballinger noted that some local men formed a Lone Star Association to encourage people to support this possibility and stand against a Southern confederacy. He refused to join this group because he thought, as many did, that "if the Union must be broken up I am for the largest confederacy that can be formed—I am no Lone Star man—I think it a chimera." Eventually, Ballinger was persuaded to support secession if it meant that Texas would join a confederacy of Southern states. Still, the third possibility of regaining the lost republic proved more amendable to Sam Houston, who preferred it over secession and joining a confederacy.[29]

After South Carolina seceded on December 20, 1860, the Gulf South states quickly followed. Within the Lower South the first to go were Mississippi, Florida, Alabama, and Georgia, while Louisiana and Texas moved more slowly. When secession came to Louisiana, it quickly consumed New Orleans in the way that the U.S.-Mexican War and the filibustering craze had. Anti-Northern and secessionist sentiment was high in the Crescent City. Crowds hung Lincoln in effigy and cheered. There was a general feeling of celebration that ramped up even more when residents learned that South Carolina had finally seceded. True, New Orleanians were to some extent divided over the issue of secession. The diverse white population in New Orleans—among them European immigrants, working-class white people, and the powerful commercial class—held a variety of opinions, ranging from absolute fealty to the Union to the view that Louisiana should wait for its sister states to strong support of immediate secession. In New Orleans debate about secession included discussion over the possibility of a blockade and its impact on the city. In January 1861 the *Daily Picayune* published a letter to the editor discussing the possibility of a blockade of the Gulf ports and its effect on trade in New Orleans. The author, writing under the name "Mentor," cautioned the paper that "your remarks about blockades and embargoes may lead your readers to apprehend further embarrassments in the commerce of New Orleans than await us." "Mentor" believed that "it is not believed that those in power, or those coming into power, at Washington, in March, will resort to either, or cause a hostile gun to be fired, unless attacked. They will doubtless allow free importation as well as free exportation from the seceding States." As for Britain and France, "Mentor" claimed "their views will not be considered" on the matter of the blockade. "Our purpose," responded the editor of the *Picayune*, was "merely to notice the law and objects of embargo and blockade, at the same time to show that a seceding state did not fall within the scope of the exercises of either, unless the United States Government acknowledged its independence for blockade or reduced it by force of arms for embargo. But of this in due time."[30] But Southerners did wonder about the extent to which Britain and France might be able to keep shortages and stranded cotton at bay. The paper noted that in the city it was "stated with authority" that "in diplomatic circles here, that England and France will never permit the blockade of the Southern ports, even should that be decided upon by the coercion party."[31]

As a senator, Pierre Soulé was outspoken about his unionism. He had long professed loyalty to both his state and the United States. During his time as a senator, after he gave a speech on the African slave trade, Henry Clay denounced him by leveling charges of disunionism and claimed "this damned Frenchman does more harm to our cause than good." Soulé answered, "When the controversy breaks its walls and degenerates into collision or rupture, a profound sentiment that I owe to my adopted country orders me to abstain and to leave its destinies to its native children and Providence." During Soulé's address at the Democratic Convention in Charleston, he spoke about the issues that had arisen since the U.S.-Mexican War and how the South had handled each one by opposing the North's stance but never leaving the Union. Though Soulé personally supported the Union, he eventually sided with Louisiana when it seceded on January 26, 1861. This was true of many of the state's political figures. The *Picayune* declared "the deed is done," and "we breathe deeper and freer for it."[32]

Back in Texas, Houston worked to slow down the process by first refusing to call for a secession convention. The public meetings in Galveston were a small part of the massive demonstration of support for secession across Texas. Secessionist speeches drew enormous crowds and public support for the convention grew daily. A correspondent writing under the pseudonym Volumnia wrote to the *Austin State Gazette* in December 1860, espousing loyalty to the state of Texas and asking the state's men to look at the spectacle of their "bleeding frontier." "Do you think that the depredations there committed are only the offspring of the fiendish Indians that swarm upon our borders," she asked.[33] In doing so, Volumnia reflected the fears associated with threats to the state's borders represented by both Mexicans and Native Americans. Importantly, both unionists and secessionists emphasized the state's border troubles, though for different reasons. Where secessionists saw no help from the federal government and therefore saw no reason to remain in the Union, unionists saw the U.S. military as the only force capable of warding off these threats and establishing an order that benefited Anglo and Southern social and cultural structures.

Prominent Texans took it upon themselves to begin printing calls for an election of deligates to a secession convention in January. Houston finally called the state legislature, which he hoped would denounce any such plans for a convention. However, this was largely wishful thinking on Houston's part, even a refusal to understand the extent to which Texans supported secession. When the state legislators met, they supported the secession convention, turned over the house to it, and adjourned themselves. The convention, made up largely of slaveholders, almost immediately took a vote to endorse secession, but unlike the other states of the Lower South, the delegates voted to instead make secession contingent upon a referendum. The final decision would be left up to the voters of Texas. On February 23, 1861, Texans voted in favor of leaving the Union, and on March 2, the anniversary of Texas's first separation from Mexico, the state formally seceded. Texas's declaration of the causes of secession included similar language to that of other Southern states, including an admission that Texas seceded to protect the institution of slavery. The writers of the declaration asserted that the federal government sought to exclude Southern white citizens from the western territories in order to acquire enough political power to "use it as a means of destroying the institutions of Texas and her sister slaveholding states." The declaration went on to list many efforts by antislavery forces to spread their message through the South, the violence in Kansas, and John Brown's raid on Harpers Ferry as more evidence that the nonslaveholding states and the federal government were trying to limit the power of the slaveholding South. It was for these reasons, as well additional factors connected to events that took place in Texas, that the "delegates of the people of Texas, in the Convention assembled, have passed An Ordinance dissolving all political connection with the Government of the United States of America." The declaration also included a section in which Texans charged that the "Federal Government, while but partially under the control of these our unnatural and sectional enemies, has for years almost entirely failed to protect the lives and property of the people of Texas against the Indian savages on our border, and more recently against the murderous forays of banditti from the neighboring territory of Mexico; and when our State government has expended large amounts for such purpose, the Federal Government has refused reimbursement therefor, thus rendering our condition more insecure and harrassing than it was during the existence of the Republic of Texas."[34]

Voting for secession was not the end of the story for Texas or Sam Houston. Houston, whose loyalty to the Union was only overshadowed by his loyalty to the state he helped create, eventually relented and accepted secession. The state secession convention then demanded that all state officials swear an oath of loyalty to the Confederacy. However, Houston refused to take this oath, and for this he was pushed out of the governorship. His office was declared vacant, to be filled by Lieutenant Governor Edward Clark.[35]

Secession was no less contested in Florida, where the military's presence played a key role in the unfolding secession crisis. Animosity toward Northerners and free Black sailors had been mounting in the years leading up to election of 1860. For Pensacolians, the question of secession brought about glimmerings of the war to come and how it would play out in the Gulf Coast, where Pensacola's proposed prosperity under the U.S. navy and army stalled during the 1850s, while West Florida was hit with several yellow fever outbreaks similar to those that affected Galveston, New Orleans, and Mobile. The epidemic of 1853 proved to be especially bad, and no one could ever be sure if it was the town or the naval yard which had caused it. The outbreak of secession drove a wedge between the troops housed in the fortifications so valued by the town's boosters and the town itself.[36] Immediately after Lincoln's election, large meetings were held in Pensacola, as they were throughout the South, to determine how the citizens would address disunion. One naval officer described the fervor over secession to be such that it was as if all "men, women, and children had gone mad."[37]

During the early days of January, Lieutenant Adam J. Slemmer, then in charge of the U.S. Army forces housed at Fort Barrancas, quickly recognized that nearby Fort Pickens was much more easily defensible and a prime target for secessionists. William Chase, who had overseen construction at the forts and helped to bolster the Pensacola economy, resigned from the U.S. Navy and quickly moved to take over the various military installations in Pensacola. On January 8, 1861, a group of local men under Slemmer's command attacked Fort Barrancas. The Union soldiers within the fort repelled them, and Slemmer pulled his forces back to Fort Pickens. On that same day, Slemmer destroyed twenty thousand pounds of gunpowder at Fort McRee, spiked the guns at Barrancas, and evacuated fifty-one soldiers and sailors to Pickens. In an ironic twist, the Gulf South had once lobbied hard for federal government appropriations to improve the forts and naval yard in Pensacola; now, however, secessionist forces were intent on removing one of the region's most vital defense posts from Union hands and viewed the men within the fort as enemies. Pensacolians' support of secession may had been lessened had the federal government funded improvements to the forts and naval yard to the townsfolks' satisifaction during the antebellum period. Their frustration had taken on early sectionalist aspects in the regional newspapers, a factor doubtless on the minds of secessionists in 1861.[38]

Amid all of this, West Floridians waited to hear what would come of the secession convention in Tallahassee. Even considering the size and enthusiasm of the secessionist meetings, West Florida provided the largest number of delegates to the secession convention, who urged postponing the final decision until other Southern states seceded. Going against convention delegates who urged patience, the more ardent secessionists dominated the proceedings, and Florida seceded on January 10, 1861. After secession, pressure mounted on Slemmer to surrender Fort Pickens. On two separate occasions, January 15, 1861, and January 18, 1861, Slemmer refused locals' demands to surrender the fort. He managed to hold onto it until April, when it was reinforced by other U.S. forces. The nearby naval yard did not remain in Union hands and was eventually shelled by secessionists. The dry dock that Pensacolians had advocated for so strongly was taken out into the bay and destroyed.[39]

Reaction to secession within the coastal communities quickly morphed into worries over the possibility of a blockade as war seemed imminent. In many ways, the blockade would create a different relationship with foreign powers such as Great Britain, and their presence in the Caribbean did not seem as threatening as it had been in the 1840s and 1850s. Prior to the outbreak of the Civil War, Gulf Coast writers and intellectuals argued that the presence and interests of countries such as France and Great Britain made increased naval and military power necessary for protection of their trade from possible foreign encroachment. Now the prospect of British and French ships patrolling the waters desperate for Southern cotton and sugar became a bargaining chip and a way to denounce the impending Union blockade, which also demonstrated the economic and strategic importance of the Gulf Coast ports to the new Confederate States of America.

RUNNING TO THE CARIBBEAN

The outbreak of war signaled a new reality for coastal communities in the Gulf of Mexico. In New Orleans, Maria Craig wrote a letter to her sister Fanny Leverich in which she observed, "Our streets are filled with large Military Companies; and composed of the very Flower and Chivalry of Louisiana." Craig joined in with the other white women of New Orleans, like their counterparts throughout the South, to help equip the volunteer companies that milled about their streets with the uniforms and equipment they might need. They organized a military fair, the "biggest ever given in the city," which raised ten thousand dollars intended for poorer soldiers and their families.⁴⁰

In July, after the Battle of Bull Run, some of the first bodies came back to New Orleans, and Pierre Soulé received a letter that requested his presence at the funeral of a dear friend. James Trudeau wrote him, asking that he be there as a representative of "all those who are united in purpose to see triumphant the ideas and principles of our Confederate States, in one word all the true patriots of the South, to render a last tribute of respect to him who shed his blood in defense of the Sacred Rights of our Country."⁴¹ There is no word on whether or not Soulé attended his friend's funeral, but it was the first of many that took place in New Orleans and signaled that the war had most definitely come. Yet, what affected the coast most of all were not the faraway battles like First Bull Run but the blockade that President Lincoln called for in the early months of the war.

Abraham Lincoln's announcement of a blockade of Southern ports from South Carolina to Texas came on April 19, 1861; it would later include North Carolina and Virginia. The blockade raised questions as to how the navy, numbering just 671 ships in March 1861, was going to accomplish this task. The length of the coastline stretched for over thirty-five hundred miles; the blockade was also to affect the Mississippi River and its tributaries, as well as all the other rivers, inlets, and bayous associated with the Gulf. This was a mammoth undertaking. Many of the larger port cities boasted heavy fortifications, and the outer banks and sand bars also added additional hurdles to creating an effective blockade. One of the other issues that Lincoln and his cabinet grappled with was whether or not imposition of a blockade might signal tacit recognition of the Confederacy's nationhood, since it did give Britain and France the opportunity to recognize the Confederacy's belligerent status. When the blockade was declared, European nations declared neutrality. The blockade declaration was enough to trigger a cavalcade of Southern writers speculating on all of these issues at the beginning of the war.⁴² The strategy for the Union blockade evolved out of part of Winfield Scott's Anaconda Plan, which sought to create a blockade of the Atlantic and Gulf ports in order to keep the Confederacy from importing military supplies and goods from European merchants and suppliers. In 1861 Secretary of the Navy Gideon Welles reported that the U.S. Navy would close the Confederacy's ports to trade and hunt down Confederate commerce raiders and blockade runners.

The *Daily Picayune* called readers' attention to the fact that the blockade had to be effective, otherwise it was little more than a "paper blockade." The Gulf South ports of Mobile and New Orleans remained open for business. "All foreign ships," the paper announced, "have perfect right to enter any rebel port, subject only to the impediment of effective blockade." In the *Navarro Express*, the editor asked whether or not the president could conduct the blockade or the war against them without the permission of Congress, and if a declaration of war was issued, would that then implicitly recognize the South's independence? For its part, the Confederacy, of course, had no navy at the start of the war. Instead, local troops busied themselves taking control of fortifications, though they were unsuccessful at gaining Forts Pickens and Sumter.

As it took over the forts and naval yards that the United States once controlled, the Confederate government outfitted several ships as commerce raiders and commandeered others along the Gulf Coast for their own use. The Confederacy's big gamble was to create a cotton embargo, in the belief that withholding cotton from the world market would pressure Britain and France into supporting the Confederate cause. In turn, the Union chose to focus on the same locations: the port cities that Confederates were most likely to use to import supplies.[43] Southerners in the Gulf South fought to keep control of their connections with the Caribbean in hopes that these would foster a trade that could keep the Confederacy supplied through what was quickly evolving into an incredibly bloody and costly war. Merchants and stores began advertising the goods and supplies that arrived through the use of a blockade runner. In February 1862 a Mobile merchant advertised many "fine nautical instruments" brought in by a blockade runner along with luxury items such as opera glasses, cigars, and tobacco. Merchants felt they could make a tidy sum on luxury goods and imported them sometimes over much needed supplies and food stuffs. The Houston *Tri-Weekly Telegraph* remarked on how the blockade gave Texans the chance to patronize a local tannery and foundry. The paper's editor thanked the owners for a "pair of elegant goat skins, from which we have had some boots made that are really splendid. Texas made boots from Texas tanned leather, better than that imported from the North, thanks to the [guerilla] blockade, will now come into general use."[44]

When the war began, the Southern states had to outfit an army and keep their citizens and soldiers fed without relying on imports from the North. This meant that they wound up buying supplies through companies and merchants in Great Britain. The Union's control of Fort Pickens shut down one of the best bays that the Confederacy could have used for blockade running through the Gulf of Mexico. This left New Orleans, Mobile, and other smaller ports such as Galveston, as well as the length of the Rio Grande, to be used for importing and exporting goods and cotton by blockade runners. The islands where these blockade runners would pick up their cargo included Nassau, Bermuda, and Havana, Cuba.[45]

The blockade of the Gulf Coast presented its own particular challenges to the Union Navy. When the first blockaders sailed into the Gulf of Mexico, they were not entirely prepared for the challenges that the geography and weather presented. In addition to the vast Mississippi Delta and bayous, they also faced massive storms and hurricanes. As the U.S. Navy steamed into the Gulf of Mexico in 1861, Southerners assured themselves that the blockade was merely a weak paper blockade and that British ships sailing for the ports could overcome the Union Navy intent on stopping them. In November the Houston *Tri-Weekly Telegraph* declared the Union's "heaviest brick, the blockade, is a perfect fizzle, a dead failure, and declare that the sooner they generally admit this fact and act upon it, the sooner they will 'begin the war.'"[46]

In the Gulf South the war began with the blockading of ports through Florida and the attack on New Orleans. Because New Orleans was such an important commercial and shipping center it was a prime place to begin a blockade-running trade; for this reason, as well as the city's position on the Mississippi, it became an important target for the Union. The Western Gulf Blockading Squadron under the command of then-Flag Officer David Farragut commenced their attack on New Orleans on April 18, 1862, with the Battle of Forts Jackson and St. Phillip. On April 24 Farragut's fleet defeated the small Confederate fleet. The three-thousand Confederate troops under General Mansfield Lovell retreated north of the city on the next day, and Farragut arrived, taking possession of it. As a result of the fall of New Orleans, blockade-running efforts shifted to Mobile as well as parts of the Texas coast.[47]

The arrival of one of the early blockade runners into Mobile demonstrates the many ways that Southerners came to see the sailors and officers who sailed aboard these ships. The C.S.S. *Florida* was first named the *Oreto* when shipwrights built her in a shipyard in Liverpool, before being purchased by the Confederacy for wartime work as a commerce raider.[48] The ship docked in Nassau to be outfitted with provisions, coal, and arms; it then moved on toward the Gulf coast. John Maffitt, the soon-to-be captain, wrote to Stephen Mallory, the Confederate secretary of the navy, and informed him of the ship's situation. Maffitt had spent nearly thirty years in the U.S. Navy serving in the U.S. Coast Survey before resigning his position and joining the Confederacy. Before joining the Confederate Navy, he spent time running the U.S. naval ships that patrolled the Gulf of Mexico. In his letter to Mallory, Maffitt estimated the blockade he'd have to run, which included "some twelve men-of-war." However, the governor of Nassau, Charles John Bayley, was suspicious that the *Florida* was, in fact, bound for the Confederate Navy and blocked it from meeting other Confederate ships at Nassau. So, they met off the coast in another bay, Green Cay, where the *Florida* took on stores, coal, and arms and was commissioned into the Confederate Navy. Disaster quickly struck the new commerce raider while still at Green Cay, when yellow fever swept through the small crew.[49]

The Southern press and the Confederate government lauded both the *Florida* and its captain, for their heroic dash through the blockade, serving as a prime example of the romanticization of blockade runners. In July Mallory wrote to Maffitt, instructing him on what he should do with the *Florida*: "I feel very great anxiety about the Florida and trust that you may be able to get her to sea safely and make a dock with her against the enemy. The difficulties in your way are serious."[50] The *Florida* ran the blockade into Mobile as Union ships unleashed a barrage of fire. For those in the city it was an exciting feat. Mallory wrote Maffitt, exclaiming, "The escape of your defenseless vessel from an overwhelming force with liberty to choose its ground and mode of attack was alone due to the handsome manner in which she was handled." The ship's defenseless state was due to a lack of munitions, and the yellow fever making its way through the crew. A month before he received Mallory's note of praise, Maffitt wrote to his daughter to tell her the story of the now-famous C.S.S *Florida* commerce raider. Of his yellow fever, Maffitt wrote, "I too, fell before this pestilential tyrant of the tropics and for 9 days, was condemned beyond all hope when recovering my mental faculties." Maffitt revealed to his daughter that the main reason that he took the risk of running the ship into Mobile Bay was because it was "impossible on account of the strict neutrality laws of Britain and Spain to obtain men, all that was left was to save the vessel and run her into a Confederate port."[51]

Blockade runners and commerce raiders evoked the same feeling of excitement and heroism that the filibusters had as transnational figures willing to risk it all to maintain the South and its institutions. Once it was safely in Mobile, crowds visited the crew of the *Florida* and celebrated their miraculous run. Maffitt claimed his cabin resembled a "flower garden and as for jellies, cakes and dulcies the young ladies seem to spend great industry and great courtesy," writing in his letter to his daughter that a ship full of ladies intent on visiting with the heroic captain came alongside the *Florida*. The *Florida*'s 1862 blockade-running episode was reported throughout the South as evidence that the Union blockade was ineffective. The Houston *Weekly Telegraph* called Maffitt a "very different sort of person, [who] evidently emulates the fame of a Paul Jones, rather than a Captain Kidd." They focused intensely on figures like Maffitt and Raphael Semmes, connecting them to the figures of the Revolution and emphasizing their bravery.[52]

Still, blockade running turned out to be not as effective through the Gulf of Mexico and the port cities there. It was far more effective out of the of Atlantic coastal communities like Charleston and Wilmington. Maffitt's famous dash across the Gulf of Mexico into Mobile drew a lot of attention, which had a negative impact on the development of a blockade-running trade. The U.S. Navy also guarded Galveston's main shipping channel, but a second pass, the San Luis Pass, provided a backdoor to Galveston for trading ships and blockade runners. Additionally, for a time Texans could export cotton through Matamoros and Brownsville on the Rio Grande. A portion of the Treaty of Guadalupe-Hidalgo in 1848 stipulated that Mexican and U.S. Naval ships could not impose a blockade one mile north and south of the opening of the river. The fact that Mexico was embroiled in a civil war of its own and an invasion by the French also made running supplies through Matamoros difficult. Furthermore, the use of wagons and railroads slowed down the movement of supplies through Texas; meanwhile, Texas officials tended to commandeer materials for their own troops. The Confederacy's tendency to commandeer ships for commerce raiders and naval ships also hampered the overall trade. In the Gulf of Mexico, the eventual attack of Galveston, plus the increasing pressure on the trade in Matamoros and the fall of Mobile in 1864, meant that the blockade-running trade in the Gulf South would never be as successful as it was along the Atlantic Coast. Even so, the Gulf South remained an important center for supplies and though it was not the location of massive battles, those living there still experienced the uncertainty of the war years, the dislocation of large numbers of white and Black Southerners, as the region continued to be an important link between the South and Latin America.[53]

CONCLUSION

In the Gulf South, the end of the filibusters, the slave trade, and issues like army protection against Native Americans incursions all fed into the debate over secession. Anglo Southerners' understanding of geopolitical borders and expansion into Latin America shaped the discourse of secession in 1861. Their unique geographic location and interests in the Caribbean and Mexico informed their perspective as they tried to understand what future lay beyond the decision to secede. The actual secession of the Southern states caused many within the Gulf Coast communities to question the relationship with the U.S. Army and Navy that they had courted and counted on for over two decades.

The growing debate over secession added a layer of paranoia and anxiety to a society already traumatized and frustrated with the failures of expansion into countries such as Cuba and the territories of the Mexican Cession. For the white residents of the Gulf South, the outbreak of the Civil War was merely the latest in a long series of fights over supremacy in the Gulf of Mexico writ large. Secessionists and unionists often asked the same questions but arrived at completely different answers. The Gulf's past, its involvement in the great westward and southward migration of people, shaped not only the issues people in the local communities cared about but also how they spoke about them. As the South birthed a nation from its regional boundaries, Southerners within the Gulf of Mexico again reimagined their community and its connections with the Caribbean and Latin America.

Despite having served in the U.S. Army through a number of armed conflicts, Albert Sidney Johnston chose to follow the state that he had made his home, Texas. Johnston had moved to Texas in the 1830s and helped found the Republic of Texas, taking up a position of secretary of war. Johnston was in San Francisco when Texas seceded. He then gathered a number of secessionist soldiers and proceeded to march to Texas. Sam Houston, on the other hand, tried to keep control of the state as the secessionists fought to take Texas out of the Union. He'd been an avowed unionist and struggled to bring the state into the United States after actively contributing to its secession from Mexico. He tried to convince his son not to join the Confederate Army, but in this he also failed, and Sam Houston Jr. joined the Second Texas Infantry Regiment. He was wounded at the Battle of Shiloh. Albert Sidney Johnston died on that battlefield on April 6, 1862. Sam Houston moved his family to Huntsville, where he succumbed to pneumonia on July 26, 1863.

The ideas and experiences of expansionists contributed to the many ways that Southerners in Gulf Coast communities understood and interpreted secession. While expansionists often talked about European nations as interlopers and competition, this changed during the Civil War. Rather than being a threat, the English presence in the Gulf of Mexico now meant possible salvation, as it offered the ability for the Confederacy to obtain weapons, ammunition, and other goods they could use to fight the war.

The Civil War also changed the way that Southerners viewed European involvement in Latin America. Race played an important part here as in all things. When the French went to war with republican factions in Mexico and Confederate diplomats attempted to link European interests with Confederate interests, those residing in Texas and along the Gulf Coast largely saw such events in a positive light—and as a way for whiteness to prevail in Mexico. The Confederate government may have still entertained the possibility of a slave empire in Latin America, but the blockade runners and Confederate troops now used the Gulf Coast communities to protect their fragile new nation. Their need for possible allies required a careful dance that began with the secession crisis.[54]

While the large armies of the Union and Confederacy marched off to fight one another in Virginia, Maryland, and the many states of the border South, Gulf Coast whites looked to the sea and the Union ships establishing a cordon around the Southern coast. These were intent on stopping Southern trade, but they were also intent on stopping Southerners from using the connections to the Caribbean and Europe they had worked to create in the decades before the Civil War. Commerce raiders and blockade runners sailed back and forth through the lines that the Union Navy established. As a result, they became famous among their Southern compatriots for taking the risk not only because they were in a position to keep the South going as the war progressed but because they flouted the power of the United States, a power and presence many Gulf South residents had once greatly supported. What's more, the Gulf South experienced the war at sea and the war on land as well as the French invasion of Mexico. In the years after the surrender of New Orleans, the communities of the Gulf South would be inundated with great swaths of people displaced by the violence of war.[55]

CHAPTER 7

Empire on the Run

When New Orleans fell into Union hands on May 2, 1862, Confederate residents remained defiant. As Union officers and marines tried to make their way to city hall to receive the city's official surrender, armed mobs attempted to hold them at bay. After the marines raised the Union flag above the U.S. Mint building in the center of town, resident William Mumford tore it down and the crowd burned it, much the same way New Orleanians had burned the emblem of the Spanish consul after the failed López expeditions. Despite all of this, the city quickly became a haven for unionist refugees from Texas, who began pouring in by the hundreds.[1] Among them were Thomas DuVal and his family, who made their way into the city on Christmas Eve in 1863. DuVal was intent on organizing a regiment of Unionist refugees to invade Texas, and at least two thousand joined up. They went to Brownsville but nothing ever came of this planned invasion. By 1865 he was back in New Orleans with his family. On April 8, 1865, DuVal wrote in his diary that he had heard that the Army of the Potomac had Lee cornered at Appomattox Courthouse and things did not look good. "This renders it certain that the great 'Southern Confederacy' which was to have been the mistress of the world through the aid of slavery and King Cotton is no more."[2] By August, a different kind of refugee arrived in the Crescent City too: ex-Confederates hoping to catch steamers bound for Latin America. They signaled the last gasp of the South's great vision of continental dominance, Latin American empire.

The enormity of the Civil War uprooted all Southerners' lives in ways that previous expansionist conflicts had not. Though the series of events discussed in the previous chapters caused migrations, both forced and voluntary, they were not nearly on the scale of the kind of movements that the Civil War would unleash. Between the Texas Revolution and the Civil War there were many other conflicts with Mexico and Native American peoples that disrupted parts of the South and various groups within the general population, but the conflict that began in 1861 affected everywhere and everyone. During the Civil War, the Gulf South played host to several different migrations and a variety of displaced people. White Southerners fleeing fighting in other parts of the South or abandoning the plantation districts of the Lower South migrated to perceived safe havens in places like Texas. Slaveholders forced the African Americans they had enslaved to move with them, often times trekking across the South to arrive in Texas. Unionists, also seeking safe havens, moved to Union-occupied parts of the region such as New Orleans. The movement of displaced people through Gulf South communities did not end in 1865. It continued for years afterward as ex-Confederates fled the United States altogether, many of them founding new colonies in Brazil and Mexico.

This chapter focuses on these many dislocated peoples as they drifted in and out of the Gulf South during the closing years of the war and the beginning of Reconstruction. It follows the movement of people through the port communities and into Texas and traces the final transformation in the long history of Southern interests in Latin America—that is, the moment when Southerners largely gave up dreams of slave empires. It will focus mostly on the white Southern refugees, enslaved African Americans forced to go to Texas, and ex-Confederates who went to Mexico, Brazil, and Cuba. Mexico and Brazil were two of the most popular destinations for Confederate expatriates, and Cuba became a stopping point for Confederates headed elsewhere. In reference to Mexico, the chapter will primarily examine the first wave of emigration that consisted largely of fleeing Confederate officers and soldiers. The exodus to Brazil started almost as early as the stream of migrants to Mexico but lasted much longer. These various migrations, while representing a continued movement of Americans into Latin America, still marked the end of the long trajectory of Southern expansionism and the imperialist fantasies that focused on Latin America and the Gulf South.

The Civil War and the onset of Reconstruction changed the context in which white Southerners in the Gulf South and throughout the former Confederacy related to the nations of Latin America. Where dreams of war, conquest, and annexation once lived in the minds of many white Southern expansionists, many Southerners who now went to Latin America sought escape and safety instead. Tracing different groups and their movements through the Gulf South and into Latin America during this period reveals some of the ways in which Southern imperialism came to an end. The Civil War unmoored Southern society in multiple ways, one of which meant the end of the notion the South was destined to be a glorious empire in its own right. Many Confederates still entertained this idea, but through the course of the war and afterward it began to fade. That long narrative arc that began with the first attempts to conquer Texas and perhaps even farther back in the South's history, ended with the surrender of Confederate armies and the collapse of the Confederacy.[3]

REFUGE FOR SOME AND A PRISON FOR OTHERS

By 1863 streams of people choked the roads of the American South, as they fled the collapse of slavery and the destruction of war. As historian Megan Kate Nelson notes, the war years provided the nation and especially the South with a new sight—the sight of ruin. In March, when Sir Arthur Fremantle, a British officer intent on making a tour of the war-ravaged South, arrived in Mexico, Union and Confederate armies had already destroyed many Southern towns and the landscape bore the scars of massive battles. Fremantle was drawn to this destruction while others fled from it.[4]

In some ways, Fremantle's trip through the wartime South was conducted in reverse. The journey that found him traveling through the South was a testament to the transnational nature of the Civil War. As thousands began to pour into the Gulf South, particularly Texas, Fremantle traveled in the opposite direction, delving deeper into the South. He began his journey in England aboard a mail steamer, leaving his home country on March 2, 1863. Aboard the *Atrato* he befriended a Texan merchant making his return who agreed to help him on his trip through Texas. Fremantle and his companion, Mr. McCarthy, first stopped in Havana, where they boarded a British naval frigate that would be able to take them through the Union Gulf Coast blockade. He was essentially "smuggled" into the Confederacy through Matamoros, Mexico, like so much war materiel. Making landfall April 2, 1863, at Bagdad, a small island at the mouth of the Rio Grande that had become a major export depot for the South's cotton, Fremantle described it as a cluster of a few "miserable wooden shanties, which have sprung into existence since the war began." He then observed the "endless bales of cotton" that stretched on for an "immense distance." Matamoros had become the primary point for exporting cotton and importing goods used to prolong the war.[5]

As early as the middle of 1862, slaveholders in the Deep South began looking to the Gulf South frontier to save a society under siege. They reasoned, quite rightly, that the advance of Union armies across the Southern landscape created a potent motivation for enslaved African Americans to abandon the plantations and run away. They were also alarmed by the Confederate armies' decision to "impress" the property of Confederate citizens, including enslaved African Americans.[6] The *Texas State Gazette* reported that "plantations have in some instances been abandoned by their owners on the approach of our [the Union] army. Others have been deserted by the negroes, who left 'old massa to take care of the cotton hisself,' and rushed to the embrace of massa 'Lincoln's folks,' as they call the armies of the United States." In the same month refugees from Louisiana began showing up on Texas's border. "The roads leading from Louisiana to Eastern Texas are said to be still filled with wagons coming into Texas," noted the *Texas Almanac*. The wagon trains carried with them upward of fifty or sixty wagons, among them "many of the Louisianans [who] were compelled to leave their crops in the field, in their haste to save their families."[7] By May, among Fremantle's traveling companions as he headed across the Texas border into Louisiana was a Confederate Army officer who intended to look for "negroes" to impress and transport back to Texas to work on the construction of further fortifications in Galveston.

As Fremantle traveled further into the South, he watched men and women pass him searching out a place to maintain their grasp on their lives, their slaves, and the world that was quickly disintegrating all around them. He experienced the great heaving movement caused by warfare. As he traveled toward the Texas-Louisiana border, he told of meeting planters on the road "who with their families and negroes were taking refuge in Texas, after having abandoned their plantations in Louisiana on the approach of Banks. One of them had as many as sixty slaves with him of all ages and sizes."[8] Many of them were fleeing the U.S. Army of the Gulf under Nathaniel P. Banks, whose men had gained a reputation for plundering the plantations.

Despite the fact that Texas was seen as a relatively calm and safe place, far removed from the seat of war, even there its effects were felt and seen. After Fremantle and his Texan guide traversed across the Rio Grande, they traveled up along the Gulf Coast toward Galveston and Houston. What they found in Galveston was desolation. The city had been largely abandoned by its residents since the start of the blockade in February 1861. Many of them went to Houston to wait out the war. They were perhaps some of Texas's first refugees, but they would not be the last. Refugees from Galveston also spoke to the dislocation that happened in places where Union domination seemed a foregone conclusion. Despite the fact that Confederate forces under John B. Magruder retook the island

and the city on New Year's Day 1863, many Galvestonians still refused to return home. Other key cites along the Gulf Coast experienced similar fates during the war.[9]

Refugees still came to Texas. They came from Missouri and Arkansas as well as Louisiana. In June 1863 the Houston *Tri-Weekly Telegraph* passed along reports on the condition in these other states. The former governor of Missouri Claiborne Fox Jackson intended to send his family to Texas as refugees to wait out the war. Many of the white refugees were Southern white women, whose arrival in Texas elicited great scrutiny. By November 1863 a group of refugees from Arkansas and Missouri arrived in Texas. J. M. Johnson wrote a letter to the editor of the Houston *Tri-Weekly Telegraph* describing the scene of female refugees in Arkansas that were bound for Texas. While discussing the death of a daughter, the child of a woman named Mary Walton, Johnson took a moment to chastise Texas women for insufficient patriotism. He praised the loyalty of the refugee women and cautioned Texas women that their plight should be a lesson to the "ladies of Texas who, as yet, have felt none of the hardships and privations of this war, especially those who are continually writing to their husbands and brothers in the army, making out their cases as dark as possible, thereby discouraging their friends, and inducing them to desert their country's flag."[10]

Many of the refugees moving into Texas were either elite planter women or others who had been forced from their homes by Union and Confederate armies. Johnson reminded Texas women that they had not experienced migrations such as these on the same scale as women in other Southern states. Yet while he praised refugee women for their forbearance, effort, and patriotism, others began to be increasingly critical of planter elites who fled the plantations of the Deep South in favor of peace in Texas. Historian Candice N. Shockley has argued that some Texans began to feel a sense of bitterness toward fleeing elites, believing it was these Southerners, and not Texas women like those Johnson spoke of, who wrote to their husbands to tell them about their troubles at home. It was the planter class who was weakening the war effort and straining the already taxed resources of Texas. In contrast, the flight of women from the yeoman class was more understandable and viewed as an act of compulsion and not of choice.[11]

While white Southerners fled to Texas seeking refuge, enslaved African Americans were forced by their enslavers to go to Texas to keep them from seeking freedom under the wing of the advancing Union Army. By May 10, 1863, Fremantle awoke to the news of the fall of Alexandria, Louisiana, and the sight of "negroes, who are being 'run' into Texas." He claimed that the road was "alive" with them, noting that his traveling party must have met "hundreds of them."[12] The war challenged the security of the South's institutions, just as expansion had, and caused white Southerners to move and take slaves and slavery with them. But as Texas became a major site of Southern movement again by 1863, its meaning changed: it was not so much a model of territorial expansion any more but a safe haven and a place where slavery could survive, largely untouched by the Union Army.

In many parts of the trans-Mississippi and western theaters like Louisiana, Mississippi, and even as far north as western Tennessee, enslavers began removing enslaved Black people in a process sometimes called "refugeeing." Essentially slaveholders forced their enslaved people to migrate to Texas so they could not escape to the Union Army. Slaveholders often viewed U.S. soldiers as stealing enslaved Black people by emancipating them, encouraging them to be more outspoken, or duping them into running away.

Many of the 1930s interviews with former slaves conducted by the Works Project Administration comment on the ways that enslavers forced the enslaved to migrate to Texas. One gentleman, Van Moore, came to Texas from Virginia as an infant with his mother, and he related the story of their journey. Moore noted that Louisiana and Texas were both prime places for refugeeing. His mother told him that when they started for Texas in wagons, slaveholders told them that in Texas there were going to be "lakes full of syrup and covered with batter cakes, and dey won't have to work so hard. Dey tells 'em dis so dey don't run away."[13] Louis Love started his life on a plantation in Louisiana, but after the fall of New Orleans his master forced him along with three hundred other enslaved people to load up in wagons and start toward Texas. He stated that "dey camps dat night at Camp Fusilier, where de 'federates have de camp. Dey make only five mile dat day. Dey stops one night at Pin Hook, in Vermilionville. My brudder die dere. Dey kep' on dat way till dey come to Trinity River. I stay dere five year." A former slave from Alabama told a similar story, explaining that "Marse Tom heared they gwine 'mancipate the slaves in Selma, so he got his things and niggers together and come to Texas. My mammy said they come in covered wagons but I wasn't old 'nough to 'member nothin' 'bout it." Another woman, Ann Ladly, remembered hearing from her sister that their master said that, in Texas, "all dey has to do is shovel up money" so they wouldn't run off, but, as Ladly tells it, when they got there all they shoveled was cotton.[14] Enslavers coerced enslaved people with stories about Texas as they saw it and in ways they thought would mollify slaves who otherwise might protest against the migration. Historians have no hard numbers on the slaves that planters forced to migrate, but estimates range from 20,000 to 150,000 individuals packed up on wagons and marched to Texas.¹⁵

Along with Texas, Florida also became a site of similar movements of white and Black Southerners. In Florida, slaves were moved from East Florida onto substitute plantations in the middle of the state. Aside from slaves and defecting soldiers, many of the refugees toward the end of the war included white women. In some cases, their husbands had, prior to the war, provided them with locations to go to in case evacuation was necessary. On March 15, 1864, one Confederate officer, Major General Washington Scott, wrote his wife a detailed letter explaining what she would have to do and where she would have to go. A woman living in Jacksonville, Maria Murphy, fled in early 1862 and took refuge in middle Florida as a teacher; prior to leaving the city she saw her husband off to war and sold off most of their property. Parts of the Florida Gulf Coast were almost entirely abandoned. Residents in Pensacola fled the area for the safety of south Alabama towns in 1862, and when it was finally taken over by the Union, it was, as one historian notes, a "ghost town." Residents and Confederate soldiers had left nothing but ransacked homes and overgrown streets when they abandoned Pensacola. The city's residents dwindled to ten men, thirty women, and thirty children. It was rendered unimportant by both sides and remained abandoned through much of the war.¹⁶

The relative stability of Texas created a refuge for Confederates, but for unionists it was an entirely different story that resulted in additional migrations to other places in the Gulf South, namely New Orleans, as Texas Confederates committed grievous acts of violence against unionists. Newspapers kept up a high feeling of alarm about Northerners. The *Austin State Gazette* as early as 1861 encouraged its readers to "destroy every element of treason in Texas by the most prompt and efficient means." New Orleans was inundated by those seeking to get out of the way of the violence in other regions, especially Texas. Confederate Texans relentlessly policed Texan communities for unionist dissenters, going so far as to execute forty settlers in Gainesville in 1862 accused of plotting to destroy arsenals in town and kill Confederate citizens. That same year, Confederates slaughtered German Texans on the Nueces River. Fearing pockets of foreign dissenters in its vulnerable Southern border region, the Confederacy imposed martial law on central Texas. German immigrants had a reputation in Texas and the Confederacy as being unionists and, at best, ambivalent on the institution of slavery. A party of German immigrants decided to flee to Mexico and then sail from either Matamoros or Veracruz to Union-held New Orleans, like many other unionists. However, they were caught before they could reach their intended destination by Confederate soldiers and managed to repulse one attack before some of the men in the German camp fled the area. The rest raced toward the Rio Grande and were finally all killed by their pursuers.[17]

By 1863 unionists fled the state, many moving through Mexico to get to New Orleans. For them as well as for Confederates hoping to smuggle cotton out of the embattled South, Mexico was the conduit through which they could obtain what they needed—for the Rebel army it was war materiel and for unionists it was escape from the isolation and terror of the Confederate milieu. By 1862 hundreds of unionists had passed through the town of Matamoros to New Orleans and others to Monterey, Mexico. On top of hundreds of unionists, nearly ten thousand emancipated African Americans were also present in and around New Orleans, while hundreds of Confederate citizens chose to evacuate the city. For example, Thomas DuVal had been a federal judge in Texas prior to the war and was able to utilize his governmental connections to provide his family with a more comfortable time in exile to New Orleans. In addition to DuVal's plans to organize a unionist regiment, the *Texas Almanac* reported that Edmund J. Davis intended to join the Texas United States Volunteers and welcomed unionist refugees from other regiments to join him. They reported that seventy-five "Texas renegades" had entered the city and joined this new regiment.[18] However, Davis and his fellow unionists lost in a skirmish with Confederate forces.

By 1864 the Texan unionists living in New Orleans had organized themselves into regiments and political associations. General Alexander Hamilton Jackson addressed the Texas Loyal League in New Orleans. He implored the crowd to "give aid to those who come here destitute—refugees from country and family; to give the necessary means to the needy; and to embody whatever information can be gathered from our distracted State, and put in a form to be made serviceable to those who are engaged in the work of bringing her back to the Union." It was New Orleans's occupation as well as its distance from the epicenter of war that gave both Confederate and unionist refugees rhetorical room to talk about the war's aims as well as find a physical space of refuge in the city. In an ironic turn of events in the Gulf South, though the war raged on throughout the rest of the South, the region was now seen as a space removed from the fighting rather than a pathway into it. However, the final moments of war and the last-ditch efforts to sustain the separatist fight would migrate into these communities too—and sustain the region's long history of almost-uninterrupted violence.

TRYING TO ESCAPE THE END

As the Civil War came to a close, and the Confederacy collapsed piece by piece, white Southerners had no idea what awaited them. Many Confederate elites believed they might be rounded up and executed for treason. Even Mary Boykin Chesnut, the famed diarist and slaveowner, joked that she did not know if her husband would be shot as a soldier or hanged as a senator. Many began making plans to escape as soon as they heard the news of Robert E. Lee's surrender, and for some, those plans focused heavily on Latin America. Like the expansionists a decade before them, Confederate generals and ordinary citizens sought salvation in the lands south of the doomed slaveholders' republic. Old dreams of Southern empire quickly morphed into a desperate plan for Southern survival. And so, as the war wound down, many in the Confederate military and political leadership first fled to Mexico.

Confederate president Jefferson Davis considered plans to pursue guerrilla warfare even as he made plans to flee the country. Mary Chesnut wrote on April 23, 1865, that he planned to offer rebel soldiers a ransom in gold if they would cross the Mississippi and continue to wage a war from the West. In Shreveport, Louisiana, citizens held a large town hall meeting at which many agreed that they should find ways to continue the war. Speakers concocted a plan in which Davis and other members of the Confederate leadership should go to Havana, regroup, and head back through the Rio Grande into what had been the Trans-Mississippi Department under the Confederacy. On the run for his own life, Davis met with his cabinet in May 1865 in Washington, Georgia, and dissolved the government. He was headed for the Trans-Mississippi Department, which was still holding out, waiting for his arrival. On May 11, 1865, Union cavalry under Brigadier General James Harrison Wilson captured Davis in Irwinsville, Georgia.[19]

Even after Davis's arrest, Confederate officers were beginning to flee to Mexico. General Edmund Kirby Smith, Joseph Shelby, and John Magruder hoped to make it to Mexico before Union forces caught up with them. Their individual travels shed light on the personal experience of upheaval at the end of war and the decision of many within the Confederate leadership to use Mexico as a place of refuge once Smith's decision to surrender firmly dashed the far-fetched plan to regroup and mount a counteroffensive.

Smith had tried to keep his army intact as long as possible until he finally signed terms of surrender in Galveston on June 2, 1865. When he did so, he proceeded to formally disband the last major field army still in existence in the Confederacy. As Smith noted, by the time he returned to Texas from Shreveport troops in Texas had already started to desert and head for home. His last act as commanding officers was to address his soldiers. In his speech, he urged his men to accept the end of the war, announcing quite simply that "it is final." He mourned the fact that he was "left a commander without an army—a General without troops" and implored his men not to resist the outcome. He asked them to return to their families and "resume the occupations of farmers. Yield obedience to the laws. Labor to restore order."[20] Yet, even as he urged his men to go home and turn their swords into plowshares once again, Smith planned a quite different denouement for himself: as soon as he could, Edmund Kirby Smith left the country.

Like the elites who had escaped the areas of the South that suffered the worst of the war's destructive power, Confederate commanders in the Trans-Mississippi had the means by which to travel to Mexico and other parts of Latin America, but they were also driven by what they perceived as necessity. Smith's decision to leave the South was not a common one, but it was not entirely rare either.[21] In his notes from the journey, he wrote about learning of Lee's indictment, admitting that it was this news that "made it prudent if not my duty to place the Rio Grande between myself and harm until the excited feelings of the people at the north had calmed down, and the government had settled upon some decided course of policy toward the south."[22]

While leaders like Edmund Kirby Smith prepared to flee, white Southerners throughout the region engaged in a contentious debate over whether or not people should leave the country. Opposition to the mounting exodus to Mexico and Brazil began during the tumult caused by Abraham Lincoln's assassination. Doubtless, the assassination and the exodus were linked, as many Southerners worried over their fate, and the uncertainty that the president's death brought only served to exacerbate the feeling that Reconstruction would mean suffering and humiliation for former Confederates.

Shortly after Smith surrendered his command, he trekked from Galveston to the U.S.-Mexico border. In a letter to his wife, Caroline Selden Smith, he wrote that he had crossed into Mexico after a "fatiguing" six-hundred-mile trip. Smith's escape to Latin America was a solitary one; he did not intend for Caroline to join him. Upon arrival in Mexico he discovered that travel out of Matamoros was going to be exceedingly difficult as it was affected by the Mexican war against the French invasion in northern Mexico. After learning of Smith's surrender, General Joseph O. Shelby refused to capitulate and told his soldiers that he would be traveling to Mexico rather than surrender. One hundred and fifty of his men went with him on his frantic ride through Texas toward the border thinking they might launch a guerilla war. On the way, Shelby helped himself to arms and ammunition in the unguarded arsenals across east Texas.[23]

On June 25 Shelby was joined by several other former Confederate commanders of Trans-Mississippi forces and set out for the border, crossing into Mexico at Piedras Negras. It was there that Shelby and the other men ultimately let their Confederate dreams drown, possibly quite literally. In a move that morphed into legend and became known as the "Grave of the Confederacy Incident," Shelby's men supposedly took their former regiment's Confederate battle flag and sank it into the Rio Grande, a symbolic act perhaps meant to mark the final end of the Confederacy. While Shelby may have cast the flag down, his actions eventually led others who chose to stay in the South to view these soldiers-turned-expatriates as undefeated Rebels. On August 9, 1865, the *Bellville Countryman* gave its readers an update on the "expatriated Confederates." The paper gave a short account of a report from a gentleman recently arrived from Monterrey that "General Kirby Smith, [Sterling] Price, [John B.] Magruder, and [William] Preston, with others, had left for the city of Mexico," while others remained in that same city.

Smith at this point moved away from this group, traveling further toward the coast. He found "the roads beset with bands of plunderers & that the travel to Matamoros has ceased." He determined to take a steamer from Matamoros to Veracruz, and from there to either Havana or on to Liverpool. Unlike other Confederate expatriates who were determined to stay in Mexico, Smith was unsure of where to go. He planned for his wife and children to join him in either Canada or Europe, if it turned out that the federal government was not feeling particularly forgiving. All of his movements and the ideas he entertained were testament to his constant vacillating—and his encounters with other fleeing Confederates reflected the great uncertainty about what Reconstruction would mean and how it would affect them.

Like many of the other expatriates now roaming through northern Mexico, Edmund Kirby Smith had to figure out what to do with himself and how best to survive. He decided to join a group of Confederates traveling to the Yucatan. During July, Smith fantasized that the city of Merida in the Yucatan could provide him, his wife, and his children with the refuge they needed from the Union. He assured his wife that "they tell me I can rent a good home in the best part of the city & support my family for forty or fifty dollars a month the hire of the best servants is from 1 to 3 dollars a month." He went on to describe the large parcels of land they could obtain for so little money and the many fruit orchards that they might have on them. Meanwhile, he wrote to a Major F. Ducayet that he had heard he was in possession of some fifty thousand dollars of back pay. Kirby Smith urged him to send it to those officers who had decided to cross the Rio Grande. Kirby Smith's sister Frances Webster wrote to his wife Cassie that she would be willing to take a few of the children until Edmund was "established in some new career." His fretting over money brought up a very real aspect of becoming an expatriate—how to pay for it.[24]

What was evident was that Edmund Kirby Smith, like many of the expatriates, continued to harbor fantasies as much as any of the expansionists before them ever had. Cut loose from the society and the army he was familiar with, he was set adrift on the possibility of refuge to be found in Mexico or beyond. For Smith, his flight was temporary and he was concerned with the state of his family in the U.S. It was in late July that Edmund finally sent word to Cassie that he had made it safely to Havana. Smith explained his situation again to his wife, and he noted that Pierre Gustave Toutaunt Beauregard had been with him until he chose to return to the states and settle in Louisiana. Eventually, Union officers came knocking on Beauregard's door in New Orleans, looking for Smith. Smith, however, remained in Cuba. He again urged his wife to collect on their debts and ask friends to donate money that he might use to travel to Europe. He dreamed that this might be the time when Cassie and their children would finally join him, yet he also advised her to keep some of the collected money to live on. Several days prior to the arrival of Edmund's letter to Cassie, she received a letter from his sister, Frances, asking about Edmund's location and the state of their family.

Letters from Frances and Edmund concerning the well-being of the family lend yet another dimension to the choices that ex-Confederate leaders made in the immediate aftermath of the war. Their absence stretched families across the ocean in uncertain times. Amid discussion of the execution of Mary Surrat earlier in July, Cassie wrote Frances Webster that she was "hoping yet dreading to hear that Edmund was with you. It certainly seems to me that it would be very much wiser for him to go to Europe," or remain in Cuba. She also reported that a number of ex-Confederates had already returned and were living in Brooklyn. In many ways the war did not just subvert the connections and relationships that existed between Southern whites and the space of Latin America—the Confederate defeat also changed the relationship they had with the North.[25]

While Smith hid out in Cuba, his family back in the United States continued to fret over what would happen to their Edmund. His mother, Frances, wrote her daughter that "I should have advised him to go to France instead of Andalusia which he speaks of in his letter to me, and certainly cannot advise him to return to the U.S. much as I long to see him, unless positively and reliably assumed of a proper and unmolested reception and sojourn here."[26] Smith spent several months in Cuba and did not go to Europe, though many other Confederates did make their way to the continent.

The movement of refugees may not have been new in the communities of the Gulf South, but the size of these postwar movements, amid the loss of the war, was certainly novel. Antebellum filibusters may have been unsuccessful in their efforts too, but their numbers were miniscule by comparison. Postwar refugees' experiences emphasized the level of uncertainty in these new transnational movements. Confederate officers' rides through Louisiana and Texas also illuminated the way the war wound down in the Gulf region, and how it continued to play a part in the quickly evolving idea that places like Mexico might provide a kind of last stand for the Confederacy. This was not about gaining new territory for a Southern empire, however. For some it was about finding some way to keep fighting, but for most it was an escape and a way to bide time in relative safety.

Even as ex-Confederates traveled into Mexico after the end of the Civil War, that country remained heavily mired in its own war between the Juaristas under Benito Juarez and those fighting for the French-installed Emperor Maximilian I. Maximilian's advisors had suggested to him that the Confederate troops now streaming into Mexico might be able to help stave off the Juaristas, and it was widely reported that the Confederates were coming with the express purpose of offering to fight for the embattled emperor.[27] When Shelby and his fellow Confederates did finally arrive in Mexico City and offer their services as soldiers of fortune, Maximilian refused their offer and instead welcomed them as immigrant settlers, effectively turning them back into mere refugees, fleeing their collapsed government and nation. The pill was only mildly sweetened when he offered them not a place in his army but land for a colony.

On the heels of Confederate soldiers came white Southerners—civilians—eager to escape the devastation of the South and the changes that were rapidly taking shape there. For Confederate officers the choice to stay or return to the United States was also driven by the way that events unfolded in the early days of Reconstruction. The uncertainty of what might happen to the Confederate leadership once the war was over kept men like Edmund Kirby Smith from returning. However, once it became obvious that there would be no trials for treason and few hangings, some Confederates did return. Smith eventually sailed back to the United States and moved North for a time before finally making his way back down to the South.[28]

It was an unavoidable irony that the white Southerners who actually went to places like Brazil and Mexico were not there to perpetuate a grand Southern empire. They lived in colonies, which struggled from the beginning and ultimately failed. Before the war Southern newspapers and expansionists hailed settlers traveling into new territory or different countries like Mexico, but after the war, many fretted that such movements would hurt the region's rebuilding instead of improving the situation. What emerged was a struggle on the part of those who remained to keep the ones that were determined to leave from actually doing so.

RUNNING FROM RECONSTRUCTION

Former Confederate officers and soldiers did participate in colonization efforts, but the majority of the population of these colonies were civilians. Confederate colonies popped up in several different places but the main sites were in Mexico and Brazil. Many of the ships carrying Confederate expatriates to Brazil left from the wharves of Gulf South communities, especially New Orleans and Galveston. Colonization efforts emerged at the very end of the war and sparked a multisided conversation that involved not only Southern newspapers but also Northerners and unionists who wanted to see the South's planter class, the ones they viewed as responsible for secession, punished. All of the questions that came at the end of the war—questions about what to do with ex-Confederates, how to rebuild the South, and even what the place of freed African Americans might be—took on additional dimensions because of the possibility that the colonies, even the idea of the colonies, held out to people. Some historians put the number of Confederates at twenty thousand in Brazil alone, and others note that hundreds of thousands fled the U.S. South rather than contend with Reconstruction and possible execution for treason.[29]

Each option came with its own drawbacks and complications. As historian Todd Wahlstrom points out, the initial wave of Southerners may have been mostly made of the leadership of the Confederacy, but this would shift over the Reconstruction era. The colonists who did make it to Mexico in the years between 1865 and 1867 never numbered more than a few thousand. Toward the end of May 1865, the Houston *Tri-Weekly Telegraph* asked, "What are the duties of the hour?" The paper answered its own question: "First and foremost, then, we consider it the duty of every man to share the fate of his country. Those who claim and hold citizenship in Texas should stand by Texas now till the momentous questions of the hour are settled." The *Tri-Weekly Telegraph* denounced those who left and charged them with avoiding responsibility, lacking in moral courage, and being deficient in manliness.

The paper went on to admonish the very idea of immigration to Mexico and Brazil by noting that "thousands" of Texans had no means to leave. There was also the problem of the ongoing war in Mexico against the French and their puppet emperor, Maximilian. There was a chance that the United States might get involved in the war on the side of Juarez, which would pit the newly restored Union against ex-Confederates. If ex-Confederates went to Mexico to fight for Emperor Maximillian, it might happen that they would be taking up arms against the very Union soldiers they had fought at home.

Brazil, the other possibility for colonization, presented its own problems, argued the author of the Houston *Tri-Weekly Telegraph* article: "That is a wild country, a poor country, a weak country, and a country in which we might hide for a generation, but in which we could never enjoys rights of any kind. Leaving our homes for political reasons, we should always be regarded with the eye of suspicion, as a dangerous element in any society, and our situation would thus be disagreeable in the extreme." The article ended by admonishing readers: "Let us not fly from unknown, and, perhaps, to some extent, imaginary ills to those we do know to be unendurable; especially, when, in doing so, we avoid a duty and a danger which others, as good as good, as we must meet."[30] The next month the Houston paper published a letter on the subject of emigration by a person calling themselves "An Old Settler." This "old settler" did not denounce the prospect of emigration to the colonies but rather laid out the easiest way to accomplish colonization: with the consent of the United States government.[31]

It may have been an escape for some, but for those who chose to stay behind emigration was also an abandonment of the very land and society that had given them life. Initially, most of the concern was centered on the planter class's potential departure from the South. Rumors concerning the exodus of the planters flew wildly. An author under the pseudonym "Trinity Cottage" wrote in to the Galveston *Civilian and Gazette*, reporting that they had heard that "many of the planters are going to leave the country; some have already sold out for nearly nothing, and others are preparing to go in the Spring. It is said that the Emperor of Brazil offers one thousand acres of land and 6 months provisions; can you inform us if it is so?" The writer worried that if that rumor proved to be true, then "thousands" would go to Brazil or Mexico, "rather than live here with a population of such a complexion as must ultimately be spread over this once happy and prosperous country." They pleaded, "Don't go. At least not yet. Things may turn out better than they promise."[32]

The development of colonies and the debate this phenomenon spurred was very much a class issue because those with means could afford to make the journey. The New Orleans *Daily Picayune* warned that immigration was "ill-judged and every way unwise." The paper estimated it cost upward of one thousand dollars to emigrate and survive for several months while getting settled in Brazil. Articles popped up in many of the nation's newspapers concerning this "rebel emigration." On June 16, 1865, the *Daily Cleveland Herald* reported that a "number of the most prominent generals and engineers of the confederate army and navy contemplate emigration to Brazil. Their example will also be followed by many privates, if they can get means of transportation."[33] Colonization projects were expensive—and potential migrants faced the fundamental issue of funding. The San Francisco *Daily Evening Bulletin* noted the class issue in July when they stated that some of the South's "first families" would "get away before legislation can be had to prevent them." The paper worried that the South's wealthier citizens, those who orchestrated the secession of the Southern states, might get away before being punished for their treason. These anxieties reflected a more general concern that the South would not be punished and that the region's wealthiest citizens would take its wealth elsewhere just when the South needed it most. This might also set a dangerous precedent in that middle and lower-class white Southerners would follow suit and drain the South of its white population. The prospect of wealthy white Southerners leaving also triggered concern that cotton production would be negatively affected.

Yet Texans looked at their own lands and saw them as a possible part of these far-flung colonization projects. They needed white Southerners as badly as some former Confederates needed a way out of the South. One writer wrote, "Let us have the State populated, cultivated, educated, and brought up to the highest standard of the civilization that is forced upon us, and we shall have no need to go to Brazil, or California, or even to New York to get within the habitable globe again. Our own country, this Texas garden spot will be the choice spot of creation. We have pointed out what we believe is to be done." The editors of the *Tri-Weekly Telegraph* commented that letters such as these "sustain us. Ranters and theorists may say what they will. We honestly believe we can save the honor, the character, the worth of this country. Let us do it."[34] With the emergence of the colonization projects, the question of how the South would be reconstructed went far beyond the boundaries of the old slave states and became a transnational discussion.

Many in the South feared that the continued exodus from the region would remove vital skills and money needed to rebuild the South. At first, the movement of white Southerners south to Latin America was reported more as a curiosity than anything else. Yet as the years passed it became obvious that thousands of Southerners were leaving to seek their fortunes and attempt to rebuild their society in Latin American countries. Robert E. Lee joined the chorus of those urging Southerners not to leave. Only a few months after he surrendered his Army of Northern Virginia, he commented on the probability of Confederate expatriation in the *Daily Evening Bulletin*. Lee argued that leniency was needed in dealing with ex-Confederate soldiers, because a more severe Reconstruction would cause the country to "lose its best people. Already they are seeking to expatriate themselves, to Brazil, to Canada, to France or elsewhere." The paper noted that Lee was often asked to help stave off this exodus. It insisted that the young men entertaining ideas of expatriation are the country's "bone and sinew, its intelligence and enterprise, its hope for the future, and wisdom demands that no effort be spared to keep them in the country and pacify them."[35] Lee wanted white Southerners to stay put and rebuild. In the years after the war Lee tried to be a model citizen to Southerners and show them the way toward reunification. Many refused to listen. A *New York Herald* correspondent reporting from Selma, Alabama, observed that planters in the surrounding area were selling plantations for three to five dollars an acre where, before the war, the land would have gone for fifty dollars or more an acre. The sellers, "last ditch men" as the correspondent referred to them, hoped to leave for Brazil or some other foreign country.[36]

Within this context, Emperor Maximilian and Matthew Fontaine Maury began devising a plan to settle Southerners in northern parts of Mexico. Maury was already a well-known figure among expansionists by the time of the Civil War, as one who had celebrated strengthening the country's navy and naval defenses. A pioneering oceanographer and U.S. naval officer, Maury, like many others, sided with his home state of Virginia when it seceded from the Union. Maury was put in charge of coastal and riverine defenses during the war and sent to Britain on a diplomatic mission as well. After the war, Maximilian made Maury a commissioner of immigration so he could begin creating colonies. In response to a letter he received in September in 1865 asking if he would return to Virginia soon, Maury wrote, "Back to what? To poverty and misery?" The ex-Confederate had other plans and knew other Southerners felt as he did. In the early months after the final surrenders, this is what many Southerners saw: a devastated landscape without much to support them. Maury envisioned a network of settlements primarily in Mexico's agricultural regions surrounding Mexico City, but also in northern Mexico around Monterey and Chihuahua. Cordoba and Jalapa became two of the main sites of colonization. By 1866 the colony was given the name of New Virginia Colony by its chief organizers, including Maury.

Yet colonists could never rebuild their antebellum society entirely: Mexico did not allow slavery and there would be none in the colonies.

The labor question was foremost in the minds of both Maury and white Southerners back in the states. Yet, Maury did not completely abandon the idea of a Black labor force. He reasoned that the new colonies would comprise both Southern whites and newly freed Black people who might come with their former owners or come searching for work. Newspapers in the South also reported the possible importation of African and Asian workers to Mexico. The *Tri-Weekly Telegraph* reported on August 23, 1865, that the "Imperial Government of Mexico has definitively reported the plan of African colonization proposed by Mr. De Costa Vianna, and the proposals of other persons, for the importation of 100,000 Chinese workmen." This search for workers mirrored many Southern planters' interests in the possibility of importing workers through the coolie trade to replace formerly enslaved African Americans in the cotton fields. Chinese contract laborers also met the demand for labor in other Latin American nations such as Peru.[37] In his writings on Mexico and colonization, Maury expounded on the richness of the Mexican soil and the ability to launch different kinds of agriculture there. Though Maury's colonies were never going to lead to annexation of additional Mexican territory into the United States, that sort of imperialist vision still popped up occasionally in discussions of the ex-Confederate movement to Mexico. For example, the Bangor *Daily Whig and Courier* argued that as soon as "these lands shall have received a certain contingent of emigrants cities will spring up, trade and industry will begin, and the whole face of Mexico will be changed."[38]

Maury looked to Jamaica for a model of postemancipation Black labor. White Southerners like him had always looked to other places, like the West Indies, to foretell what might happen to them after emancipation. It was Jamaica's own apprenticeship methods that Maury sought to replicate in Mexico. As many historians have noted, white Southerners, especially planters, looked for ways to retain as much of the old system as they could, especially when it came to their control over a subjugated workforce. That said, there was no going back to the antebellum days, so Maury, like other Southern whites, sought out ways to manage their new circumstances. In a way, he continued to use Latin America as a backdrop against which he would imagine Southern society. His ideas to transplant Southern society to Mexico were not exactly new, though he was not hoping to remake the entire country in the image of the slaveholding South either. Instead, he sought to preserve little patches of the South in parts of the country under the protection of a monarchy.

A large majority of the middling and small planters who eventually came to the colonies were from Texas and the surrounding Gulf South states. But they soon witnessed yet another loss and another bloody collapse of a government, when in 1867, Benito Juarez and the Juaristas triumphed and executed Maximilian. At the same time, while they erected homes and invested in business ventures, they were less interested in erecting Southern society wholesale and were willing to adapt to the political and social climate of Mexico. But their efforts proved largely futile. The New Virginia colony was attacked by Juarez forces, and the communities almost vanished entirely by the next year.[39] The limits that Mexico placed on the colonies and emigrants made Brazil a more appealing option for migrants due to the fact that the nation still had slavery.

The *Daily Picayune* published a poem that encapsulated a growing interest in creating colonies in Brazil:

> Oh, give me a ship with sail and with wheel
> And let me be off to happy Brazil
> Home of the sunbeam—great kingdom of heat,
> With woods evergreen and snake forty feet!
> Land of the diamond—bright nation of pearls,
> With monkeys aplenty, and Portuguese girls!
> Oh give me a ship with sail and with wheel,
> I yearn to feel her perpetual spring,
> And shake by the hand Dom Pedro her king,
> Kneel at his feet—call him, "My Royal Boss!"
> And receive in return, "Welcome Old Hoss!"[40]

Generally, Southerners saw Emperor Dom Pedro II as sympathetic to them and their cause. During the war, he had been careful to maintain Brazil's neutrality while Confederate blockade-runners used Brazilian ports as safe harbors when Union vessels pursued them. In Brazil, slavery was alive and well, with numbers close to that of the United States prior to the war. The agents hoping to galvanize support for Brazilian colonization efforts emphasized this in their writings. For many white Southerners, slavery provided a proper order in society, a sense of security in the racial order, which the ex-Confederates now hoped to find in Brazil. Yet many Confederados—as they would become known in Brazil—would never own massive numbers of enslaved Afro-Brazilians or massive plantations once they immigrated to their new home. Like the struggling colony in Mexico, they too failed at fully resurrecting what they once had in the antebellum United States.

Many questions about the place of Southerners in Brazil and the place of these immigrants within Southern culture and society floated back and forth with the ships that took them to South America. Historians such as Claire M. Wolnisty have suggested that Southerners in both the American South and Brazilian colonies became transnational families, moving back and forth across borders at will.[41] However, the choice to leave the South during Reconstruction came with a great deal of controversy, and for some a certain amount of grief at the prospect of leaving devastated communities and loved ones. This marked this as a different sort of migration than the movements to Texas and Florida back in the 1830s and '40s. In addition to the financial cost of migrating, there was the intangible cost of leaving the region that was one's home and becoming what the *Clarksville Standard* described as a "discontented wanderer." The paper warned its readers that "emigrants leaving this country individually would receive no assistance whatsoever from the Government." However, the paper did speculate that the Brazilian emperor might set aside land for the colonists in some locale.[42]

By August 1865 newspapers began reporting on talk of Brazilian colonization. A Galveston newspaper reported that several Southerners proposed to sail from New York City to establish "a settlement somewhere in the Amazon Valley provided the Emperor of Brazil has no objections."[43] On August 21, 1865, another group of would-be emigrants gathered in Edgefield, South Carolina, to form the Southern Emigration Society. The organization dedicated itself to scouting out locations in Latin America and the western territories of the United States for colonies of ex-Confederates. Two members of the society, Hugh G. Shaw and Major Robert Meriwether, arrived in Brazil soon after and spent several months making a report of the country and its prospects for settlement. In Sao Paulo, they encountered several "gentlemen of the South," who introduced them to the minister of agriculture, Paulo Susa. The minister furnished the pair with food, lodging, transport, and anything else they needed to make their report. In May 1866 the *Edgefield Advertiser* published the report in full; it was then published in newspapers through the South. Shaw and Meriwether noted the climate of different regions as being either favorable to their "people" or not and reported that in the region around Sao Paulo "is grown the best quality of upland cotton. Sugar and tobacco and all the Tropical fruits are grown in great perfection."[44] A young man who had recently gone to Texas was staying with a friend of his brothers', a Colonel Woodward, who planned to go to Brazil and the young man anticipated he would follow him there.[45] Rumors such as these hinted at the many ways in which the onset of Reconstruction would alter everything about the South, including the direction of expansion.

On April 6, 1867, the Keyes family of Montgomery, Alabama, began their own exodus as they prepared to set sail for New Orleans. During this early phase of ex-Confederate emigration to Brazil, people usually left in large groups, and many left from New Orleans and Galveston as these were two main ports in the South where ships arrived regularly from Latin American countries. Many had never visited Brazil and were worried about what they would find on the other end of the voyage. Would they arrive in a metropolitan city like the one from which they embarked? Or would it be a barbaric world far removed from the one they left? Julia Keyes, the eldest daughter, recorded in her memoirs that some of her friends "who went down to see us off, believed that ours was a fearful undertaking and thought we would have cause to regret the move." Certainly, their efforts in Brazil sought to recreate the South they had left behind. Keyes wrote that her father purchased property when they arrived and named it "Dixie Island." In 1868 he wrote to his brother, who had visited his family in Brazil and had expressed interest in the Dixie Island property. He asked if his brother would want to come and invest in the property with them, and informed him that he was involved in several economic ventures that were intended to help the family get back up on its feet. In addition to Dixie Island, he built a small dentistry business and grew sugarcane. The elder Keyes was interested in buying a larger property near a "Confederate neighbor" who had the means to grind the cane.

Many moved to Brazil because they could not fathom living under Union control and alongside emancipated African Americans. The Edgefield report had compared the Amazon to the Mississippi River in terms of climate and the possibility of cotton growth. Organizations like the Southern Emigration Society packaged Brazil for them as a kind of new South, one untouched by the losses of the Southern states, and one that was ready to welcome them despite what the Southern newspapers claimed. Many of the colonists in Brazil came from the Deep South states. While some Confederados made their home in the urban areas of Sao Paulo and Rio de Janeiro, others journeyed into the northern Amazon or farther south. The majority remained located in and around the cities in two communities named Santa Bárbara d'Oeste and Americana. The new immigrants usually arrived with no real clue as to which colony they would join and most wound up picking one as soon as they arrived. Once they arrived in Brazil, Dom Pedro sold lands in the colonies or anywhere the Confederados wanted to plant their flags along with passage to another seaport in Brazil if they wished to undertake it. After purchasing land and living there for two years, Confederados could become Brazilian citizens, and if they petitioned the legislature, they could rush the process and become citizens shortly after arrival.[46]

In her memoirs, Keyes offered romantic images of the early days of the Confederados' time in Rio de Janeiro. Emperor Dom Pedro II was eager to encourage further cotton cultivation in Brazil and felt that an infusion of cotton growers from the United States would help him accomplish this goal. To begin luring disaffected and dissatisfied former Confederates, Dom Pedro's administration created agents whose job it was to meet with prospective colonists in immigration offices created in the Brazilian embassy in Washington, D.C., and in New York City. The emperor offered them subsidized transport to Rio de Janeiro; upon arrival, they would be put in an immigrants' hotel while they waited to go on to their colonies. Julia Keyes and her family arrived in Rio de Janeiro, "a picture of beauty in its softest light." Julia recorded in her diary that the Brazilian government chartered a large steamer to transport them at the cost of forty thousand dollars. Once they arrived in Brazil, Keyes described the hotel as a palatial building adorned with "rows of Imperial palms" and marble. They were greeted by a former Confederate officer who owned the hotel, Colonel Broome. Keyes's ex-Confederates "were a happy band of emigrants," who felt they had "reached a place of rest, among kind, generous people, who gave us a welcome we did not expect." She estimated that along with her family there were possibly as many as three hundred other guests staying at the guesthouse.[47]

Julia Keyes's experiences in Brazil foreshadowed, in some ways, the evolution of the South's most enduring vision of itself, the Lost Cause. Her time as a Confederate expatriate also served as a reminder that the Southerners who did actually immigrate to Latin American nations after the Civil War did not arrive as the conquerors they once envisioned themselves to be. When she did arrive she noted that Brazil had a welcoming atmosphere, in part because it recalled the world they had seen destroyed. What Julia did not mention were the servants that doubtless also populated the hotel, most of whom would have been enslaved. This omission recalled earlier omissions in the writings of Southerners who encountered Latin America—they did not always mention the enslaved—as well as later omissions in Lost Cause literature. Keyes did note that naturalized citizens enjoyed the same civil rights as other Brazilians. She recorded that the "government of Brazil is stable" and that its "laws and authorities protect all without distinction or classes; and the distribution of civil and criminal justice is made with equality." Further contributing to the sense of stability, Brazilians had established regular steamship lines to the Confederado colonies that sprouted up throughout the Amazon and outside of the capital city in the wake of the Civil War.

Southerners in these colonies benefited the cotton industry of Brazil by bringing newer cultivation practices and technology. Yet as in the Southern states and in Mexico of the 1830s, they could not fully escape the onset of emancipation. As Reconstruction took hold in the South, Confederados worked to improve their lot in Brazilian society, though many of the communities remained incredibly insular. Many of them though eventually gave up, and due to homesickness or frustration, made the trip back to the United States. Most ex-Confederates did not become large scale planters and did not gain much status in Brazil or Brazilian politics. As Reconstruction gave way to white supremacist Redemption, republicanism took hold in Brazil. In an effort to stave off a possible coup d'état, Dom Pedro II's government instituted emancipation in 1888. Yet emancipation led to a revolution, and his government was toppled soon after. This had dramatic effects for the Confederados, as the new government revoked their land grants. According to William Clark Griggs, two Southern men with mining interests in Brazil lost large tracts of land and had to sue the new government to get them back. Despite antebellum fantasies about Latin America, Brazilian culture proved alien to them. It just wasn't home. As a result, many Confederados went home to a Southern society that had changed even as white Southerners lashed out violently in an effort to regain control of state governments and squash the rights of Black people.[48]

CONCLUSION

The Confederados may have attempted to preserve aspects of antebellum Southern society by choosing to leave behind the trials of Reconstruction for what seemed to be a more sympathetic society but the larger transnational forces of abolition that the South had fought against with its conception of imperialism followed them to their new home. Even in Brazil, their dreams were ultimately thwarted as the long arc of the narrative of an expansionist South came to an end. The population of the colonies never numbered more than several thousand and they struggled throughout the latter half of the nineteenth century. Additionally, they failed in their efforts to provide a buffer against the changes happening in South America and the American South. Americana, the largest colony, morphed into a city that still exists today. Many ex-Confederates stuck it out, unwilling to think of going back to the Southern states; however, their descendants remain an incredibly small part of the Brazilian population. They essentially became similar to other immigrant communities within Brazil, and today they are curiosity occasionally covered in major American newspapers.[49]

The Confederacy was the final and most important test of the viability of a hemispheric Southern slave-based empire. As with all the other conflicts that affected the Gulf South port communities, the Civil War shaped the lives of their residents in unprecedented ways. However, with the Civil War, white Southerners outside of the Gulf South viewed it as a space of refuge and relative peace, far removed from the real destruction experienced in places like the Upper South. The end of the Civil War set off yet another migration that also affected the region—the movement of ex-Confederates to places like Mexico, Cuba, and Brazil. Some hoped to keep fighting either by regrouping and launching a guerilla war or by fighting for someone like Emperor Maximilian in Mexico. Others hoped to find some place to wait out the aftermath of the war, wondering if Union troops were going to round up Confederate officers and hang them for treason. Later, other Southerners left the country to escape a South that was changing. Many hoped to start over in some place that bore a resemblance to the pre-emancipation South. Whether in Mexico or Brazil, the colonies they founded ultimately collapsed and Southerners in Brazil witnessed emancipation again.

The Southern refugees and ex-Confederate colonists represent the end of a long trajectory of expansionism into Latin American that was connected to the imperialistic notion of an ever-expanding South. They used the links that others once established between the American South and Latin America nations to leave the Gulf South. Southerners who stayed retreated from the view that Latin America could save their society and make it prosperous. Rather than seeing Southern ex-patriots as the vanguard of a vast empire, they often saw them as foolish and the choice to leave as a betrayal, giving up on the region at a time when it needed them the most.

By the turn of the century, Southerners may not have spread their society out beyond the borders of the United States, but the racist visions of Latin American nations and their peoples as well as the dreams of conquest, war, and annexation remained and fed into the nation's imperialist goals well into the twentieth century. Gulf South communities continued to be a part of this story of American empire, and to be shaped, as ever, by the wars waged in its name.

CONCLUSION

What Comes after Southern Imperialism?

Sam the "Banana Man" Zemurray was buried in Metarie Cemetery in 1961 amid the centennial anniversary of the American Civil War. He had spent most of his adult life as one of the central figures in the nation's late nineteenth- and early twentieth-century efforts to establish itself as a major economic and political power in the hemisphere. Zemurray was a Russian immigrant who first lived in Selma, Alabama, before finding himself at age eighteen selling bananas from a street cart in Mobile in 1895, the same year that Cuba began its Independence War against Spain. The story of Cuban struggle and American turn-of-the-century imperialism were as deeply entwined with the communities of the Gulf South as the Civil War–era wars of conquest had been. Eventually, the United States interceded in the Cuban Independence War, and Zemurray's Cuyamel Fruit Company became one of the major American corporations to dominate the economies and the politics of many Central American nations. Zemurray eventually became the head of the infamous United Fruit Company (UFC) and bought a big house on St. Charles Avenue in New Orleans. In his lifetime, U.S. warships and the gleaming white UFC fleets sailed back and forth across the Gulf of Mexico to do what slaveholding Southerners never managed to accomplish—achieve the spread of American power into Latin America.[1]

While the Confederacy had failed to produce the slave empire that white Southern expansionists had wanted, the idea of an American empire did not die in the mid-nineteenth century. The continuation of westward expansion through the Civil War and afterward via the encouragement of white settlers to move West and the continuation of war against various Native American nations proved that settler colonialism continued at a ferocious pace. The United States sought empire in both the West and in the Caribbean, Central, and South America. Even though slavery had been abolished, racism toward Native Americans, African Americans, and Latinx peoples played crucial roles in the way white Americans thought about empire moving forward. For the people of the Gulf Coast, the question remained—what role would their communities play in these postwar movements? Such questions were partially answered through Reconstruction and the awful violence of white Southern Redemption.[2]

Even decades after the end of slavery, the Southern communities of the Gulf Coast could not avoid being entangled in the simultaneous emergence of segregation, settler colonialism in the West, and American empire. Each of the communities and states covered in this book were touched by these various forces. Shelled by Union artillery during the Battle of Galveston, the city set about rebuilding after the war. Galveston remained an essential port for Texas's exports and a gateway of immigration for the state. As for Texas's Black residents, they experienced most of the opportunities of Reconstruction and the violence that came with its end. And for their part, Texans of Mexican descent did not escape unscathed from the violence of the white South's "redemption." They too were disenfranchised and segregated in ways similar to African Americans. On the Great Plains and in western Texas, the Union Army, tested by the battles of the Civil War fought against the plains nations, among them the Comanche.

In Louisiana in particular, African Americans fought for equality and freedom during Reconstruction and experienced the horrors of a white South hell-bent on resurrecting white power. New Orleans was rocked by the New Orleans Massacre of 1866, one of several bloody massacres (such as the Colfax Massacre in 1873) in the state during Reconstruction. Along with the physical violence came the black codes and laws that came to serve as the framework for segregation. Louisiana's segregation policy on train cars led to the eventual Supreme Court decision in *Plessy v. Ferguson* that condoned the region's laws under the doctrine of "separate but equal" in 1896. Amid all this the New Orleans waterfront continued to play host to a cast of characters from all over the world. Immigrants from Europe, the Caribbean, Mexico, and Central and South America arrived in the Gulf South to work in its fields and in its ports.[3]

In Florida, in the aftermath of the Civil War, different communities like Tampa took on more importance than places like Pensacola. The Pensacola Naval Yard was largely inactive after the war. As the United States gained the ability to build a base at Guantanamo Bay after the Spanish American War in 1898, the need for a navy yard in Pensacola receded. In the

1890s Tampa's Cuban cigar workers created a multiracial and very political community known as Ybor City that was heavily involved in supporting the Cuban Revolutionary movement. Cuban Revolutionary clubs repeatedly hosted the exiled Cuban nationalist and writer José Martí and helped fund the revolution itself. They did this at the same time they battled against southern segregation and racism. Tampa was also a major embarkation point for the U.S. soldiers who went to fight the Spanish American War.[4]

When the United States annexed Texas in 1845, few understood how the seeds planted in this new territory might grow. Yet white Southerners felt confident that expansion represented the path to prosperity and security, so long as the nation continued to use its military power to pursue their interests in Latin America. The annexation of Texas and the U.S.-Mexican War had secured immense tracks of land. After the war with Mexico it seemed as though Cuba would become the next slave state in the Union; even Central America appeared within reach. However, the failure of filibustering called this imagined future into question. Through secession and Civil War, white Southern efforts to sustain the Confederacy relied on Gulf communities and places in the Caribbean that those filibusters had once tried to conquer. The Gulf South's many connections with the outside world defined the local communities' experiences of all these events and shaped how many people viewed and talked about the events covered in this book.

Expansionism gave voice to all the possibilities, imagined futures, hopes, and fears Southerners—white Southerners in particular—could muster in the years of the Civil War era. The conflicts that plagued the region quickly became a fundamental part of that experience, shaping the national movement for more territory. Beyond the standard argument that more land meant more room for excess enslaved populations and yeoman farmers lay the belief that gaining more territory meant securing the South's borders and for some, providing a bridge to a more commercial South with influence along the Gulf rim and the Pacific.

Throughout the mid-nineteenth century, white Southerners living in these communities consistently imagined and reimagined Latin American people and spaces and in so doing they also reimagined themselves. Those living in the Gulf South created racial constructions of Native Americans, Mexicans, and Cuban Creoles to further the project of expansion.

Secession called into question the region's relationship with U.S. military presence. As Southerners throughout the Gulf South shared in the difficulties and anxieties brought about by war, they were forced to evaluate fundamental aspects of their society in much the same way that Gulf Coast communities had throughout the various conflicts of the previous twenty years. The Civil War decided the nation's course in terms of territorial expansion and imperialism.[5] As the Civil War came to a close and the Confederacy collapsed piece by piece, old dreams of Southern empire morphed into a desperate plan for Confederate survival. In the aftermath of the war, some Southerners did manage to escape to Latin America rather than surrender. They wound up in Mexico, Cuba, and Brazil, where many tried to resurrect their decimated society, ultimately with little success. The long story of Southerners' dreaming of empire in Latin America came to a close when would-be conquerors became refugees.[6]

After the Civil War, the United States took on the linked mantels of imperialism and westward expansion, though the imperialism that the nation pursued involved the expansion of political and economic control as much as it did the pursuit of physical territory. The use of race to support Anglo American dominance at home and abroad was defined during the earlier territorial expansion of the Civil War era. Within the Gulf of Mexico, this later stage of U.S. empire building and race making was also founded on white Southerners' attempts to secure their society's place in the ever-changing world that lay beyond the water's edge.[7]

NOTES

INTRODUCTION. Wanting a Southern Empire

1. Olmsted, *Journey through Texas*, foreword, 456.

2. Other historians who have turned their attention to the Gulf South in the Civil War era and beyond. Some of these books focus on the Deep South, which is perhaps a better-known name for the region, but even these histories note the confluence of different worlds. See for example Jack E. Davis, *Gulf Sea*; Sledge, *Gulf of Mexico*; Smith, *Louisiana*; Adam Rothman, *Slave Country*; Langley, *Struggle for the American Mediterranean*; Langley, "Whigs and the Filibustering Expeditions to Cuba"; Lamp, "Empire for Slavery."

3. The South's role as a site of Latinx history and the construction of racism toward Latinx peoples has, at times, been treated as largely tangential to the more well-established histories of Latinx peoples in the West. Historians who examine these various interpretations of white manhood and imperialism in conjunction with racism against Latin American people include Reséndez, *Changing National Identities*; Greenberg, *Manifest Manhood*; Gomez, *Manifest Destinies*; Montejano, *Anglos and Mexicans*; and Ramos, *Beyond the Alamo*.

4. Downs, *Second American Revolution*; May, *Southern Dream*; West, "Reconstructing Race."

5. Thalen, "Nation and Beyond"; Nagler, Doyle, and Gräser, *Transnational Significance*; Gleeson and Lewis, *Civil War as Global Conflict*; Armitage et al., "Interchange"; Schoen, *Fragile Fabric of Union*; Doyle, *Cause of All Nations*; Karp, *This Vast Southern Empire*.

6. In truth, the Gulf South was a transnational space since the beginning of European invasion and colonization. For more on the Gulf South in the colonial era, see Richmond F. Brown, *Coastal Encounters*; Strang, *Frontiers of Science*; and Weber, *Spanish Frontier in North America*, 31–41, 147–171.

7. Latin American people were not a single race even if white southerners often treated them as such. The literature concerning race and racism in Latin American societies is immense. I offer here a few works upon which this study draws: Fuente and Gross, *Becoming Free, Becoming Black*; Sartorius, *Ever Faithful*; Gomez, *Manifest Destinies*; Montejano, *Anglos and Mexicans*.

8. Kaye, "Second Slavery," 627; Cohen, "South and the Caribbean," 155–156; Adams, Bibler, and Accilien, *Just below South*, 2–6; Dessens, *Myths of the Plantation Society*; Haynes, *Unfinished Revolution*, 1–2.

9. Isenberg, *White Trash*, 143–149.

10. Morrison, *Slavery and the American West*; Greenberg, *Manifest Manhood*, 4–5; Downs, "Mexicanization of American Politics," 387–388; Freehling, *Road to Disunion*, 353–440; Silbey, *Storm over Texas*; Steven Hahn, *Nation without Borders*.

11. Holt, *Political Crisis of the 1850s*; Potter, *Impending Crisis*; Lacy K. Ford, *Origins of Southern Radicalism*; Link, *Roots of Secession*; McCurry, *Masters of Small Worlds*; Sinha, *Counterrevolution of Slavery*; Dew, *Apostles of Disunion*; Varon, *Disunion!*

12. Hämäläinen and Truett, "On Borderlands," 353. Works on the Southwest and U.S.-Mexico borderlands include Reséndez, *Changing National Identities*; Weber, *Mexican Frontier*; Weber, *Spanish Frontier in North America*; Truett and Young, *Continental Crossroads*; Alonzo, *Tejano Legacy*; Baud and van Schendel, "Toward a Comparative History of Borderlands;" and James David Miller, *South by Southwest*.

For studies that view the Gulf South as a borderland see Richmond F. Brown, *Coastal Encounters*; Usner, *Indians, Settlers, and Slaves*; Smith, *Louisiana*; and Narrett, *Adventurism and Empire*.

13. Kolchin, "South and the World"; Fleche, *Revolution of 1861*, 154–156; Smith and Cohn, *Look Away!*; Rugemer, *Problem of Emancipation*, 200–242; Guterl, *American Mediterranean*.

CHAPTER 1. **The Possibilities of Texas**

1. C. M. Haile, "Letter from Pardon Jones on the Texas Question," *Daily Picayune*, June 6, 1844; Benjamin and Marquez, "War between the United States and Mexico."

2. Schroeder, "Annexation or Independence"; Morrison, "Westward the Curse of Empire."

3. Sibley, *Storm over Texas*, xvii–xix; Freehling, *Road to Disunion*, 1:353–355. These books focus primarily on secession and Civil War causation, but the idea that Texas is a turning point is central to both. Hahn, *Nation without Borders*, 37–42.

4. Edward L. Miller, *New Orleans and the Texas Revolution*, 3–5.

5. Billington, *Land of Savagery*; Truettner and Anderson, *West as America*; Slotkin, *Regeneration through Violence*; Pike, *United States and Latin America*; Spurgeon, *Exploding the Western*; LeMenager, *Manifest and Other Destinies*; Gannon, *Florida*, 32; Terry G. Jordan, "Imprint of the Upper and Lower South."

6. Weber, *Mexican Frontier*; Reséndez, *Changing National Identities*, 339, 340; Bazant, *Concise History of Mexico*, 50–55; Stevens, *Origins of Instability*, 5–7: Lewis, *American Union and the Problem*, 35–40.

7. Dupre, *Alabama's Frontiers*, 225, 250–274; Jack E. Davis, *Gulf Sea*, 98–105; Johnson, *Soul by Soul*, 23–52.
8. Leclerc, *Texas and Its Revolution*, 6.
9. Cortés, Jarratt, and Saunders, *Mexican Experience in Texas*; Alanso, *Thread of Blood*; Alonzo, *Tejano Legacy*, 130, 143; Rodríguez O., *Independence of Mexico*.
10. Torget, *Seeds of Empire*, 148–188, 204–206, 191.
11. Hunt and Forsyth, *Annexation of Texas*.
12. General Memucan Hunt to John Forsyth, August 4, 1837, in Hunt and Forsyth, *Annexation of Texas*.
13. Langley, *Struggle for the American Mediterranean*, 39, 60–61.
14. Memucan Hunt, "Annexation of Texas to the United States," *Telegraph and Texas Register*, December 6, 1837.
15. Houstoun, *Texas and the Gulf*, 243–244.
16. *Telegraph and Texas Register*, October 13, 1838; Torget, *Seeds of Empire*, 4–5, 7–8.
17. Shelton, "On Empire's Shore," 717–20; Beasley, *Alleys and Back Buildings*, 194.
18. "Lamar on Annexation," *Texas National Register*, March 1, 1845.
19. Mirabeau B. Lamar to Chief Bowles, May 26, 1839, in Winfrey and Day, *Indian Papers of Texas*, 62–65.
20. Winfrey and Day, *Indian Papers of Texas*, x.
21. *Texas Sentinel*, May 1, 1840; *City Gazette*, May 20, 1840.
22. *Texas Sentinel*, November 14, 1840.
23. Hämäläinen, *Comanche Empire*, 223–225; DeLay, *War of a Thousand Deserts*, 76–77.
24. Lee, *Three Years among the Comanches*, 13–18.
25. *Texas Sentinel*, May 27, 1841.
26. *Texas Sentinel*, May 27, 1841.
27. *Houston Telegraph and Texas Register*, August 25, 1841; *Houston Telegraph and Texas Register*, December 22, 1841; Denton, "Count Alphonso De Saligny."
28. Haynes, *Unfinished Revolution*, 230–237; *Houston Telegraph and Texas Register*, September 12, 1842.
29. Edward L. Miller, *New Orleans*.
30. *Houston Telegraph and Texas Register*, February 9, 1842.
31. *Houston Telegraph and Texas Register*, January 13, 1841.
32. Reséndez, *Changing National Identities*.
33. George Wilkins Kendall, "The Texan Santa Fe Expedition," *Clarksville Northern Standard*, taken from the *Daily Picayune*, August 27, 1842; Kendall, Quaife, and Quaife, *Narrative*; Houstoun, *Texas and the Gulf*, 75.
34. George B. Wallis, "Arabella," *Southern Literary Messenger* 6 no. 10 (November 1840): 766.
35. Ibid., 766–769.
36. Fehrenbach, *Lone Star*, 252–254, 262–263.
37. *Daily Picayune*, January 17, 1841; Ramos, *Beyond the Alamo*, 177–190.
38. Jonathan W. Jordan, *Lone Star Navy*.

39. *Northern Standard*, August 27, 1842; Reagan, *Memoirs*, 33–35; *Daily Picayune*, January 16, 1842; Sam Houston, "Proclamation for the Blockade of Mexican Ports," March 31, 1842, in Houston, *Writings of Sam Houston*, 2:257; *Daily Picayune*, January 27, 1842.

40. *New Orleans Bulletin*, November 11, 1843; Pletcher, *Diplomacy of Annexation*.

41. *Daily Picayune*, April 11, 1844.

42. *Houston Telegraph*, February 10, 1844; *Daily Picayune*, February 14, 1844; Rice Ballard to Albert Sidney Johnston, April 17, 1844, Albert Sidney and William Preston Johnston papers; Joshua D. Rothman, *Ledger and the Chain*.

43. Johnston, *Life*, 92–95.

44. Johnston, *Life*, 67–68; H. Clay Davis to Albert Sidney Johnston, March 27, 1844, Albert Sidney and William Preston Johnston Papers; J. S. Mayfield to Johnston, March 8, 1845, Johnston Papers; James Love to Johnston, March 30, 1845, Johnston Papers.

45. Walker, *Letter of Mr. Walker*, 8.

46. Ibid., 15.

47. Roemer, *Roemer's Texas*, 26–27, 35–36.

48. Ibid., 29, 37, 77, 61.

49. Gambrell, *Anson Jones*.

50. *Daily Picayune*, April 11, 1844; ibid., January 10, 1845.

51. Roemer, *Roemer's Texas*, 36.

52. Pablo, "The Texan Soldier," *Southern Literary Messenger* 11, no. 11 (November 1845): 684.

53. Manuel Rincon, *El Ciudadano Manuel Rincon*, 1836. Translation my own.

54. These interactions form a large part of Chicana/o and borderlands historiography. For a selection see Alonzo, *Tejano Legacy*; Montejano, *Anglos and Mexicans*; De Leon, *They Called Them Greasers*; Guiterrez, *Walls and Mirrors*; Ramos, *Beyond the Alamo*; Résendez, *Changing National Identities*.

CHAPTER 2. **The Possibilities of Pensacola**

1. Sanders and Mason, *Memoirs on the Military Resources*, 3.

2. Cusick, *Other War of 1812*; Owsley, *Struggle for the Gulf Borderlands*.

3. Belko, "Epilogue," 9.

4. Fitch Waterman Taylor, *Broad Pennant*, 83–84; Nathan Miller, *U.S. Navy*, 83–87.

5. Baptist, *Creating an Old South*, 156–158; Monaco, *Second Seminole Indian War*.

6. Karp, *This Vast Southern Empire*, 32–50.

7. Diaz, "To Conquer the Coast;" Hulse, "Military Slave System."

8. Doherty, "Ante-Bellum Pensacola," 339.

9. Rachel Jackson to Eliza Kingsley, 1821, quoted in Clune and Stringfield, *Historic Pensacola*, 137; Dysart, "Another Road to Disappearance," 39; Gould, "In Full Enjoyment," 40–41; Amos, *Cotton City*, 6–7, 11–12.

10. Hildreth, "Railroads Out of Pensacola."
11. Clune and Stringfield, *Historic Pensacola*, 50–51.
12. Dibble, *Ante-Bellum Pensacola*, 9–10; Cannon, *Florida*, 27–28.
13. Dibble, *Ante-Bellum Pensacola*, 8, 37–40; Baptist, *Creating an Old South*, 17–19, 34; Larson, *Internal Improvement*, 11–14.
14. Nathan Miller, *U.S. Navy*, 85; Pearce, "United States Navy Comes"; *Pensacola Gazette*, August 18, 1843.
15. Ellisor, *Second Creek War*, 371–415; Rucker, "Forgotten Struggle."
16. Edward Clifford Anderson Diary, January 1, 1844.
17. Strang, *Frontiers of Science*, 287–324.
18. Edward Clifford Anderson Diary, Edward Clifford Anderson Papers, University Archives and West Florida History Center, John C. Pace Library, University of West Florida, Pensacola, Fla.; Cameron B. Strang, *Frontiers of Science: Imperialism and Natural Knowledge in the Gulf South Borderlands, 1500–1850* (Chapel Hill: University of North Carolina Press, 2018), 287–321.
19. *Pensacola Gazette*, July 5, 1840.
20. Quoted in *Pensacola Gazette*, February 28, 1846; Konvitz, *Cities and the Sea*, 4, 73–79.
21. Sanders and Mason, *Memoirs of Military Resources*, 4–6; Karp, "Slavery and American Sea Power."
22. Dibble, *Ante-Bellum Pensacola*, 3–5; *Pensacola Gazette*, April 25, 1843.
23. Dibble, *Ante-Bellum Pensacola*, 4–6; Haynes, *Unfinished Revolution*, 224; United States Congress and Benton, *Abridgement of the Debates*, 38.
24. *Pensacola Gazette*, August 12, 1843.
25. Frances Webster to Lucien Webster, November 3, 1845, quoted in Webster and Webster, *Websters*, 65–66.
26. *Pensacola Gazette*, August 12, 1843; Fitch Waterman Taylor, *Broad Pennant*, 204; *Pensacola Gazette*, July 4, 1846.
27. Rugemer, *Problem of Emancipation*; "News from Vera Cruz," *Daily Picayune*, January 23, 1845.
28. *Pensacola Gazette*, August 18, 1843.
29. Fitch Waterman Taylor, *Broad Pennant*, 197–198.
30. Ibid., 194–195.
31. Rialto House advertisement, *Pensacola Gazette*, November 6, 1847.
32. *Daily Picayune*, January 21, 1846; Arthur W. Thompson, "Massachusetts Mechanic in Florida," 130–132.
33. Secretary of the Navy, *Register*, 76; *Daily Picayune*, January 21, 1846.
34. *Daily Picayune*, February 11, 1846.
35. Hamersly, *Records of Living Officers*, 80; Force, *Army and Navy Chronicle*, 242; *Daily Picayune*, May 17, 1846; *Pensacola Gazette*, January 9, 1847.
36. *Charleston Mercury*, December 30, 1846; *Pensacola Gazette*, January 9, 1847; *Daily Picayune*, June 16, 1847.
37. *Daily Picayune*, July 31, 1847.

38. *Pensacola Gazette*, September 7, 1847.

39. Alfred N. Proctor to Brother, April 11, 1847, Alfred N. Proctor Letters, Library of Florida History, George Smathers Libraries, University of Florida, Gainesville, Fla.

40. Dibble, *Ante-Bellum Pensacola*, 9–11.

41. John Innerarity, letter, Innerarity-Hulse Family Papers.

42. *Pensacola Gazette*, August 6, 1853.

CHAPTER 3. **Making Meaning of the U.S.-Mexican War**

1. *Pensacola Gazette*, March 21, 1846; *Daily Picayune*, March 27, 1846; Santa Anna, *Eagle*, 4–5, 88–89.

2. Guardino, *Dead March*, 5–6.

3. Crisp, *Sleuthing the Alamo*, 35, 116–118.

4. Fitz, *Our Sister Republics*; Appleby, *Liberalism and Republicanism*; Wilentz, *Chants Democratic*, 14.

5. Greenberg, *Wicked War*, 16–17; Wilentz, *Rise of American Democracy*, 562–563; Hietala, *Manifest Design*, 215.

6. Johannsen, *To the Halls of the Montezumas*, 39–40; McCaffrey, *Army of Manifest Destiny*, 13–16.

7. J. D. B. De Bow, "Oregon and California," *De Bow's Review* 1, no. 1 (January 1846): 65; Howe, *Transformation of America*, 667–669, 699.

8. Henderson, *Glorious Defeat*, 40, 151; Woodworth, *Manifest Destinies*, 78–79.

9. Guardino, *Dead March*, 35.

10. James K. Polk, "Message from the President of the United States to the Two Houses of Congress at the Commencement of the First Session of the Twenty-Ninth Congress," University of North Texas Libraries, 4, available at https://texashistory.unt.edu/ark:/67531/metapth2365/; Merry, *Country of Vast Designs*, 186–187, 256–257.

11. Polk, "Message from the President," 14–15.

12. Polk, "Message from the President," 7–24; Freehling, *Road to Disunion*, 1:353–371; Tutorow, *Texas Annexation*. While this emphasizes the Northwest rather than the old Southwest as being interested in the annexation of Texas, the connection between the two cannot be underestimated in terms of the American borderlands' interests in Texas. They present different reasons for doing so and the Southern slaveholders of the old Southwest frontier states promoted both annexation and war with more fervor than many within the United States.

13. Polk, "Message from the President," 4–6.

14. Henderson, *Glorious Defeat*, 151–155; Merry, *Country of Vast Designs*, 188–189.

15. *Daily Picayune*, February 13, 1846; *Pensacola Gazette*, July 7, 1846; *American Flag*, November 28, 1846.

16. Payne, "Camp Life in the Army," 326–328; O'Rear, *Storm over the Bay*, 12.

17. *Daily Picayune*, January 18, 1846.

18. Johannsen, *To the Halls of the Montezumas*, 8.
19. Pinheiro, *Manifest Ambition*, 43–45.
20. Johannsen, *To the Halls of the Montezumas*, 176–183.
21. Baptist, *Half Has Never Been Told*; Kendi, *Stamped from the Beginning*; Winthrop Jordan, *White Over Black*; Gómez, *Manifest Destinies*, 17–22, 146–155.
22. Franchot, *Roads to Rome*, 38–39; Restall, *When Montezuma Met Cortés*.
23. Gustavus Schmidt, "Mexico, Its Social and Political Condition," *De Bow's Review* 1, no. 2 (February 1846): 116.
24. *Civilian and Gazette*, December 5, 1846; *Pensacola Gazette*, July 7, 1846; Johannsen, *To the Halls of the Montezumas*, 16–20.
25. William E. Bard, "Fleeson, Isaac Neville," *Handbook of Texas Online*, https://www.tshaonline.org/handbook/entries/fleeson-isaac-neville.
26. Theodore Eckerson, "The 'Lone Star,'" *Republic of the Rio Grande, and Friend to the People*, June 30, 1846.
27. *Republic of the Rio Grande, and Friend of the People*, June 6, 1846.
28. Lander, *Trip to the Wars*, 7–9.
29. *Austin Texas Democrat*, October 21, 1846; *Civilian and Gazette*, December 7, 1846; Crisp, *Sleuthing the Alamo*.
30. *Austin Texas Democrat*, October 21, 1846; *Civilian and Gazette*, December 7, 1846.
31. Guardino, *Dead March*, 24–28, 216–217.
32. Semmes, *Service Afloat and Ashore*, 25; Houstoun, *Texas and the Gulf*, 144; Santa Anna, *Eagle*, 89–90.
33. Santa Anna, *Eagle*; Lange, *Antonio López de Santa Anna*; Santa Anna, "Mis memorias, Escritas de mi puño y letra sin ayuda de nadie, en mi ultimo destierro," memoir, box G546, Antonio López de Santa Anna Collection.
34. Stevens, *Origins of Instability*, 107–109.
35. Leclerc, *Texas and Its Revolution*, 107; Mariano Paredes, "Address of General Don Mariano Paredes, to the Mexican Nation. Recovery of the Territory of Texas," *Telegraph from Texas Register*, December 25, 1844; Santa Anna, *Eagle*, 89.
36. Fitch Waterman Taylor, *Broad Pennant*, 255.
37. "Late from Mexico," *American Flag*, September 26, 1846.
38. "More of the Mexican News," *Daily Picayune*, September 16, 1846
39. Guardino, *Dead March*, 186–192.
40. Bauer, *Surfboats and Horse Marines*.
41. "Departure of Volunteers," *Daily Picayune*, May 13, 1846.
42. G. R. W, "Letter to the Editors of the Delta," *New Orleans Daily Delta*, September 6, 1846; Foos, *Short, Offhand, Killing Affair*, 62–63, 68–69.
43. "Speech of Mr. Douglas," *Northern Standard*, June 3, 1848.
44. "American Commerce in the Gulf of Mexico," *Washington National Intelligencer*, August 9, 1845.
45. Semmes, *Service Afloat and Ashore*, 74; Spencer, *Raphael Semmes*, 10–13.
46. Semmes, *Service Afloat and Ashore*, 74–76.

47. Ibid., 93.
48. *Barbados Globe*, June 4, 1846, published in the *Daily Picayune*, July 4, 1846.
49. Semmes, *Service Afloat and Ashore*, 77–78.
50. Albert Sidney Johnston to George Hancock, July 10, 1846, Albert Sidney and William Preston Johnston papers.
51. Charles G. Bryant to Albert Sidney Johnston, July 10, 1846, Johnston Papers.
52. Johnston to Hancock, July 30, 1846, Albert Sidney and William Preston Johnston papers.
53. Weber, *Mexican Frontier*, 86; Guardino, *Dead March*, 71.
54. Johnston, *Life of General Sydney Johnston*, 148–149.
55. May, *John A. Quitman*, 1–200; Rousey, "Friends and Foes of Slavery"
56. Eisenhower, *So Far from God*, 110.
57. John A. Quitman to Eliza Quitman, August 14, 1846, Quitman Family Papers no. 616; John A. Quitman to Children, August 18, 1846, ibid.
58. Eliza Quitman to John A. Quitman, October 29, 1846, Quitman Family Papers.
59. May, *John A. Quitman*; Francis Collins, "Memoir Manuscript," n.d., Francis Collins Papers, box 2C482.
60. Johnston to George Hancock, November 1, 1846, Albert Sidney and William Preston Johnston papers.
61. William Preston, November 11, 1847, Diary of Lieutenant Colonel William Preston, Mexico, 1847–1848, Albert Sidney and William Preston Johnston papers.
62. Preston, Diary of Lieutenant Colonel William Preston, November 27, 1847.
63. Preston, Diary of Lieutenant Colonel William Preston, November 29, 1847.
64. May, *John Quitman*, 187–200.
65. Reilly, *War with Mexico!* 214–217.

CHAPTER 4. **Annexing the Gem of the Antilles**

1. Thrasher, *Addresses Delivered*.
2. Narrett, *Adventurism and Empire*; McMichael, *Atlantic Loyalties*. In the past few decades, scholarship on the filibustering expeditions has undergone a significant transformation. The filibusters were often thought of as curious side stories to the larger narrative of American antebellum history. Robert E. May has been instrumental in rethinking their importance, motivations, and consequences. His work, and the work of other scholars, has revealed the crucial part that these expeditions played in the history of territorial expansion, which provides a foundation for my inquiries here. May, *Southern Dream*, 4–6; May, *Manifest Destiny's Underworld*; Franklin, *Militant South*, 105–15; Charles H. Brown, *Agents of Manifest Destiny*; Chaffin, *Fatal Glory*; Greenberg, *Manifest Manhood*, 31–32, 148–151; Guterl, *American Mediterranean*, 85–86, 90–113; Villafana, *Expansionism*; Langley, "Whigs and the Filibustering Expeditions."

3. Norman, *Norman's New Orleans and Environs*, 71; Rightor, *Standard History of New Orleans, Louisiana*, 127. In 1836 the city council and mayor's office separated New Orleans's various neighborhoods into three main municipalities. The city was split up into the first, second, and third municipality. The first being the French Quarter, the second the Faubourg St. Mary, and the third Faubourg St. Marigny.

4. Alexander Jones, *Cuba in 1851*, 11–12.

5. J. D. B. De Bow, "New Orleans and Charleston," *De Bow's Review* 1, no. 1 (January 1846): 49; Jones, *Cuba in 1851*, 154.

6. Russell, "Intermarriage and Intermingling"; Karp, *Vast Southern Empire*, 190–194.

7. Lazo, *Writing to Cuba*; Walter Johnson, *River of Dark Dreams*, 330–366; Gruesz, "Gulf of Mexico System," 468–495.

8. Norman, *New Orleans and Environs*, 67–68.

9. Klein, *Creole*, xiii–xv; Thompson and King, *Creole Families of New Orleans*; Dormon, *Creoles of Color*; Hall, *Africans in Colonial Louisiana*; Landers, *Atlantic Creoles*; Hanger, *Bounded Lives, Bounded Places*; McHatton-Ripley, *Social Life in New Orleans*, 173–174; Guterl, *American Mediterranean*, 28–29, 90–91.

10. Norman, *New Orleans and Environs*, 65–78.

11. "Old Creole Mansion," *San Antonio Ledger*, October 16, 1851.

12. "M. Pierre Soule," *Illustrated Magazine of Art* 3, no. 17 (1854): 317–318.

13. F. Galliardet, "Pierre Soule who died in New Orleans, was the most remarkable Frenchman of the New World. He was the only one of our compatriots who came to be so popular in the United States that he became a Senator at Washington, having declaimed with the most eminent orators, and having been given the honor of representing his adopted country as Special Envoy and Plenipotentiary minister in a strange court," *Louisiana Liberte*, no. 19, p. 25, Pierre Soulé Papers, April 22, 1870.

14. Ibid., 26.

15. *Trenton State Gazette*, November 18, 1850.

16. Alfred Mercier, trans., Marietta Millet, *Biographie*, 44–50, Pierre Soulé Papers.

17. Lazo, *Writing to Cuba*, 150–157. Most work covering the filibuster movement or the Cuban annexation movement does not often focus on the extent to which Creole elites themselves were involved in orchestrating annexation. Lazo points the way toward much needed work on this subject.

18. Phillip Thomas Tucker, *Cubans in the Confederacy*, 20–21; Chaffin, *Fatal Glory*, 72–73.

19. Garcia, *Abduction of Juan Francisco Rey*, 8–12.

20. *Texas State Gazette*, October 20, 1849; "The South; Cuban Affairs—Lieut. Marcy—Mr. Bradford—News from Havana—The Cotton Crops.& c," *New York Times*, August 30, 1852.

21. *New Orleans Daily True Delta*, December 16, 1849.

22. *New Orleans Daily True Delta*, December 22, 1849.
23. Lazo, *Writing to Cuba*; Johnson, *River of Dark Dreams*, 330–366.
24. Chaffin, *Fatal Glory*, 2; Wilson, *Authentic Narrative*, 1.
25. Muller, *Cuban Émigrés and Independence*, 22–27; Chaffin, *Fatal Glory*, 78–79.
26. Baptist, *Half Has Never Been Told*, 56–66. Some of the participants in the Haitian Revolution were later taken as slaves to the German Coast south of New Orleans, where they rose up and marched toward New Orleans, threatening to take the city before the rebellion was finally broken by military forces.
27. Boggess, *Veteran of Four Wars*.
28. Greenberg, *Manifest Manhood*, 12–13; May, *Manifest Destiny's Underworld*, 108–109; Boggess, *Veteran of Four Wars*, 20.
29. *New Orleans Daily True Delta*, April 13, 1850; *Daily Picayune*, May 1, 1850.
30. Chaffin, *Fatal Glory*, 110–113.
31. John Quitman to Mansfield Lovell, March 15, 1850, Quitman Family Papers.
32. Claiborne, *John A. Quitman*, 2:53–57; *Daily Picayune*, April 24, 1850; Freehling, *Road to Disunion*, 1:23–25; Louisa R. Quitman to John Quitman, March 3, 1850, Quitman Family Papers, no. 616.
33. *New Orleans Daily True Delta*, May 12, May 17, 1850.
34. Narciso López, "Address to the Patriots," *Tennessean*, May 28, 1850.
35. Chaffin, *Fatal Glory*; Johnson, *River of Dark Dreams*; May, *Manifest Destiny's Underworld*, 28–29.
36. Filibustero, *Life of General Narciso Lopez*, 13–14.
37. Boggess, *Veteran of Four Wars*, 24–25.
38. *Diario de la Marina*, May 18, 22, and 30, 1850. Translation my own.
39. *Daily Picayune*, May 29, 1850.
40. Eliza Quitman, July 4, 1850, Quitman Family Papers.
41. Louisa to John Quitman, August 5, 1850, Quitman Family Papers.
42. John to Louisa Quitman, September 21, 1850, Quitman Family Papers.
43. John to Louisa, March 14, 1851, Quitman Family Papers.
44. James D. B. DeBow, "The Late Cuban Expedition," *De Bow's Review* 9, no. 2 (August 1850): 164–177.
45. J. C. Davis, *History of the Late Expedition*, 2–3.
46. John Henderson to John A. Quitman, November 6, 1850, Quitman Family Papers; *Daily Picayune*, April 15, 1851; *Mobile Daily Register*, April 18, 1851.
47. Carrie Gibson, *Empire's Crossroads*, 203–204; Chaffin, *Fatal Glory*, 196–199.
48. *Pensacola Gazette*, August 20, 1851; *Daily Picayune*, August 19, 1851; *Alabama Daily Journal*, August 25, 1851.
49. Boggess, *Veteran of Four Wars*, 30; Johnson, *River of Dark Dreams*, 330–331.
50. Author unknown, letter, August 22, 1851, Riot in New Orleans Letter, Howard-Tilton Memorial Library, Tulane University, New Orleans, Louisiana; *Daily Picayune*, August 22, 1851; *Alabama Daily Journal*, August 25, 1851; Kendall, *History of New Orleans*, 171–172; Charles Colcock Jones to Parents, letter, August 1851, box 10, folder 6, Charles Colcock Jones Collection.

51. Filibustero, *Life of General Narciso Lopez*, 29.

52. Boggess, *Veteran of Four Wars*, 31; *San Antonio Ledger*, August 19, 1852; William Perkins to Editor of the *Daily Picayune*, 1855, Southern Filibuster Collection, Mss. 2260.

53. Moore, "Pierre Soulé."

54. Karp, *This Vast Southern Empire*; May, *Southern Dream*, 67–70.

55. Thrasher, *Addresses Delivered*, 3–4,6.

56. Halcombe, *Free Flag of Cuba*.

CHAPTER 5. **Galveston and the Fight for the Texas Borderlands**

1. *Houston Telegraph and Texas Register*, April 19, 1848.

2. Cartwright, *Galveston*; Fornell, *Galveston Era*, 193–194; St. John, *Line in the Sand*, 12–18.

3. St. John, *Line in the Sand*, 12–18.

4. Montejano, *Anglos and Mexicans*, 30–34, 77–89; Torget, *Seeds of Empire*, 255–257.

5. Berlin, *Many Thousands Gone*; Baum, *Shattering of Texas Unionism*; Campbell, *Empire for Slavery*; Hammond, *Slavery, Freedom, and Expansion*; Johannsen, Haynes, and Morris, *Manifest Destiny and Empire*.

6. McComb, *Galveston*, 11.

7. *Indianola Bulletin*, October 19, 1853.

8. Cartwright, *Galveston*, 71–84.

9. *Texas Planter*, November 11, 1845; *Texas Almanac, for 1858*, 182.

10. Campbell, *Empire for Slavery*, 50–66.

11. Beasley, *Alleys and Back Buildings*, 13–14; Rankin, *Texas in 1850*, 157–158.

12. *Daily Picayune*, January 1 and February 20, 1846.

13. Fornell, *Galveston Era*, 23–24; *Indianola Bulletin*, October 19, 1853.

14. *Galveston Weekly Journal*, December 24, 1850, March 27, 1851, March 13, 1851, July 22, 1851; *Civilian and Gazette*, August 23, 1851; Fornell, *Galveston Era*, 151–152.

15. Shelton, "On Empire's Shore," 717–720; Beasley, *Alleys and Back Buildings*, 194.

16. Hayes, *Galveston* (Austin: Jenkins Garrett Press, 1974), 1:334; W. D. Richardson, *Galveston Directory* (Galveston: News and Job Office, 1859), Galveston and Texas History Center, Galveston, Texas, 40.

17. Roemer, *Roemer's Texas*, 28.

18. Fornell, *Galveston Era*, 200–202.

19. Calvert, De Leon, and Cantrell, *History of Texas*, 115–116.

20. Beasley, *Alleys and Back Buildings*, 16–17; "Texas: Climate, Rivers, Lands, Productions, Animals, Minerals, Populations, Government, Emigration, etc.," *De Bow's Review* (June 1851): 641–642.

21. Machann and Mendl, *Czech Voices*; Fornell, *Galveston Era*, 85–86; "Texas," *De Bow's Review* 10, no. 6 (June 1851): 638–640.

22. Rodney Ferry Boat, Natchez Trace Steamboat Collection; Fornell, *Galveston Era*, 27–28; *Galveston News*, March 27, 1848; *Civilian and Gazette*, April 28, 1848; Baughman, "Evolution of Rail-Water Systems."

23. Stephen F. Austin to Wiley Martin, May 30, 1833, quoted in Campbell, *Empire for Slavery*, 20; Cantrell, Stephen F. Austin, 6–9.

24. Kelley, *Los Brazos de Dios*.

25. The historiography of slavery is mammoth, and for purposes of space, I cite here those works that have been most influential in my thinking on the evolution of slavery in the Texas borderlands. Kelley, *Los Brazos de Dios*, 20–21; Berlin, *Many Thousands Gone*; Baumgartner, *South to Freedom*; Camp, *Closer to Freedom*, xvii, xviii; Hammond, *Slavery, Freedom, and Expansion*; Quintard Taylor, *In Search of the Racial Frontier*.

26. Josephine Ryles, WPA Slave Narratives, Texas, District 6; Mintie Maria Miller, WPA Slave Narratives, Texas District 7; Johnson, *Soul by Soul*, 5–7.

27. *Civilian and Gazette*, 1839, January 4, 1843, January 25, 1845; *Houston Democratic Telegraph and Texas Register*, May 25, 1857; Fornell, *Galveston Era*, 112–113; Olmsted, *Journey through Texas*, 230–231.

28. Campbell, *Empire for Slavery*, chap. 1; *Civilian and Gazette*, December 24, 1850; *Galveston Weekly Journal*, May 13, 1851; *Galveston Weekly Journal*, May 27, 1851; *Galveston Weekly Journal*, July 22, 1851; *Civilian and Gazette*, September 23, 1851.

29. Zelia Husk, "Petition to the Republic of Texas Congress," Harris County, December 14, 1840, Texas State Library-Archives Division, Records of the Legislature, Memorials and Petitions, Record Group 100.

30. Fanny McFarland, "Petition to the Republic of Texas Congress," Harris County, October 30, 1840, Memorials and Petitions.

31. Olmsted, *Journey through Texas*, 229–231.

32. Lewis Jenkins and John White, in Baker and Baker, *Till Freedom Cried Out*, 39–42.

33. Jenkins and White, in Baker and Baker, *Till Freedom Cried Out*, 39–42, 120–128.

34. Van Moore, District 7, Tarrant County, Slave Narratives, Works Progress Administration Records, Dolph Briscoe Center for American History, University of Texas at Austin; Ann Ladly, WPA Slave Narratives, Texas, District 7; Jim Johnson, WPA Slave Narratives, Texas, District 6; Lu Lee, WPA Slave Narratives, Texas, District 6; Isabella Jackson, WPA Slave Narratives, Louisiana; Baptist, *Creating an Old South*, 191–219.

35. Kelley, "Mexico in His Head," 709–710, 717; Mulroy, *Freedom on the Border*; Baumgartner, *South to Freedom*, 4, 165–174.

36. Baumgartner, *South to Freedom*, 1.

37. Reynolds, *Texas Terrors*, 24; Quintard Taylor, *In Search of the Racial Frontier*, 54–57; *Galveston Weekly News*, October 7, 1856; David Richardson, *Texas Almanac*, 92.

38. Campbell, *Empire for Slavery*, 62–64; John Solomon Ford, *Rip Ford's Texas*; "Wild Cat and the Seminoles," *Texas State Gazette*, April 1856; Franklin, *Militant South*.

39. Baumgartner, *South to Freedom* is a full-length treatment of the subject of African Americans escaping slavery by running away to Mexico.

40. *Galveston Weekly News*, May 13, 1851.

41. Olmsted, *Journey through Texas*, 454–455.

42. Johannsen, *To the Halls of the Montezumas*; Perez, *On Becoming Cuban*; Perez, *War of 1898*. These works all discuss similar trends in race and class in Anglo outlooks toward Latin American peoples.

43. "Seguin," *El Bejareno*, April 25, 1855.

44. The article in the *San Antonio Ledger* was found in the *Texas State Gazette*, February 24, 1855; *Texas State Gazette*, October 14, 1854, and April 7, 1855; Ramos, *Beyond the Alamo*, 227–229; *El Bejareno*, February 7, 1855; "Know Nothing Convention," *Texas State Gazette*, June 23, 1855; *Texas State Gazette*, September 9, 1854; "Origins of the Know Nothing Party," *San Antonio Ledger*, July 7, 1854; "Indignacion, Junta De Know-Nothings," *El Ranchero*, July 28, 1856.

45. Baum, *Shattering of Texas Unionism*, 9; Sam Houston, "Synopsis of Speech at Washington, Texas, August 2, 1855"; "Speech Delivered at a Know-Nothing Mass Barbecue at Austin, November 23, 1855," in Houston, *Writings of Sam Houston*, 5:6, 201, 209–234; *Texas Ranger and Lone Star*, August 11, 1855.

46. Hämäläinen, *Comanche Empire*, 313–315.

47. *Houston Telegraph and Texas Register*, April 2, 1848.

48. Roland, Robbins, and Johnston, "Diary of Eliza," 462–463"; Roland, *Albert Sidney Johnston*, 117–119, 122, 162.

49. Eliza Johnston to ———, August 8, 1855, Johnston Papers.

50. Buenger, *Secession and the Union*, 106–111; Fehrenbach, *Lone Star*; U.S. House of Representatives and U.S. Senate, "An Act for the Better Protection of the Frontier," January 27, 1858, Correspondence 1857–1865, Frontier Protection Records, box 2B41, Dolph Briscoe Center for American History, University of Texas, Austin, Texas.

51. Rubin, *Shattered Nation*, 2–3.

52. "President's Message," *Civilian and Gazette*, December 15, 1858.

53. "Texas and the Union," *Civilian and Gazette*, January 25, 1859.

54. *Houston Tri-Weekly Telegraph*, October 12, 1859; Jerry Thompson, *Cortina*.

55. *Daily Picayune*, October 19, 1859, November 18, 1859.

56. Montejano, *Anglos and Mexicans*, 32–33; De Leon, *They Called Them Greasers*, 53–55; "Savages on the Borders," *San Antonio Ledger*, March 9, 1860; Jerry D. Thompson, *Vaqueros in Blue and Gray*, 17–23; "Texas and Mexican Frontier," *San Antonio Ledger*, November 19, 1860.

57. "Texas Items," *Houston Weekly Telegraph*, January 4, 1860.

58. "Governor's Message," *Texas State Gazette*, November 12, 1859; Marten, *Texas Divided*, 15.

59. "A Foul Document," *Civilian and Gazette*, September 4, 1860.

60. Oakes, *Scorpion's Sting*; Ettinger, *Mission to Spain of Pierre Soulé*.

61. *Civilian and Gazette*, August 14, 1860.

CHAPTER 6. Launching a New Nation

1. Louisa Lovell Claiborne to John. A Quitman, August 5, 1850, in the Quitman Family Papers no. 616.

2. Dew, *Apostles of Disunion*; May, *Slavery, Race, and Conquest*.

3. Haynes, *Unfinished Revolution*, 278–279; May, *Manifest Destiny's Underworld*, 216; May, *Southern Dream*; Freehling, *Road to Disunion*, 2:2, 148–186; Takaki, *Pro-Slavery Crusade*; Barney, *Road to Secession*; Fehrenbacher, *Slaveholding Republic*; Younge, "Liberia," 430; Walter Johnson, *River of Dark Dreams*, 395–422.

4. Wise, *Lifeline of the Confederacy*; Symonds, *Civil War at Sea*; Spencer C. Tucker, *Blue and Gray Navies*; Buker, *Blockaders, Refugees, and Contrabands*; Surnam, "Union Navy's Blockade Reconsidered."

5. Greenberg, *Manifest Manhood*.

6. Hicks, "Some Letters Concerning the Knights"; Keehan, *Knights of the Golden Circle*.

7. Walter Johnson, *River of Dark Dreams*, 406–418, Robert E. May, *Slavery, Race, and Conquest*, 205–206.

8. Freehling, *Road to Disunion*, 1:456–458; 2:157.

9. Freehling, *Road to Disunion*, 2:155–158; Greenberg, *Manifest Manhood*, 172–173.

10. Albert Sidney Johnston to William Preston Johnston, September 9, 1856, Albert Sidney and William Preston Johnston Papers.

11. Johnston, *Life of General Sidney Johnston*, 196; May, *Manifest Destiny's Underworld*, 47–50; *Civilian and Gazette*, December 21, 1858.

12. "Hon. J. H. Reagan, on Filibustering and the African Slave Trade," *Civilian and Gazette*, April 26, 1859.

13. Houston, *Writings of Sam Houston*, 5:419–420.

14. Houston, *Writings of Sam Houston*, 7:84–85; Haley, *Sam Houston*, 322–327; 354–355.

15. E. W. Cave, *Nacogdoches (Tex.) Campaign Chronicle* 2, no. 4, ed. 1, July 5, 1859, University of North Texas Libraries, the Portal to Texas History, https://texashistory.unt.edu/ark:/67531/metapth713316/; Houston, *Writings of Sam Houston*, 7:304–305.

16. "Speech of Hon. Sam Houston at Nacogdoches, Saturday July 9, 1859," *Civilian and Gazette*, July 26, 1859.

17. Johnson, *River of Dark Dreams*, 437; J. D. B. De Bow, "The African Labor Supply Association," *De Bow's Review* 27, no. 2 (August 1859): 231–235.

18. Campbell, *Empire for Slavery*, 46–48, 52–53; Torget, *Seeds of Empire*, 44–45; Freehling, *Road to Disunion*, 2:168–169; Johnson, *River of Dark Dreams*, reopening slave trade chapter.

19. "False Position," *Daily Picayune*, April 17, 1859.

20. Ibid.

21. "Annual Examination and Commencement in Texas Monument and Military Institute," *Houston Weekly Telegraph*, June 2, 1858.

22. "Speech to the Baconian Literary Society," 1858, Ashbel Smith Papers, box 2G237.
23. *Houston Weekly Telegraph*, July 14, 1858.
24. "Speech of the Hon. James Chestnut, Jr. of South Carolina," *Galveston Crisis!*, September 9, 1860; T. J. Semmes quoted in Freehling, *Road to Disunion*, 2:273–274.
25. "Speech of Hon. Jefferson Davis," *Galveston Crisis!*, August 27, 1860.
26. William Pitt Ballinger, Diary of William Pitt Ballinger April 2, 1860–August 22, 1860, Personal Diary, Galveston, Texas January 1 to December 31, 1860, William Pitt Ballinger Papers 1832–1947 MSS # 50-0001, Rosenberg Library, Galveston, Texas. The diaries are also held at the Dolph Briscoe Center for American History at the University of Texas. See: William Pitt Ballinger Papers.
27. J. E. B. De Bow, "The South's Power of Self-Protection," *De Bow's Revie (November 1860): 545–561.*
28. *Bellville Countryman*, November 21, 1860; *Indianola Courier*, November 24, 1860; James Marten, *Texas Divided*.
29. "What Shall Be Done?" *Houston Weekly Telegraph*, January 11, 1860; William Pitt Ballinger, Diary of William Pitt Ballinger, Personal Diary, Galveston, Texas, November 8–December 21, 1860, William Pitt Ballinger Papers.
30. *Daily Picayune*, January 17, 1861.
31. *Daily Picayune*, February 5, 1861.
32. F. Gaillardet, "Pierre Soule," *Louisiana Liberte*, no. 19, Pierre Soulé Papers, April 22, 1870, 33–35; Braden and Soulé, "Secession Means Disunion," 82; *Daily Picayune* quotes in Roland, "Louisiana and Secession."
33. Volumnia, "From a Texas Lady," *Austin State Gazette*, December 29, 1860.
34. Wrinkler, *Journal of the Secession Convention of Texas 1961*, 61–65.
35. Buenger, *Secession and the Union*; Texas Convention, Declaration of the causes which impel the state of Texas to secede from the Federal Union: also the ordinance of secession, Austin, Tex.: Herald office, Austin, 1861, https://www.loc.gov/item/95139713/; Haley, *Sam Houston*, 390–391; Rozelle, *Exiled*, 146–148.
36. Coleman and Coleman, *Guardians on the Gulf*, 36–37.
37. Quoted in Revels, *Grander in Her Daughters*, 10.
38. Buker, *Blockaders, Refugees, and Contrabands*.
39. Thompson, "Rights, Causes, and Necessity"; Pearce, *Pensacola during the Civil War*; Driscoll, *Civil War on Pensacola Bay*; Dibble, *Ante-Bellum Pensacola*, 115–141.
40. Maria to Fanny, Fanny Leverich Eshleman Craig Collection.
41. James Trudeau to Pierre Soulé, July 8, 1861, Pierre Soule Papers, Mss. 401,1044,2028.
42. Symonds, *Civil War at Sea*, 33–35; Spencer C. Tucker, *Blue and Gray Navies*, 80, 81; Wise, *Lifeline of the Confederacy*, 24–25.
43. Wise, *Lifeline of the Confederacy*.
44. *Mobile Daily Register*, February 5, 1862.

45. *Daily Picayune*, January 17, 1861; *Navarro Express*, May 1, 1861; Wise, *Lifeline of the Confederacy*, 20–21.
46. Houston *Weekly Telegraph*, November 13, 1861.
47. Wise, *Lifeline of the Confederacy*, 74–89; Browning, *Lincoln's Trident*, 6–7.
48. Owsley, *C.S.S. Florida*, 20–21.
49. Stephen Mallory to John Maffitt, August 1, 1862, John Newland Maffitt Papers no. 1761; Cleland, "Between King Cotton," 30–31, 55–59; Shingleton, *High Seas Confederate*, 39–54.
50. Stephen R. Mallory to John Maffitt, July 14, 1862, John Newland Maffitt Papers no. 1761.
51. John Newland Maffitt Papers no. 1761.
52. *Houston Weekly Telegraph*, March 30, 1863.
53. Browning, *Lincoln's Trident*, 163–167; Daddysman, *Matamoros Trade*, 29–39.
54. Doyle, *American Civil Wars*.
55. Karp, *This Vast Southern Empire*, 173–199; Doyle, *Cause of All Nations*, 186–187.

CHAPTER 7. **Empire on the Run**

1. Winters, *Civil War in New Orleans*, 94–95.
2. Thomas Howard DuVal, April 8, 1865, Diary of Thomas DuVal, Thomas Howard DuVal Papers; Freehling, South vs. the South.
3. Wahlstrom, *Southern Exodus to Mexico*; Jarnagin, *Confluence of Transatlantic Networks*. Confederates went to many different places after the war finally came to an end. My work focuses primarily on those in Latin America, but some Confederates also went to Europe and Canada and places even further afield.
4. Sternhell, *Routes of War*, 3–6; Megan Kate Nelson, *Ruin Nation*, 2–3.
5. Fremantle, *Three Months in the Southern States*, vii–2.
6. Martinez, *Slave Impressment in the Upper South*.
7. *Texas Almanac*, December 18, 1862.
8. Fremantle, *Three Months in the Southern States*, 43.
9. Cutrer, *Theater of a Separate War*, 168–210.
10. Levine, *Fall of the House of Dixie*, 194–195; *Texas State Gazette*, December 10, 1862; *Houston Tri-Weekly Telegraph*, November 16, 1863.
11. Shockley, "They Call Us All Renegades," 229–231.
12. Fremantle, *Three Months in the Southern States*, 45–46.
13. Van Moore, District 7, Tarrant County, Slave Narratives, Works Progress Administration Records, Dolph Briscoe Center for American History, University of Texas at Austin.
14. Louis Love, WPA Slave Narratives, Texas, District 7; Ann Ladly, WPA Slave Narratives, Texas, District 7.
15. Sternhell, 99–101; W. Caleb McDaniel, "How Many Slaves Were Refugeed to Confederate Texas," http://wcaleb.org/blog/how-many-refugeed-slaves-in

-texas, accessed July 15, 2023. W. Caleb McDaniel argues that the often-cited number of 150,000 slaves "refugeed" to Texas is perhaps too high, explaining the possible origins of the number. I've chosen to use the range of estimates in part to emphasize that the story of refugeed slaves needs much more investigation.

16. Revels, *Grander in Her Daughters*, 117–121; Gannon, *Florida*, 40–46.
17. Bailey, *Invisible Southerners*, 1–23.
18. Marten, "Wearying Existence"; Cutrer, *Theater of a Separate War*, 312–313.
19. McPherson, *Ordeal of Fire*, 475.
20. Address of General Smith to his troops, n.d., in the Edmund Kirby-Smith Papers, folder 48, box 4, no. 404.
21. Edmund Kirby Smith to J. O. Webster, June 10, 1865, Edmund Kirby-Smith Papers, folder 48, box 4, no. 404.
22. Diary of Flight from Mexico to Cuba, June–July 1865, Edmund Kirby-Smith Papers, folder 48, box 4, no. 404.
23. Purashkin, *A Crisis in Confederate Command*, 215–216.
24. O'Flaherty, *General Jo Shelby*.
25. Caroline Seldon Smith to Francis Webster, July 24, 1865, Edmund Kirby-Smith Papers.
26. Francis to Sister, August 12, 1865, Edmund Kirby-Smith Papers.
27. Doyle, *Cause of All Nations*, 299–313; Arthur, *General Jo Shelby's March*.
28. Wahlstrom, *Southern Exodus to Mexico*, xxvi–xxvii, 117–127.
29. Harter, *Lost Colony of the Confederacy*, 16–17.
30. *Houston Tri-Weekly Telegraph*, May 26, 1865.
31. *Houston Tri-Weekly Telegraph*, June 21, 1865.
32. *Civilian and Gazette*, August 23, 1865.
33. *Daily Cleveland Herald*, June 16, 1865.
34. *Houston Tri-Weekly Telegraph*, July 24, 1865.
35. *Daily Evening Bulletin*, June 9, 1865.
36. *Flake's Daily Bulletin*, August 9, 1865.
37. *Houston Tri-Weekly Telegraph*, August 23, 1865.
38. *Bangor Daily Whig and Courier*, June 19, 1865.
39. Wahlstrom, *Southern Exodus to Mexico*.
40. *Daily Picayune*, March 18, 1866.
41. Wolnisty, *Different Manifest Destiny*, 80.
42. *Clarksville Standard*, September 9, 1865.
43. *Flake's Daily Bulletin*, August 15, 1865.
44. *Edgefield Advertiser*, May 2, 1866.
45. *Flake's Daily Bulletin*, August 16, 1865; Transcript of Letter from W. M. Yandell to Maud C. Fentress, October 29, 1865, letter, October 29, 1865, University of North Texas Libraries, UNT Libraries Special Collections, the Portal to Texas History, texashistory.unt.edu/ark:/67531/metapth182741/m1/1/?q=brazil.
46. Harter, *Lost Colony of the Confederacy*.

47. "On Life in Brazil," Julia Louisa Hentz Keyes Reminiscence #1672-z, Southern Historical Collection, Wilson Library, University of North Carolina at Chapel Hill.

48. Griggs, *Elusive Eden*.

49. Lesser, *Immigration, Ethnicity, and National Identity*, 44–45.

CONCLUSION. What Comes after Southern Imperialism?

1. Chapman, *Bananas*; Grandin, *Empire's Workshop*.

2. Richardson, *West from Appomattox*, 5–7, 31–37; West, *Continental Reckoning*, xx–xxi, 142, 170–73; Love, *Race over Empire*, 1–26; Langley, *Struggle for the American Mediterranean*, 135–165.

3. Foner, *Reconstruction*, 262–264.

4. Ferrer, *Insurgent Cuba*, 179–181; Scott, *Degrees of Freedom*; Adams, Bibler, and Accilien, *Just below South*; Ayers, *All Over the Map*; Richmond F. Brown, *Coastal Encounters*; Dessens, *Myths of the Plantation Society*; Fernandez-Armesto, *Americas*; Kelley, *Los Brazos de Dios*.

5. Oakes, *Ruling Race*; Roark, *Masters without Slaves*; Manning, *What This Cruel War*; Faust, *Mothers of Invention*; Camp, *Closer to Freedom*.

6. McPherson, *Battle Cry of Freedom*, 313–314, 378–383; Guterl, *American Mediterranean*, 73–113; Dawsey and Dawsey, *Confederados*.

7. Perez, *War of 1898*, 3–7, 39–40; Jacobson, *Barbarian Virtues*, 6–7; Foley, *White Scourge*, 3–7.

Bibliography

Primary Sources

MANUSCRIPTS AND ARCHIVES

Benson Latin American Collection, University of Texas Libraries, University of Texas at Austin

Antonio López de Santa Anna Collection

Dolph Briscoe Center for American History, University of Texas at Austin, Austin Texas

William Pitt Ballinger Papers
Francis Collins Papers
Thomas Howard DuVal Papers
Frontier Protection Records
Natchez Trace Collection
Ashbel Smith Papers

Howard-Tilton Memorial Library, Tulane University, New Orleans Louisiana

Fanny Leverich Eshleman Craig Collection
Albert Sidney and William Preston Johnston Papers
Charles Colcock Jones Collection
Riot in New Orleans letter

Galveston and Texas History Center, Rosenberg Library, Galveston, Texas

William Pitt Ballinger Papers

Hill Memorial Library, LSU Libraries, Baton Rouge, Louisiana

Southern Filibuster Collection
Pierre Soulé Papers

Southern Historical Collection, Wilson Library, University of North Carolina at Chapel Hill

Julia Louisa Hentz Keyes Reminiscence, 1874
John Newland Maffitt Papers

Quitman Family Papers
Edmund Kirby-Smith Papers
Waddy Thompson Papers

University Archives and West Florida History Center, John C. Pace Library, University of West Florida

Edward Clifford Anderson, Portion of Diary 1844
Innerarity-Hulse Family Papers

Periodicals

Alabama Daily Journal
American Flag
Austin State Gazette
Austin Texas Democrat
Barbados Globe
El Bejareno
Bellville Countryman
Charleston Mercury
Clarksville Standard
Daily Cleveland Herald
Daily Evening Bulletin
De Bow's Review
El Diario de la Marina
Edgefield Advertiser
Flake's Daily Bulletin
Galveston Civilian and Galveston Gazette
Galveston Crisis!
Galveston Weekly Journal
Galveston Weekly News
Houston Democratic Telegraph and Texas Register
Houston Tri-Weekly Telegraph
Indianola Bulletin
Indianola Courier
Mobile Daily Register
Nacogdoches Chronicle
Navarro Express
New Orleans Daily Delta
New Orleans Daily Picayune
New Orleans Daily True Delta
New York Times
Northern Standard
Pensacola Gazette
El Ranchero

Republic of the Rio Grande and Friend to the People
San Antonio Ledger
Southern Literary Messenger
Tennessean
Texas Almanac
Texas Planter
Texas Ranger and Lone Star
Texas State Gazette
Trenton State Gazette

Printed Primary Sources

Boggess, Francis Calvin Morgan. *A Veteran of Four Wars, the Autobiography of F. C. M. Boggess: A Record of Pioneer Life and Adventure, and Heretofore Unwritten History of the Florida Seminole Indian Wars.* Arcadia, Fl.: Champion Job Rooms, 1850.
Braden, Waldo W., and Pierre Soulé. "Secession Means Disunion." *Louisiana History: The Journal of Louisiana Historical Association* 6 (Winter 1965): 77–82.
Claiborne, J. F. H. *John A. Quitman: Life and Correspondence.* Vol. 2. New York: Harper and Brothers, 1860.
Davis, J. C. *"The History of the Late Expedition to Cuba," by One of the Participants.* New Orleans: Job Office of the Daily Delta, 1850.
Filibustero, A. *Life of General Narciso Lopez: Together with a Detailed History of the Attempted Revolution of Cuba, from Its First Invasion at Cardinas, Down to the Death of Lopez, at Havana.* New York: Dewitt and Davenport, 1851.
Force, William Queruea. *Army and Navy Chronicle, and Scientific Repository.* Vol. 8. N.p.: William Q. Force, 1839.
Fremantle, Arthur James Lyon. *Three Months in the Southern States, April–June 1863.* Edinburgh: William Blackwood and Sons, 1863.
Garcia, Juan Rey. *Abduction of Juan Francisco Rey: Narrative of Events from His Own Lips, from the Time He Left Havana, in Company with Villaverde and Fernandez, Until His Return to the United States, Embracing a Relation of What Occurred on His First Departure from Havana; the Intrigues and Violence by which His Abduction Was Accomplished in New Orleans; His Voyage Back to Havana on the Mary Ellen; and His Imprisonment There, and His Release and Return to the United States, Together with a Compilation of the Testimony in the Preliminary Investigation before Judge Bright and Commissioner Cohen, a Review of the Same.* Translated by Daniel Scully. New Orleans: New Orleans True Delta Office, 1844.
Hamersly, Lewis R. *The Records of Living Officers of the U.S. Navy and Marine Corps.* Philadelphia: J. B. Lippincott, 1870.
Hicks, Jimmie. "Some Letters Concerning the Knights of the Golden Circle, 1860–1861." *Southwestern Historical Quarterly* 65, no. 1 (1961): 80–86.
Houstoun, Matilda Charlotte. *Texas and the Gulf of Mexico, or, Yachting in the New World.* London: John Murray, Albemarle Street, 1844.

Houston, Sam. *The Writings of Sam Houston, 1813–1863*. Edited by Amelia W. Williams and Eugene C. Barker. 8 vols. Austin: University of Texas Press, 1938–1943.

Hunt, Memucan, and John Forsyth. *Annexation of Texas to the United States. Message from the President of the United States, in compliance with a resolution of the House of Representatives of the 13th instant, respecting an annexation of Texas to the United States*, 1837, University of North Texas Libraries, the Portal to Texas History, https://texashistory.unt.edu/ark:/67531/metapth498484/.

Johnston, William Preston. *The Life of General Sidney Johnston*. New York: D. Appleton, 1878.

Jones, Alexander. *Cuba in 1851 Containing Authentic Statistics of the Population, Agriculture and Commerce of the Island for a Series of Years, with Official and Other Documents in Relation to the Revolutionary Movements of 1850 and 1851*. New York: Stringer & Townsend, 1851.

Jones, Anson. *Letters Relating to the History of Annexation*. Philadelphia, n.d.

Kendall, George Wilkins, and Milo Milton Quaife. *Narrative of the Texan Santa Fé Expedition*. Chicago: Lakeside Press, 1929.

Lander, Alexander. *A Trip to the Wars, Comprising the History of the Galveston Riflemen, Formed April 28, 1846, at Galveston, Texas; Together with the History of the Battle of Monterey; Also, Descriptions of Mexico and its People*. Monmouth, N.J.: Printed at the "Atlas Office," 1847.

McHatton-Ripley, Eliza. *Social Life in Old New Orleans, Being Recollections of My Girlhood*. New York: D. Appleton, 1912.

Lee, Nelson. *Three Years among the Comanches: The Narrative of Nelson Lee, the Texas Ranger*. Norman, Okla: University of Oklahoma Press, 1991.

Norman, Benjamin Moore. *Norman's New Orleans and Environs, Containing a Brief Historical Sketch of the Territory and State of Louisiana, and the City of New Orleans, from the Earliest Period to the Present Time: Presenting a Complete Guide to All Subjects of General Interest in the Southern Metropolis; with a Correct and Improved Plan of the City, Pictorial Illustrations of Public Buildings, Etc*. New Orleans: B. M. Norman, 1845.

Olmsted, Frederick Law. *A Journey through Texas: Or, a Saddle-Trip on the Southwestern Frontier*. Austin: University of Texas Press, 1978.

Pickens, Lucy Halcombe. *The Free Flag of Cuba, or, the Martyrdom of Lopez: A Tale of the Liberating Expedition of 1851*. New York: DeWitt & Davenport, 1855.

Rankin, Melinda. *Texas in 1850*. Boston: Damrell and Moore, 1852.

Reagan, John Henninger. *Memoirs, with Special Reference to Secession and the Civil War*. New York: Neale Publishing, 1906.

Richardson, David. *Texas Almanac, Giving Annual Statistics of the State, and the Progress of Improvements in Agriculture, Commerce and Manufactures; the Increase of Population, Wealth and Revenue; of Churches, Schools, Charitable Institutions, & C.; Lives of Distinguished Texians; History of Texas, Continued annually, and Designed to Embrace Many Original Documents and Important Historical Facts,*

Furnished by Living Witnesses, Never Before Published. Galveston: Richardson & Co., at the "News" Office, 1857.

Rightor, Henry. *Standard History of New Orleans, Louisiana, Giving a Description of the Natural Advantages, Natural History, Settlements, Indians, Creoles, Municipal and Military History, Mercantile and Commercial Interests, Banking, Transportation, Struggles against High Water, the Press, Educational, Literature and Art, the Churches, Old Burying Grounds, Bench and Bar, Medical, Public and Charitable Institutions, the Carnival, Amusements, Clubs, Societies, Associations, etc*. Chicago: Lewis Publishing, 1900.

Rincon, Manuel. *El Ciudadano Manuel Rincon, General de Division y Gobernador Constitucional del Departmento de Mexico*. June 4, 1845.

Roemer, Ferdinand. *Roemer's Texas*. Boerne, Tex.: Mockingbird Press, 1935.

Roland, Charles P., Richard C. Robbins, and Eliza Johnston. "The Diary of Eliza (Mrs. Albert Sidney) Johnston: The Second Cavalry Comes to Texas." *Southwestern Historical Quarterly* 60, no. 4 (1957): 463–500.

Sanders, John, and James Louis Mason. *Memoirs on the Military Resources of the Valley of the Ohio, as Applicable to Operations on the Gulf of Mexico; and on a System for the Common Defence of the United States. With a Review of the Same, Concisely Exhibiting the Proper Functions and True Relations of Forts and Ships, Their Mutual Dependence and Harmonious Action, When Properly Combined*. Washington, D.C.: C. Alexander, Printer, 1845.

Santa Anna, Antonio Lopez de. *The Eagle: The Autobiography of Santa Anna*. Edited by Ann Fears Crawford. Austin, Tex.: Pemberton Press, 1967.

Secretary of the Navy. *Register of the Commissioned and Warrant Officers of the Navy of the United States Including Officers of the Marine Corps and Others for the Year, 1846*. Washington, D.C.: Alexander Printers, 1846).

Taylor, Fitch Waterman. *The Broad Pennant, or, A Cruise in the United States flagship of the Gulf Squadron, during the Mexican Difficulties*. New York: Leavitt, Trow, 1848.

Thrasher, J. S. *Addresses Delivered at the Celebration of the Third Anniversary in Honor of the Martyrs for Cuban Freedom*. New Orleans: Sherman, Wharton, 1854.

United States Congress and Thomas Hart Benton. *Abridgement of the Debates of Congress, from 1789 to 1856: From Gales and Seaton Annals of Congress; From Their Register of Debates; And from the Official Reported Debates, by John C. Rives*. New York: D. Appleton, 1861.

Walker, Robert J. *Letter of Mr. Walker, of Mississippi, Relative to the Annexation of Texas: In Reply to the Call of the People of Carroll County, Kentucky, to Communicate His Views on That Subject*. Washington, D.C.: Printed at the Globe Office, 1844.

Webster, Frances Marvin Smith, and Lucien Bonaparte Webster. *The Websters: Letters of an American Army Family in Peace and War, 1836–1853*. Edited by Van R. Baker. Kent, Oh.: Kent State University Press, 2000.

Wilson, Thomas W. *An Authentic Narrative of the Piratical Descents upon Cuba Made by Hordes from the United States by Narciso Lopez, a Native of South America; To Which Are Added Some Interesting Letters and Declarations from the Prisoners, with a List of Their Names.* N.p.: Havana, 1851.

Winfrey, Dorman H., and James M. Day. *The Indian Papers of Texas and the Southwest 1825–1916*, vol. 1. Denton, Tex., 2017. https://texashistory.unt.edu/ark:/67531/metapth846140/: University of North Texas Libraries, The Portal to Texas History, https://texashistory.unt.edu.

Secondary Sources

Adams, Jessica, Michael P. Bibler, and Cécile Accilien. *Just below South: Intercultural Performance in the Caribbean and the U.S. South.* New World Studies. Charlottesville: University of Virginia Press, 2007.

Alanso, Ana María. *Thread of Blood: Colonialism, Revolution, and Gender on Mexico's Northern Frontier.* Tucson: University of Arizona Press, 1995.

Alonzo, Armando C. *Tejano Legacy: Rancheros and Settlers in South Texas, 1734–1900.* Albuquerque: University of New Mexico Press, 1998.

Amos Doss, Harriet E. *Cotton City: Urban Development in Antebellum Mobile.* Tuscaloosa: University of Alabama Press, 1985.

Appleby, Joyce Oldham. *Liberalism and Republicanism in the Historical Imagination.* Cambridge, Mass.: Harvard University Press, 1992.

Armitage, David, Thomas Bender, Leslie Butler, Don H. Doyle, Susan-Mary Grant, Charles S. Maier, Jörg Nagler, Paul Quigley, and Jay Sexton. "Interchange: Nationalism and Internationalism in the Era of the Civil War," *Journal of American History* 98, no. 2 (2011): 455–489.

Arthur, Anthony. *General Jo Shelby's March.* New York: Random House, 2010.

Ayers, Edward L., ed. *All Over the Map: Rethinking American Regions.* Baltimore: Johns Hopkins University, 1996.

Bailey, Anne J. *Invisible Southerners: Ethnicity in the Civil War.* Athens: University of Georgia Press, 2006.

Baker, T. Lindsay, and Julie P. Baker, eds. *Till Freedom Cried out: Memories of Texas Slave Life.* College Station: Texas A&M University Press, 1997.

Baptist, Edward E. *Creating an Old South: Middle Florida's Plantation Frontier before the Civil War.* Chapel Hill: University of North Carolina Press, 2002.

———. *Half Has Never Been Told: Slavery and the Making of American Capitalism.* New York: Basic Books, 2016.

Barney, William. *The Road to Secession: A New Perspective on the Old South.* New York: Praeger, 1972.

Baud, Michiel, and Willem van Schendel. "Toward a Comparative History of Borderlands." *Journal of World History* 8, no. 2 (1997): 211–242.

Baughman, James P. "The Evolution of Rail-Water Systems in the Gulf Southwest, 1836–1890." *Journal of Southern History* 34, no. 3 (August 1968): 357–381.

Bauer, Jack K. *Surfboats and Horse Marines; U.S. Naval Operations in the Mexican War, 1846–48*. Annapolis: U.S. Naval Institute, 1969.

Baum, Dale. *The Shattering of Texas Unionism: Politics in the Lone Star State During the Civil War Era*. Baton Rouge: Louisiana State University Press, 1998.

Baumgartner, Alice L. *South to Freedom: Runaway Slaves to Mexico and the Road to the Civil War*. New York: Basic Books, 2020.

Bazant, Jan. *A Concise History of Mexico from Hidalgo to Cardenas, 1805–1940*. New York: Cambridge University Press, 1977.

Beasley, Ellen. *The Alleys and Back Buildings of Galveston: An Architectural and Social History*. College Station: Texas A&M University, 2007.

Bederman, Gail. *Manliness and Civilization: A Cultural History of Gender and Race in the United States, 1880–1917*. Chicago: University of Chicago Press, 1995.

Belko, William S. "Epilogue to the War of 1812: The Monroe Administration, American Anglophobia, and the First Seminole War." In *America's Hundred Years War*, 54–103.

Belko, William S., ed. *America's Hundred Years War: U.S. Expansion to the Gulf Coast and the Fate of the Seminole, 1763–1858*. Gainesville: University Press of Florida, 2011.

Benjamin, Thomas, and Jesus Velasco Marquez. "The War between the United States and Mexico, 1846–1848." In *Myths, Misdeeds, and Misunderstandings: The Roots of Conflict in U.S.-Mexican Relations*, edited by Jaime E. Rodríguez O. and Kathryn Vincent, 112–114. Wilmington: SR Books, 1997.

Berlin, Ira. *Many Thousands Gone: The First Two Centuries of Slavery in North America*. Cambridge, Mass.: Belknap Press, 2000.

Billington, Ray Allen. *Land of Savagery / Land of Promise: The European Image of the American Frontier in the Nineteenth Century*. New York: W. W. Norton, 1981.

Buker, George E. *Blockaders, Refugees, and Contrabands: Civil War on Florida's Gulf Coast, 1861–1865*. Tuscaloosa: University of Alabama Press, 1993.

Brown, Charles H. *Agents of Manifest Destiny: The Lives and Times of Filibusters*. Chapel Hill: University of North Carolina Press, 1980.

Brown, Richmond F. *Coastal Encounters: The Transformation of the Gulf South in the Eighteenth Century*. Lincoln: University of Nebraska Press, 2007.

Browning, Robert. *Lincoln's Trident: The West Gulf Blockading Squadron during the Civil War*. Tuscaloosa: University of Alabama Press, 2015.

Buenger, Walter L. *Secession and the Union in Texas*. Austin: University of Texas Press, 1984.

Calvert, Robert A., Arnoldo De Leon, and Greg Cantrell. *The History of Texas*. 3rd ed. Wheeling, Ill.: Harlan Davidson, 2002.

Camp, Stephanie M. H. *Closer to Freedom: Enslaved Women and Everyday Resistance in the Plantation South*. Chapel Hill: University of North Carolina Press, 2004.

Campbell, Randolph B. *An Empire for Slavery: The Peculiar Institution in Texas, 1821–1865*. Baton Rouge: Louisiana State University Press, 1989.

Cannon, Michael. *Florida: A Short History*. Gainesville: University Press of Florida, 2003.

Cantrell, Gregg. *Stephen F. Austin, Empresario of Texas*. New Haven: Yale University Press, 1999.

Cartwright, Gary. *Galveston: A History of the Island*. Fort Worth, Tex.: TCU Press, 1991.

Cash, W. J. *The Mind of the South*. New York: Alfred A. Knopf, 1941.

Chaffin, Tom. *Fatal Glory: Narciso López and the First Clandestine U.S. War against Cuba*. Charlottesville: University Press of Virginia, 1996.

Chapman, Peter. *Bananas: How the United Fruit Company Shaped the World*. New York: Grove Press, 2014.

Cleland, Beau Darl. "Between King Cotton and Queen Victoria: Confederate Informal Diplomacy and Privatized Violence in British America during the Civil War." PhD diss., University of Calgary, 2019.

Clune, John J., Jr., and Margo S. Stringfield. *Historic Pensacola*. Gainesville: University Press of Florida, 2008.

Cohen, Deborah. "The South and the Caribbean: A Review Essay." *Southern Quarterly: A Journal of the Arts in the South* 42, no. 3 (Spring 2004): 151–156.

Coleman, James C., and Irene Coleman. *Guardians on the Gulf: Pensacola Fortifications, 1698–1980*. Pensacola, Fla.: Pensacola Historical Society, 1982.

Cortés, Carlos E., Rie Jarratt, and Lyle Saunders. *The Mexican Experience in Texas*. New York: Arno Press, 1976.

Crisp, James E. *Sleuthing the Alamo: Davy Crockett's Last Stand and Other Mysteries of the Texas Revolution*. New York: Oxford University Press, 2005.

Cusick, James G. *The Other War of 1812: The Patriot War and the American Invasion of Spanish East Florida*. Gainesville: University of Florida Press, 2002.

Cutrer, Thomas W. *Theater of a Separate War: The Civil War West of the Mississippi River, 1861–1865*. Chapel Hill: University of North Carolina Press, 2017.

Daddysman, James W. *The Matamoros Trade: Confederate Commerce Diplomacy and Intrigue*. Newark: University of Delaware Press, 1984.

Davis, Jack E. *The Gulf Sea: The Making of an American Sea*. New York: Liveright, 2018.

Dawsey, Cyrus B., and James M. Dawsey. *The Confederados: Old South Immigrants in Brazil*. Tuscaloosa: University of Alabama Press, 1995.

DeLay, Brian. *War of a Thousand Deserts: Indian Raids and the U.S.-Mexican War*. New Haven: Yale University Press, 2008.

De Leon, Arnoldo. *They Called Them Greasers: Anglo Attitudes toward Mexicans in Texas, 1821–1900*. Austin: University of Texas Press, 1983.

Denton, Bernice Barnet. "Count Alphonso De Saligny and the Franco-Texienne Bill." *Southwestern Historical Quarterly* 45 (July 1941–April 1942): 136–146.

Dessens, Nathalie. *Myths of the Plantation Society: Slavery in the American South and the West Indies*. Gainesville: University Press of Florida, 2003.

Dew, Charles B. *Apostles of Disunion: Southern Secession Commissioners and the Causes of the Civil War*. A Nation Divided: New Studies in Civil War History. Charlottesville: University Press of Virginia, 2001.

Diaz, Maria Angela. "To Conquer the Coast: Pensacola, the Gulf of Mexico, and the Construction of American Imperialism, 1820-1848." *Florida Historical Quarterly* 95, no. 1 (2016): 1–25.

Dibble, Ernest F. *Ante-Bellum Pensacola and the Military Presence, The Pensacola Series Commemorating the American Revolution Bicentennial*. Pensacola: University of West Florida, 1974.

Doherty, Herbert J. Jr. "Ante-Bellum Pensacola: 1821–1860." *Florida Historical Quarterly* 37, no. 34 (January–April 1959): 348–353.

Dormon, James H. *Creoles of Color of the Gulf South*. Knoxville: University of Tennessee Press, 1996.

Downs, Gregory P. "The Mexicanization of American Politics: The United States' Transnational Path from Civil War to Stabilization." *American Historical Review* 117, no. 2 (2012): 387–388.

———. *The Second American Revolution: The Civil War-Era Struggle over Cuba and the Rebirth of the American Republic*. Chapel Hill: University of North Carolina Press, 2019.

Doyle, Don Harrison. *American Civil Wars: The United States, Latin America, Europe, and the Crisis of the 1860s*. Chapel Hill: University of North Carolina Press, 2017.

———. *The Cause of All Nations: An International History of the American Civil War*. New York: Basic Books, 2014.

Driscoll, John K. *The Civil War on Pensacola Bay, 1861–1862*. Jefferson, N.C.: McFarland, 2007.

Durham, Marvin L. "American Expansionism into Mexico, 1848–1862." PhD diss., Tufts University, 1962.

Dupre, Daniel. *Alabama's Frontiers and the Rise of the Old South*. Bloomington: Indiana University Press, 2018

Dysart, Jane E. "Another Road to Disappearance: Assimilation of Creek Indians in Pensacola, Florida during the Nineteenth Century." *Florida Historical Quarterly* 61, no. 1 (July 1982): 37–48.

Eisenhower, John D. *So Far from God: The U.S. War with Mexico, 1846–1848*. Norman: University of Oklahoma Press, 2000.

Ellisor, John T. *Second Creek War: Interethnic Conflict and Collusion on a Collapsing Frontier*. Lincoln: University of Nebraska, 2010.

Ettinger, Amos Aschbach. *The Mission to Spain of Pierre Soulé, 1853–1855; a Study in the Cuban diplomacy of the United States*. New Haven: Yale University Press, 1932.

Faust, Drew Gilpin. *The Creation of Confederate Nationalism: Ideology and Identity in the Civil War South*. Baton Rouge: Louisiana State University Press, 1989.

Fehrenbach, T. R. *Lone Star: A History of Texas and the Texans*. New York: American Legacy Press, 1991.

Fehrenbacher, Don E. *The Slaveholding Republic: An Account of the United States Government's Relations to Slavery*. New York: Oxford University Press, 2001.

Fernandez-Armesto, Felipe. *The Americas: A Hemispheric History*. New York: Modern Library, 2005.

Ferrer, Ada. *Insurgent Cuba: Race, Nationalism, Revolution, 1868–1898*. Chapel Hill: University of North Carolina Press, 1999.

Fitz, Caitlin. *Our Sister Republics: The United States in an Age of American Revolution*. New York: W. W. Norton, 2016.

Fleche, Andre M. *The Revolution of 1861: The American Civil War in the Age of National Conflict*. Chapel Hill: University of North Carolina Press, 2012.

Foley, Neil. *The White Scourge: Mexicans, Blacks, and Poor Whites in Texas Cotton Culture*. Berkeley: University of California Press, 1999.

Foos, Paul. *A Short, Offhand, Killing Affair: Soldiers and Social Conflict during the Mexican-American War*. Chapel Hill: University of North Carolina Press, 2002.

Ford, John Solomon. *Rip Ford's Texas*. Austin: University of Texas Press, 1978.

Ford, Lacy K. *Origins of Southern Radicalism: The South Carolina Upcountry, 1800–1860*. New York: Oxford University Press, 1988.

Fornell, Wesley. *The Galveston Era: The Texas Crescent on the Eve of Secession*. Austin: University of Texas Press, 1976.

Franchot, Jenny. *Roads to Rome: The Antebellum Protestant Encounter with Catholicism*. Berkeley: University of California Press, 1994.

Franklin, John Hope. *The Militant South, 1800–1861*. Cambridge, Mass.: Belknap Press, 1956.

Freehling, William W. *Road to Disunion*. Vol. 1, *Secessionists at Bay, 1776–1854*. New York: Oxford University Press, 1991.

———. *Road to Disunion*. Vol. 2, *Secessionists Triumphant, 1854–1861*. New York: Oxford University Press, 2007.

———. *The South vs. The South: How Anti-Confederate Southerners Shaped the Course of the Civil War*. New York: Oxford University Press, 2002.

Fry, Joseph A. *Dixie Looks Abroad: The South and U.S. Foreign Relations, 1789–1973*. Baton Rouge: Louisiana State University Press, 2002.

Fuente, Alejandro de la, and Ariela Julie Gross. *Becoming Free, Becoming Black: Race, Freedom, and Law in Cuba, Virginia, and Louisiana*. Cambridge: Cambridge University Press, 2020.

Gambrell, Herbert Pickens. *Anson Jones: The Last President of Texas*. Garden City, N.Y.: Doubleday, 1948.

Gannon, Michael. *Florida: A Short History*. Columbus Quincentenary Series. Gainesville: University Press of Florida, 2003.

Gleeson, David T., and Simon Lewis, eds. *The Civil War as Global Conflict: Transnational Meanings of the American Civil War*. Columbia: University of South Carolina, 2014.

Gómez, Laura. *Manifest Destinies: The Making of the Mexican American Race*. New York: NYU Press, 2018.

Gould, Lois Virginia Meacham. "In Full Enjoyment of Their Liberty: The Free Women of Color of the Gulf Ports of New Orleans, Mobile, and Pensacola, 1769–1860." PhD diss., Emory University, 1998.

Grandin, Greg. *Empire's Workshop: Latin America, the United States, and the Rise of the New Imperialism*. New York: Holt Paperbacks, 2007.

Greenberg, Amy S. *Manifest Manhood and the Antebellum American Empire*. New York: Cambridge University Press, 2005.

———. *A Wicked War: Polk, Clay, Lincoln, and the 1846 U.S. Invasion of Mexico*. New York: Alfred A. Knopf, 2012.

Griggs, William Clark. *The Elusive Eden: Frank McMullan's Confederate Colony in Brazil*. Austin: University of Texas Press, 1987.

Guardino, Peter. *The Dead March: A History of the Mexican-American War*. Cambridge, Mass.: Harvard University Press, 2017.

Guiterrez, David. *Walls and Mirrors: Mexican Americans, Mexican Immigrants, and the Politics of Ethnicity*. Berkeley: University of California Press, 1995.

Gruesz, Kirsten Silva. "The Gulf of Mexico System and the Latinness of New Orleans." *American Literary History* 18, no. 3 (Fall 2006): 468–495.

Guterl, Matthew Pratt. *American Mediterranean: Southern Slaveholders in the Age of Emancipation*. Cambridge, Mass.: Harvard University Press, 2008.

———. Hahn, Steven. *A Nation without Borders: The United States and Its World in an Age of Civil Wars, 1830–1910*. New York: Penguin Books, 2016.

Haley, James L. *Sam Houston*. Norman: University of Oklahoma Press, 2002.

Hall, Gwendolyn Midlo. *Africans in Colonial Louisiana: The Development of Afro-Creole Culture in the Eighteenth-Century*. Baton Rouge: Louisiana State University Press, 1992.

Hämäläinen, Pekka. *The Comanche Empire*. New Haven: Yale University Press, 2008.

Hämäläinen, Pekka, and Samuel Truett. "On Borderlands." *Journal of American History* 98, no.2 (2011): 338–361.

Hammond, John Craig. *Slavery, Freedom, and Expansion in the Early American West*. Jeffersonian America. Charlottesville: University of Virginia Press, 2007.

Hanger, Kimberly S. *Bounded Lives, Bounded Places: Free Black Society in Colonial New Orleans, 1769–1803*. Durham, N.C.: Duke University Press, 1997.

Harter, Eugene C. *The Lost Colony of the Confederacy*. Jackson: University Press of Mississippi, 1985.

Hayes, Charles W. *Galveston: History of the Island and the City*. 2 vols. Austin, Tex.: Jenkins Garrett Press, 1974.

Haynes, Sam W. *Unfinished Revolution: The Early American Republic in a British World*. Charlottesville: University of Virginia Press, 2010.

Henderson, Timothy J. *A Glorious Defeat: Mexico and Its War with the United States*. New York: Hill and Wang, 2007.

Hietala, Thomas R. *Manifest Design: American Exceptionalism and Empire*. Rev. ed. Ithaca, N.Y.: Cornell University Press, 1985.

Hildreth, Charles H. "Railroads Out of Pensacola, 1833–1883." *Florida Historical Quarterly* 37, nos. 3/4 (January–April 1959): 397–417.

Holt, Michael F. *The Political Crisis of the 1850s*. New York: John Wiley and Sons, 1978.

Horsman, Reginald. *Race and Manifest Destiny: The Origins of American Racial Anglo-Saxonism*. Cambridge, Mass.: Harvard University Press, 1981.

Howe, Daniel Walker. *The Transformation of America, 1815–1848*. New York: Oxford University Press, 2007.

Hulse, Thomas W. "The Military Slave System and the Construction of Army Fortifications along the Antebellum Gulf Coast Mobile Point and Pensacola, 1818–1854." M.A. thesis, University of South Alabama, 2003.

Jacobson, Matthew Frye. *Barbarian Virtues: The United States Encounters Foreign Peoples at Home and Abroad, 1876–1917*. New York: Hill and Wang, 2000.

Jarnagin, Laura. *A Confluence of Transatlantic Networks: Elites, Capitalism, and Confederate Migration to Brazil*. Tuscaloosa: University of Alabama Press, 2014.

Johannsen, Robert Walter. *To the Halls of the Montezumas: The Mexican War in the American Imagination*. New York: Oxford University Press, 1985.

Johannsen, Robert Walter, Sam W. Haynes, and Christopher Morris. *Manifest Destiny and Empire: American Antebellum Expansionism*. College Station: Texas A&M University Press, 1997.

Johnson, Walter. *Soul by Soul: Life Inside the Antebellum Slave Market*. Cambridge, Mass.: Harvard University Press, 2001.

———. *River of Dark Dreams: Slavery and Empire in the Cotton Kingdom*. Cambridge, Mass: Belknap Press, 2013.

Jordan, Jonathan W. *Lone Star Navy: Texas, the Fight for the Gulf of Mexico, and the Shaping of the American West*. Lincoln, Neb.: Potomac Books, 2005.

Jordan, Terry G. "The Imprint of the Upper and Lower South in Mid-Nineteenth-Century Texas." *Annals of the Association of Geographers* 57, no. 4 (December 1967): 667–690.

Jordan, Winthrop. *White Over Black: American Attitudes toward the Negro, 1550–1812*. 2nd ed. Chapel Hill: Omohundro Institute and University of North Carolina Press, 2012.

Karp, Matthew J. "Slavery and American Sea Power: The Navalist Impulse in the Antebellum South." *Journal of Southern History* 77, no. 2 (2011): 283–324.

———. *This Vast Southern Empire: Slaveholders at the Helm of Foreign Diplomacy*. Cambridge, Mass.: Harvard University Press, 2016.

Kaye, Anthony E. "The Second Slavery: Modernity in the Nineteenth Century South and the Atlantic World." *Journal of Southern History* 75, no. 3 (August 2009): 627–650.

Keehan, David C. *Knights of the Golden Circle: Secret Empire, Southern Secession, Civil War.* Baton Rouge: LSU Press, 2013.

Kelley, Sean. *Los Brazos de Dios: A Plantation Society in the Texas Borderlands, 1821–1865.* Baton Rouge: Louisiana State University Press, 2010.

———. "Mexico in His Head: Slavery and the Texas-Mexico Border, 1810–1860." *Journal of Social History* 37, no. 3 (Spring 2004): 709–723.

Kendall, John. *History of New Orleans.* New York: Lewis Publishing, 1922.

Kendi, Ibram X. *Stamped from the Beginning: The Definitive History of Racist Ideas in America.* New York: Bold Type Books, 2016.

Klein, Sybil, ed. *Creole: The History and Legacy of Louisiana's Free People of Color.* Baton Rouge: Louisiana State University Press, 2000.

Kolchin, Peter. "The South and the World." *Journal of Southern History* 75, no. 3 (2009): 565–580.

Konvitz, Josef W. *Cities and the Sea: Port City Planning in Early Modern Europe.* Baltimore: Johns Hopkins University Press, 1978.

Lamp, Kimberly Ann. "*Empire for Slavery: Economic and Territorial Expansion, 1830–1860.*" PhD diss., Harvard University, 1991.

Lander, Alexander. *A Trip to the Wars, Comprising the History of the Galveston Riflemen, Formed April 28, 1846, at Galveston, Texas; Together with the History of the Battle of Monterey; Also, Descriptions of Mexico and its People.* Monmouth, N.J.: Printed at the "Atlas Office," for the Publisher, 1847.

———. *Atlantic Creoles in the Age of Revolutions.* Cambridge, Mass: Harvard University Press, 2010.

Lange, Brenda. *Antonio López de Santa Anna.* New York: Chelsea House, 2010.

Langley, Lester D. "The Whigs and the Filibustering Expeditions to Cuba, 1849–1851: A Chapter in Frustrating Diplomacy." *Revista de Historia de América* 71 (January–June 1971): 9–22.

———. *Struggle for the American Mediterranean: United States-European Rivalry in the Gulf-Caribbean, 1776–1904.* Athens: University of Georgia Press, 1976.

Larson, John Lauritz. *Internal Improvement: National Public Works and the Promise of Popular Government in the Early United States.* Chapel Hill: University of North Carolina Press, 2001.

Lazo, Rodrigo. *Writing to Cuba: Filibustering and Cuban Exiles in the United States.* Chapel Hill: University of North Carolina Press, 2005.

Leclerc, Frederick. *Texas and Its Revolutions.* Houston, Texas: Anson Jones Press, 1950.

LeMenager, Stephanie. *Manifest and Other Destinies: Territorial Fictions of the Nineteenth-Century United States.* Lincoln: University of Nebraska Press, 2004.

Lesser, Jeffrey. *Immigration, Ethnicity, and National Identity in Brazil, 1808 to the Present.* Cambridge U.K.: Cambridge University Press, 2013.

Levine, Bruce. *The Fall of the House of Dixie: The Civil War and the Social Revolution That Transformed the South*. New York: Random House, 2013.

Lewis, James E. *American Union and the Problem of Neighborhood: The United States and the Collapse of the Spanish Empire, 1783–1829*. Chapel Hill: University of North Carolina Press, 1998.

Link, William A. *Roots of Secession: Slavery and Politics in Antebellum Virginia*. Chapel Hill: University of North Carolina Press, 2003.

Love, Eric Tyrone Lowery. *Race over Empire Racism and U.S. Imperialism, 1865–1900*. Chapel Hill: University of North Carolina Press, 2004.

Machann, Clinton, and James W. Mendl. *Czech Voices: Stories from Texas in the Amerikán Národní Kalendář*. College Station: Texas A&M University Press, 1991.

Manning, Chandra. *What This Cruel War Was Over: Soldiers, Slavery, and the Civil War*. New York: Vintage Books, 2007.

Marten, James. *Texas Divided: Loyalty and Dissent in the Lone Star State, 1856–1874*. Lexington: University Press of Kentucky, 1990.

———. "Wearying Existence." *Louisiana History: The Journal of the Louisiana Historical Society* 28, no. 4 (August 1997): 343–356.

Martinez, Jaime Amanda. *Slave Impressment in the Upper South*. Chapel Hill: University of North Carolina Press, 2015.

May, Robert E. *John A. Quitman: Old South Crusader*. Southern biography series. Baton Rouge: Louisiana State University Press, 1985.

———. *Manifest Destiny's Underworld: Filibustering in Antebellum America*. Chapel Hill: University of North Carolina Press, 2002.

———. *Slavery, Race, and Conquest in the Tropics: Lincoln, Douglas, and the Future of Latin America*. Cambridge, UK: Cambridge University Press, 2013.

———. *The Southern Dream of a Caribbean Empire, 1854–1861*. 2nd ed. Gainesville: University Press of Florida, 2002.

McCaffrey, James M. *Army of Manifest Destiny: The American Soldier in the Mexican War, 1846–1848*. New York: New York University Press, 1992.

McComb, David G. *Galveston: A History*. Austin: University of Texas Press, 1986.

McCurry, Stephanie. *Masters of Small Worlds: Yeoman Households, Gender Relations, and the Political Culture of the Antebellum South Carolina Low Country*. New York: Oxford University Press, 1995.

McMichael, Andrew. *Atlantic Loyalties: Americans in Spanish West Florida, 1785–1810*. Athens: University of Georgia Press, 2008.

McPherson, James M. *Battle Cry of Freedom: The Civil War Era*. New York: Oxford University Press, 1988.

———. *Ordeal of Fire: The Civil War and Reconstruction*. New York: Alfred A. Knopf, 1982.

Merry, Robert W. *A Country of Vast Designs: James K. Polk, the Mexican War and the Conquest of the American Continent*. New York: Simon and Schuster Paperbacks, 2009.

Miller, Edward L. *New Orleans and the Texas Revolution*. College Station: Texas A&M University Press, 2004.
Miller, James David. *South by Southwest: Planter Emigration and Identity in the Slave South*. The American South Series. Charlottesville: University of Virginia Press, 2002.
Miller, Nathan. *The U.S. Navy: A History*. 3rd ed. Annapolis: Naval Institute Press, 1997.
Monaco, C. S. *The Second Seminole Indian War and the Limits of American Aggression*. Baltimore: Johns Hopkins University Press, 2018.
Montejano, David. *Anglos and Mexicans in the Making of Texas: 1836–1986*. Austin: University of Texas Press, 1987.
Moore, J. Preston. "Pierre Soulé: Southern Expansionist and Promoter." *Journal of Southern History* 21, no. 2 (May 1955): 204–205.
Morrison, Michael A. *Slavery and the American West: The Eclipse of Manifest Destiny and the Coming of the Civil War*. Chapel Hill: University of North Carolina Press, 1997.
———. "Westward the Curse of Empire: Texas Annexation and the American Whig Party." *Journal of the Early Republic* 10, no. 2 (1990): 221–249.
Muller, Dalia Antonio. *Cuban Émigrés and Independence in the Nineteenth-Century Gulf World*. Chapel Hill: The University of North Carolina Press, 2017.
Mulroy, Kevin. *Freedom on the Border: The Seminole Maroons in Florida, the Indian Territory, Coahuila, and Texas*. Lubbock: Texas Tech University Press, 1993.
Nagler, Jörg, Don Harrison Doyle, and Marcus Gräser, eds. *The Transnational Significance of the American Civil War*. New York: Palgrave MacMillan, 2016.
Narrett, David E. *Adventurism and Empire: The Struggle for Mastery in the Louisiana-Florida Borderlands, 1762–1803*. Chapel Hill: University of North Carolina Press, 2015.
Nelson, Megan Kate. *Ruin Nation: Destruction and the American Civil War*. Athens: University of Georgia Press, 2012.
Oakes, James. *The Ruling Race: A History of American Slaveholders*. London: W. W. Norton, 1998.
———. *The Scorpion's Sting: Antislavery and the Coming of the Civil War*. New York: W. W. Norton, 2014.
O'Flaherty, Daniel. *General Jo Shelby: Undefeated Rebel*. Chapel Hill: University of North Carolina Press, 2014.
O'Rear, Mary Jo. *Storm over the Bay: The People of Corpus Christi and Their Port*. College Station: Texas A&M Press, 2009.
Owsley, Frank Lawrence, Jr. *The C.S.S. Florida: Her Building and Operations*. Tuscaloosa: University of Alabama Press, 1987.
———. *Struggle for the Gulf Borderlands: The Creek War and the Battle of New Orleans, 1812–1815*. Tuscaloosa: University of Alabama Press, 2000.
Payne, Darwin. "Camp Life in the Army of Occupation: Corpus Christi, July 1845 to March 1846." *Southwestern Historical Quarterly* 73, no. 3 (January 1970): 326–342.

Pearce, George F. *Pensacola during the Civil War: A Thorn in the Side of the Confederacy*. Florida History and Culture Series. Gainesville: University Press of Florida, 2000.

———. "The United States Navy Comes to Pensacola." *Florida Historical Quarterly* 55, no. 1 (July 1976): 37–47.

Perez Jr., Louis A. *On Becoming Cuban: Identity, Nationality, and Culture*. Chapel Hill: University of North Carolina Press, 1999.

———. *The War of 1898: The United States and Cuba in History and Historiography*. Chapel Hill: University of North Carolina Press, 1998.

Pike, Fredrick B. *The United States and Latin America: Myths and Stereotypes of Civilization and Nature*. Austin: University of Texas Press, 1992.

Pinheiro, John C. *Manifest Ambition: James K. Polk and Civil-Military Relations during the Mexican War*. Westport, Conn.: Praeger Security International, 2007.

Pletcher, David M. *The Diplomacy of Annexation; Texas, Oregon, and the Mexican War*. Columbia: University of Missouri Press, 1973.

Potter, David M. *The Impending Crisis, 1848–1861*. New York: Harper & Row, 1976.

Prushankin, Jeffrey S. *A Crisis in Confederate Command: Edmund Kirby Smith, Richard Taylor, and the Army of the Trans-Mississippi*. Baton Rouge: Louisiana University Press, 2005.

Ramos, Raul A. *Beyond the Alamo: Forging Mexican Identity in San Antonio, 1821–1861*. Chapel Hill: University of North Carolina Press, 2008.

Reilly, Tom. *War with Mexico!: America's Reporters Cover the Battlefront*. Lawrence: University Press of Kansas, 2010.

Reséndez, Andrés. *Changing National Identities at the Frontier: Texas and New Mexico, 1800–1850*. New York: Cambridge University Press, 2005.

Restall, Matthew. *When Montezuma Met Cortés*. New York: Harper Collins, 2018.

Revels, Tracy J. *Grander in Her Daughters: Florida's Women during the Civil War*. Columbia: University of South Carolina Press, 2004.

Richardson, Heather Cox. *West from Appomattox: The Reconstruction of America after the Civil War*. New Haven: Yale University Press, 2007.

Roark, James L. *Masters without Slaves: Southern Planters in the Civil War and Reconstruction*. New York: Norton Press, 1977.

Rodríguez O., Jaime E. *The Independence of Mexico and the Creation of the New Nation*. Los Angeles: UCLA Latin American Center Publications, University of California, 1989.

Rodríguez O., Jaime E., and Kathryn Vincent, eds. *Myths, Misdeeds, and Misunderstandings: The Roots of Conflict in U.S.-Mexican Relations*. Wilmington, Del.: SR Books, 1997.

Roland, Charles P. *Albert Sidney Johnston: Soldier of Three Republics*. Lexington: University of Kentucky Press, 2001.

Rothman, Adam. *Slave Country: American Expansion and the Origins of the Deep South*. Cambridge, Mass.: Harvard University Press, 2005.

Rothman, Joshua D. *The Ledger and the Chain : How Domestic Slave Traders Shaped America*. New York: Basic Books, 2021.

Rousey, Dennis C. "Friends and Foes of Slavery: Foreigners and Northerners in the Old South." *Journal of Social History* 35, no. 2 (Winter 2001): 373–396.

Rozelle, Ron. *Exiled : The Last Days of Sam Houston*. College Station: TexasA&M University Press, 2017, 146–148.

Rubin, Anne Sara. *A Shattered Nation: The Rise and Fall of the Confederacy, 1861–1868*. Chapel Hill: University of North Carolina Press, 2005.

Rucker, Brian. "Forgotten Struggle: The Second Creek War in West Florida, 1837–1854." In Belko, *America's Hundred Years' War*, 237–261.

Rugemer, Edward Bartlett. *The Problem of Emancipation: The Caribbean Roots of the American Civil War*. Baton Rouge: Louisiana State University Press, 2009.

Russell, Sarah. "Intermarriage and Intermingling: Constructing the Planter Class in Louisiana's Sugar Parishes, 1803–1850." *Louisiana History: The Journal of the Louisiana Historical Association* 46, no. 4 (2005): 407–434.

Sartorius, David. *Ever Faithful: Race, Loyalty and the Ends of Empire in Spanish Cuba*. Durham, N.C.: Duke University Press, 2014.

Scheina, Robert L. *Santa Anna: A Curse upon Mexico*. Washington, D.C.: Brassey's, 2002.

Schoen, Brian D. *The Fragile Fabric of Union: Cotton, Federal Politics, and the Global Origins of the Civil War*. Baltimore: Johns Hopkins University Press, 2011.

Scott, Rebecca J. *Degrees of Freedom: Louisiana and Cuba after Slavery*. Cambridge, Mass.: Harvard University Press, 2008.

Schroeder, John H. "Annexation or Independence: The Texas Issue in American Politics, 1836–1845." *Southwestern Historical Quarterly* 89, no. 2   (October 1985): 137–164.

Semmes, Raphael. *Service Afloat and Ashore during the Mexican War*. Cincinnati: Wm. H. Moore, 1851.

Shelton, Richard S. "On Empire's Shore: Free and Unfree Labor in Galveston, Texas, 1840–1860." *Journal of Social History* 40, no. 3 (Spring 2007): 717–730.

Shingleton, Royce. *High Seas Confederate: The Life and Times of John Newland Maffitt*. Columbia: University of South Carolina, 1994.

Shockley, Candice N. "They Call Us All Renegades in Tyler." *Women in Civil War Texas: Diversity and Dissidence in the Trans-Mississippi*, edited by Deborah M. Liles and Angela Boswell, 229**n**>258. Denton: University of North Texas Press, 2016.

Silbey, Joel H. *Storm over Texas: The Annexation Controversy and the Road to the Civil War*. New York: Oxford University Press, 2005.

Sinha, Manisha. *The Counterrevolution of Slavery: Politics and Ideology in Antebellum South Carolina*. Chapel Hill: University of North Carolina, 2000.

Sledge, John S. *The Gulf of Mexico: A Maritime History*. Columbia: University of South Carolina Press, 2019.

Slotkin, Richard. *Regeneration through Violence: The Mythology of the American Frontier, 1600–1860*. Norman: University of Oklahoma Press, 2000.
Smith, F. Todd. *Louisiana and the Gulf South Frontier, 1500–1821*. Baton Rouge: Louisiana State University Press, 2014.
Smith, Jon, and Deborah N. Cohn. *Look Away!: The U.S. South in New World Studies*. New Americanists. Durham, N.C.: Duke University Press, 2004.
Spencer, Warren F. *Raphael Semmes: The Philosophical Mariner*. Tuscaloosa: University of Alabama Press, 1997.
Spurgeon, Sara L. *Exploding the Western: Myths of Empire on the Postmodern Frontier*. College Station: Texas A&M University Press, 2005.
St. John, Rachel. *Line in the Sand: A History of the Western U.S.-Mexico Border*. Princeton: Princeton University Press, 2012.
Sternhell, Yael. *Routes of War: The World of Movement in the Confederate South*. Cambridge, Mass.: Harvard University Press, 2012.
Stevens, Donald Fithian. *Origins of Instability in Early Republican Mexico*. Durham, N.C.: Duke University Press, 1991.
Strang, Cameron B. *Frontiers of Science : Imperialism and Natural Knowledge in the Gulf South Borderlands, 1500–1850*. Williamsburg, Va.: Omohundro Institute of Early American History and Culture, 2018.
Surnam, David G. "The Union Navy's Blockade Reconsidered." *Naval War College Review* 51, no. 4 (1998): 85–107.
Symonds, Craig L. *The Civil War at Sea*. Oxford: Oxford University Press, reprint, 2012.
Takaki, Ronald. *A Pro-Slavery Crusade: The Agitation to Reopen the African Slave Trade*. New York: Free Press, 1971.
Taylor, Quintard. *In Search of the Racial Frontier: African Americans in the American West 1528–1900*. New York: W. W. Norton, 1998.
Thalen, David. "The Nation and Beyond: Transnational Perspectives on United States History." *Journal of American History* 86, no. 3 (1999): 965–975.
Thompson, Arthur W. "A Massachusetts Mechanic in Florida and Mexico, 1847." *Florida Historical Quarterly* 33, no. 2 (October 1954): 130–141.
Thompson, Jerry D. *Vaqueros in Blue and Gray*. Austin, Tex.: State House Press, 2000.
———. *Cortina: Defending the Name in Texas*. College Station: Texas A&M University Press, 2007.
Thompson, Lauren K. "'The Rights, Causes, and Necessity for Secession': The Interplay of Race, Class, and Politics in Antebellum Florida." In *A Forgotten Front: Florida during the Civil War Era*, edited by Seth A. Weitz and Jonathan C. Sheppard, 42–59. Tuscaloosa: University of Alabama Press, 2019.
Thompson, Shirley Elizabeth, and Grace Elizabeth King. *Creole Families of New Orleans*. New York: McMillan, 1921.
Torget, Andrew J. *Seeds of Empire: Cotton, Slavery, and the Transformation of the Texas Borderlands, 1800–1850*. Chapel Hill: University of North Carolina Press, 2015.

Truett, Samuel, and Elliott Young, eds. *Continental Crossroads: Re-mapping U.S.-Mexico Borderlands History*. Durham, N.C.: Duke University Press, 2004.

Truettner, William H., and Nancy K. Anderson. *The West as America: Reinterpreting Images of the Frontier, 1820–1920*. Washington, D.C.: Published for the National Museum of American Art by the Smithsonian Institution Press. 1991.

Tucker, Phillip Thomas. *Cubans in the Confederacy: José Agustín Quintero, Ambrosio José Gonzales, and Loreta Janeta Velazquez*. Jefferson, N.C.: McFarland, 2002.

Tucker, Spencer C. *Blue and Gray Navies: The Civil War Afloat*. Annapolis: Naval Institute Press, 2006.

Tutorow, Norman A. *Texas Annexation and the Mexican War: A Political Study of the Old Northwest*. Palo Alto, Calif.: Chadwick House Press, 1978.

Usner, Daniel E., Jr. *Indians, Settlers and Slaves in a Frontier Exchange Economy: The Lower Mississippi Valley before 1783*. Chapel Hill: University of North Carolina, 1992.

Valerio-Jiménez, Omar S. *River of Hope: Forging Identity and Nation in the Rio Grande Borderlands*. Durham, N.C.: Duke University Press, 2013.

Varon, Elizabeth R. *Disunion!: The Coming of the American Civil War, 1789–1859*. Chapel Hill: University of North Carolina, 2008.

Villafana, Frank R. *Expansionism: Its Effects on Cuba's Independence*. New Brunswick, N.J.: Transaction Publishers, 2012.

Wahlstrom, Todd W. *The Southern Exodus to Mexico: Migration across the Borderlands after the American Civil War*. Lincoln: University of Nebraska Press, 2015.

Weber, David J. *The Mexican Frontier, 1821–1846: The American Southwest Under Mexico*. Albuquerque: University of New Mexico Press, 1982.

———. *The Spanish Frontier in North America*. New Haven: Yale University Press, 1992.

West, Elliott. *The Contested Plains: Indians, Goldseekers, and the Rush to Colorado*. Lawrence: University Press of Kansas, 1998.

———. *Continental Reckoning: The American West in the Age of Expansion*. Lincoln: University of Nebraska Press, 2023.

———. "Reconstructing Race." *Western Historical Quarterly* 34, no. 1 (Spring 2003): 6–26.

Wilentz, Sean. *Chants Democratic: New York City and the Rise of the American Working Class, 1788–1850*. New York: Oxford University Press, 2004.

———. *The Rise of American Democracy: Jefferson to Lincoln*. New York: W. W. Norton, 2005.

Winters, John D. *The Civil War in New Orleans*. Baton Rouge: Louisiana State Press, 1963.

Wise, Stephen R. *Lifeline of the Confederacy: Blockade Running during the Civil War*. Columbia: University of South Carolina Press, 1988.

Wolnisty, Claire M. *A Different Manifest Destiny: U.S. Southern Identity and Citizenship in Nineteenth-Century South America*. Lincoln: University of Nebraska Press, 2020.

Woodworth, Steven E. *Manifest Destinies: America's Westward Expansion and the Road to the Civil War.* New York: Vintage Books, 2010.

Wrinkler, Ernest William, ed. *Journal of the Secession Convention of Texas 1861, Edited From the Original in the Department of State.* Austin: Texas Library and Historical Commission, 1912.

Younge, Karen Fisher. "Liberia and the Last Slave Ships." *Civil War History* 54, no. 4 (December 2008): 424–442.

Index

Abolitionism and antislavery, 10, 13, 15, 23, 30, 40, 49, 83, 92, 97, 104, 115, 132, 127, 145, 177; colonization movement and, 32; southern fears of, 33–34; in Texas, 8, 16–17

African Americans and Black people: Confederate emigration and, 168, 172; Confederate forced labor and, 157–159; in Cuba, 89; emancipation, 162, 175; enslaved and free women, 115; escaping slavery, 29, 44, 157; escaping slavery in Mexico, 76, 118–119, 195n39; expansion and, 32; forced migration to Texas of (refugeeing), 8, 156, 160–161; in Galveston, 109–110, 111; in Gulf South, 2, 3, 4, 6, 46, 132, 146; labor in Reconstruction, 172, 177, 180; in New Orleans, 87; in Pensacola, 40, 48, 146; resistance to slavery in Texas, 114, 119, 127; under segregation, 180; in Texas, 1, 11, 17, 32, 107, 113, 114, 119, 121; WPA slave narratives, 160–161

Agüero y Sanchez, Joaquín de, 99

Alabama, 2, 8, 38, 41–43, 48, 171, 175, 179; as place for surplus slaves, 12; mentioned, 93, 116, 141, 143, 160

Alabama State Legislature, 41

Anderson, Edward Clifford, 44–47, 124

Anglo Americans and white southerners, 1, 14, 16, 20, 22, 26, 82; Anglo Texans, 11–13, 22, 26, 27, 58, 105, 107, 118 145; as "civilizing" force, 16, 33, 69, 107; depictions and relations of Creoles, 82, 85–88, 90, 92, 93, 101, 193; protection of slavery and, 16, 117, 119; racist views and conflicts with Mexicans, 1–2, 19, 21–26, 28, 43, 56–57, 67, 119–121; racist views and conflicts with Native Americans, 36, 38, 43, 46, 56, 78; racist views of Native Americans in Texas, 18–19, 21, 28, 29, 32; as settlers, 18, 82, 105, 113, 127; U.S.-Mexico border and, 105; views of Spanish empire, 91, 101

Apache, 20, 76, 118

Armijo, Gov. Manuel, 25

Austin, Stephen F., 21, 119

Ballard, Rice, 30
Ballinger, William Pitt, 140–143
Bancroft, George, 61
Banks, Nathaniel P., 158
Basterrèche, Jean Pierre Hippolyte, 23
Bayley, Charles John, 150
Beauregard, Pierre Gustave Toutaunt, 166
Bell, Peter Hansborough, 106
Benjamin, Judah P., 71
Bickley, George, 131
Blockade runners. *See* Confederacy
Boggess, Francis Calvin, 93, 95, 96, 101
Bolivar, Simon, 92
Brazil, 156. *See also* Confederacy
Brown, John, and raid on Harper's Ferry, 125, 145
Bryan, Guy, 125
Bryant, Charles G., 75
Buchanan, James, 102, 104; president's message and, 125–126
Bustamante, Carlos María de, 68
Butler, William Orland, 75

Calhoun, John C., 47–48, 58, 132
California, 18, 58, 84, 170; Bear Republic, 130; U.S. attempts to purchase, 59–61
Canada, 29, 30, 165, 171, 192n3

Index

Chase, William, 146
Cherokee, 18–19, 21, 43; Chief Bowl, 19
Chesnut, James, 139
Chesnut, Mary Boykin, 163
Cisneros, Gaspar Betancourt, 103
Civil War, 1, 5, 8, 147; blockade of southern ports (*see* U.S. Navy); in Gulf South, 4, 129, 156, 178; southern imperialism, 4, 6, 153, 179, 182; trans-Mississippi theater (department), 160, 163; transnational aspects of, 5, 157; unionists during, 155, 161–162; western theater, 160
—battles: First Bull Run, 148; Fort Jackson, 150; Fort St. Philip, 150; Galveston, 158; Mobile Bay, 152
—refugees, 155–157, 176; class divisions among, 159; Florida refugees in Alabama, 161; southern white women as, 159–160
Clark, Edward, 146
Comanche, 19–20, 26, 36, 43, 56, 66; conflict with settlers, 76, 135; conflict with U.S. Army, 118, 123, 124, 182; Great Raid of 1840, 10, 20; Linnville and, 20
Compromise of 1850, 97, 98
Confederacy: blockade runners and, 130–132, 149–152, 154, 173; colonies of, 168–177; commerce raiders and, 131, 148–152, 154; Confederate fears of being executed for treason, 163–164; cotton embargo and, 149; cotton trade through Mexico, 150, 152, 157, 162; C.S.S. *Florida* and, 150–151; dissolution and Grave of the Confederacy Incident, 165; end of, 156, 157, 163, 167; Ex-confederate officers in Europe, 165; Ex-confederate officers in Latin America, 163–168; of government, 163; imperialist fantasies and, 4, 8, 129; Lost Cause and, 176; navy of, 149, 150, 151; relations with European nations, 143, 144, 147, 148–151, 171; use of Gulf ports, 131
Conner, David, 61–62
Constitutional Union Party, 140
Cordova Rebellion, 19
Cortés, Hernán, 64, 78, 79
Cortina, Juan Nepomuceno, and the First Cortina War, 126, 145
Cotton production, 3, 5, 11, 14, 21, 23–24, 29, 136, 144, 147; cotton sold in Great Britain, 73; expansion of, 58; growth in Brazil, 174–177; loss of, 170
Craig, Maria, 147
Creek, 1, 36, 54; Creek War, 37; Second Creek War (Creek rebellion), 8, 38, 43–45, 48
Creoles: of color, 7, 85; in Cuba, 80, 82, 83, 84–85, 90–97, 99–101, 181; definition of white, 7, 40, 84, 86; French and Spanish, 40, 80, 85, 88–89; in Gulf South, 8, 104; in New Orleans, 80, 84–91; in Pensacola, 40–41
Crittenden, John, 100, 101
Crittenden, William, 100
Crossman, Abdiel, 89
Cuba, 3, 4, 8, 21, 56, 57; Americans living in, 98; Cuban War of Independence, 180; European threats to, 50, 51; exiles in United States, 83, 84, 85, 88, 92, 102; fears of abolition of slavery, 92, 102; Havana, 16, 81, 84, 89–91, 108, 131, 150, 163; as refuge for Ex-Confederates, 8, 156; reopening slave trade (*see* Slavery); Spanish rule, 15, 90, 97; uprisings, 99
Cuban annexation, 57, 80–85, 89–94, 99–103, 106, 133–134, 139; armed expeditions (*see* Filibusters); pro-annexation newspapers, 91; purchasing Cuba, 102–103, 131; Rey Case, 90–91; support in Cuba, 92, 93
Cushing, Edward H., 143

Davis, Edmund J., 162
Davis, Henry Clay, 31
Davis, J. C., 91
Davis, Jefferson, 122, 123; as president, 163
De Bow, James D. B., 59, 98, 136–137, 141
De Bow's Review, 58, 59, 64, 71, 98, 112, 136, 141
Democratic Party, 33, 59, 122, 134; Democratic Convention, 140, 144
Douglas, Stephen, 140
Dryden, William G., 65, 66
DuVal, Thomas, 155, 162

Eckerson, Theodore, 65–66; "Lone Star" poem, 66
Elliot, Charles, 23
England. *See* Great Britain
España, Carlos de, 89–91
Europe, 5, 20, 22, 24, 44, 67, 165, 180; Caribbean

presence of, 50–51, 154; policies and political philosophies toward United States, 60–61
—travelers from, in Gulf South: Fremantle, Arthur, 157–159; Houstoun, Matilda, 16–17, 23; Leclerc, Frederick, 12–13; Roemer, Ferdinand, 32, 33
Expansion: American, 3, 11, 12, 17, 30, 31, 47, 57, 66, 83; displacement of Native Americans; 17–19, 44–46; division between American expansion and southern imperialism, 83, 129; divisions between United States and southern expansion, 98, 99; end of southern imperialism, 157, 162–170, 180–182; failure of southern, 3, 4, 97, 101, 104, 157, 181; into Mexican territory, 12, 59, 60–61; rhetoric of, in Mexican War, 60–66; role of military in, 26, 39, 42, 65–66, 146; role of small port towns in, 39, 115, 149; secession crisis, 131; southern, and imperialism, 1–4, 26, 33, 39, 45–47, 57–58, 81, 83, 116, 118; southern fears and nightmares concerning, 3, 12, 15–17, 29, 30–32, 37, 50–51, 62, 101, 141; wars of, 2, 66
—fantasies of, 2–4, 8, 58, 60–66, 83, 156, 157; regarding Texas, 34, 56–57; regarding West Florida and Pensacola, 36–38, 46

Farías, Valentín Gómez, 70
Farragut, David, 150
Farrow, Betty, 116
Filibusters, 31, 131, 133, 190n3, 191n17; blockade runners compared with, 151; expectations of wealth, 93; expeditions during early Republic, 82–83; expeditions framed by U.S.-Mexican War, 93, 94; failure and, 97, 101–102, 118, 133, 152, 167; first expedition to Cuba, 94–97; Galveston support for, 106; López trial and, 98–99; Nicaragua takeover, 132; participants and, 93–96; rejection of, 131, 132–133; second expedition to Cuba, 84, 94, 99–104; support from Cubans, 93; viewed as pirates, 97, 133
Fisher, Samuel Rhodes, 28
Fleeson, Isaac Neville, 65–66
Florida, 2, 12, 34, 45, 50; American acquisition of, 39; east Florida, 43, 82; Florida Straits, 37, 38, 51; Fort Marion, 45; middle Florida, 41, 161; similarities with Texas, 34, 37–38, 40, 43, 46, 57, 61, 104; in Southern imaginary, 38, 39; St. Augustine, 45; Tampa and Ybor City, 39, 180; as territory, 32, 37–38, 39, 40, 41; West Florida, 7, 12, 36, 38–39, 42, 43, 44
Forsyth, John, 13, 15
Fort Sumter, 149
France, 60, 143, 144, 147–149; comparisons with Pensacola, 48; interest in Latin America, 15, 50–51; interests in Mexico, 60; relations with Texas Republic, 22–23; viewed as threat, 51, 61
Franco-Texian Bill, 22
Free Flag of Cuba (Holcombe), 107
Fremantle, Sir Arthur, 157–159

Galveston, 8, 23, 26, 40, 168, 175, 180; Baconian Society of, 138; Black population of (*see* African Americans and Black people); during Civil War, 149, 152, 158, 163, 164; development of slave codes and ordinances in, 108–111; development of slave markets in, 110–111, 114; development of trade and, 109–110; Galveston Bay and, 28; Houston, Texas, and, 24, 114, 115, 119, 122; Indianola, Texas, and, 24, 108; presence of immigrants in, 109–110; relation to western counties, 111–112
Galveston Brazos Navigation Company, 113
Galveston, Houston, and Henderson Railroad, 111
Galveston Riflemen, 67
German Coast Uprising, 93
Goliad Massacre, 58, 67
Gonzales, Ambrosio, 96
Great Britain, 9, 22, 23, 25; abolitionism of, 9, 10–11, 23, 49, 50, 139; fears concerning, 37, 47–50, 54; interests in Mexico, 32, 50, 60; naval power of, in Gulf South, 14–15, 36, 37, 49, 147, 149; relations with Texas Republic, 22, 23, 24, 29, 30–33, 61
Gulf Coast. *See* Gulf South
Gulf of Mexico and the Caribbean, 1, 2, 9, 14, 16, 20, 22, 51, 52, 79, 179, 182; as American Mediterranean, 41, 48, 49, 82, 138; Bermuda and, 148; as center of expansion, 2, 3, 10, 14, 24, 62, 68, 70; challenges of Civil War

Gulf of Mexico and the Caribbean (*continued*) blockade, 150–151, 152; connection to West, 36, 127; Nassau and, 148–152; U.S. defense of, 36–37, 38, 39, 61, 62, 104; warfare in, 28, 50, 67, 72, 151–152

Gulf South, 1–3; as American Mediterranean, 48–49; desire for military protection, 3, 29, 38, 47, 83, 98, 104, 111, 138; European threats to, 14, 28, 37, 43, 49, 51, 61, 90, 104, 138, 153; fears of being blockaded, 27, 50, 140; impact of Mexican War on, 70–71; internal relations among port communities, 11, 29, 24, 38, 39, 41, 61, 109, 111, 114, 116, 128, 138, 149; pirates and privateers in, 28, 42; as refuge during Civil War, 155, 157–160; rejection of U.S. military, 130, 145, 146–148; relationship with federal government, 4, 6, 39, 48, 91, 98, 123–127, 130, 132, 136, 146–147; in relation to Cuba, 21, 34, 83–85; in relation to Lower South (Deep South), 10, 12, 21, 38, 92, 130, 132, 142, 143, 145, 156–157, 175, 183n2; as southern coast of Confederacy, 2, 129, 130, 147, 154; support of Texas Revolution and Republic, 11, 29; support of U.S.-Mexican War, 58–59; surplus slaves in, 12, 29; trade within, 3, 11, 24, 29, 37, 38, 40, 48, 74, 83–84, 102, 104, 109, 143

Gutierrez-Magee Expedition, 31

Haile, C. M., and Pardon Jones, 9
Haiti and San Domingo, 87, 93, 102; Haitian Revolution, 93, 192n26
Henderson, James Pinckney, 22, 33, 74
Henderson, John, 94–95, 99
Henderson, Richard, 139
Henshaw, David, 49
History of the Conquest of Mexico (Prescott), 64
Holcombe, Lucy, 103–104
Hood, John Bell, 123
Houston, Sam, 3, 10, 17, 19, 22, 28, 58, 76, 122; opposition to filibusters, 135; opposition to Kansas-Nebraska Bill, 122, 134–135; as president of Texas, 10, 14, 16, 18–29, 31; on reopening the slave trade, 136; support of Cuban annexation, 106; unionism and, 134, 142–146, 153; U.S. Army on Texas frontier and, 135–136

Houston, Tex., 24
Houstoun, Matilda, 16–17, 23
Hunt, Memucan, 13–16, 19
Husk, Emily and Zelia, 115, 194

Immigrants, 17, 68, 83, 87, 106, 107–110, 112, 115, 119, 124, 143; Germans in Texas, 32, 107, 110, 161–162; tensions between Germans and Anglos, 121–122
Iturbide, Agustín, 69

Jackson, Alexander, 162
Jackson, Andrew, 16–17, 40
Jackson, Claiborne Fox, 159
Jackson, Rachel, 40
Jenkins, Lewis, 116–117
Johnston, Albert Sidney, 3, 18, 30–31, 133; return to U.S. Army in 1850s, 123–124; secession and, 153; during U.S.-Mexican War, 74–77, 78, 79, 140
Johnston, Eliza, 123–124
Johnston, William Preston, 133
Jones, Alexander, 83–84
Jones, Anson, 31, 33
Jones, Charles Colton, 101
Juarez, Benito, 165

Kansas-Nebraska Act, 102, 104, 122, 134
Kendall, George Wilkins, 25
Keyes, Julia, 175–176
Kingsley, Eliza, 40
Kinney, Henry, 62
Kirkwood, James P., 52
Knights of the Golden Circle, 131
Know-Nothing Party, 121–123

Ladly, Louis, 160
Lamar, Mirabeau Bonapart, 10, 14, 17–21, 22, 31
Lander, Alexander, 67
Lassaulx, Pierre François de, 23
Latimer, William K., 53
Latin America, 2, 4–6, 8, 94, 103, 141, 156, 198n3; Gulf of Mexico, 53, 153; in relation to Europe, 15, 153; as site of southern expansion, 33–34, 66, 80, 83, 94, 120, 125, 129–130, 138, 154, 179, 181; U.S. slavery and, 32–33, 152
Leclerc, Frederick, 12–13

Lee, Robert E., 123, 155, 164
Leverich, Fannie, 147
Lincoln, Abraham, 8, 130, 142, 143, 146, 148, 158, 164
López, Narciso, 7, 84, 91–101, 104; execution of, 100; memorials for, 81–82; transformation into martyr, 101, 131, 132, 155
Louisiana, 2, 12, 22, 49, 59, 71, 160, 163, 180; Confederate refugees in, 158–159, 167; secession and, 143; as territory, 82, 86, 93
Louisiana state legislature, 86
Love, James, 31
Love, Louis, 160
Lovejoy, Owen, 125
Lovell, Mansfield, 95, 150

Madison, James, 20
Maffitt, John, 150–152
Magruder, John B., 158–159, 163, 165
Mallory, Stephen, 150–151
Manifest Destiny, 2, 67
Marcy, William, 61
Martí, José, 180
Mason, John, 102
Maury, Matthew Fontaine, 171
Maximillian I, 167
Mayfield, J. S., 31
McCall, George, 40
McCulloch, Benjamin, 135
McFarland, Fanny, 115
Meriwether, Robert, 174
Mexican army, 13, 27, 56, 63, 67, 120
Mexicans, 1, 3, 4, 7; antislavery sentiments, 107; in Mexico, 57, 60, 69, 70; in New Mexico, 25–26; in Texas, 9–10, 12–13, 18, 19, 43, 46, 106, 116, 119–121; views of Anglos, 67–68; violence between Anglos and, 12, 32, 120, 121, 124, 126
Mexico: anti-Mexican laws and ordinances, 120–121; as antislavery nation, 9, 76; Camargo, 71, 75, 76; centralism and, 56, 65, 70; Chihuahua, 25, 171; confederate exiles and colonies, 8, 156, 168, 169, 170–172, 178; federalism and, 65, 112; French invasion and, 152, 154, 164, 167, 169; government of, 18, 25, 28, 59, 60, 70, 118; importation of Chinese laborers and, 172; invasion of Texas in 1842, 26, 29; Mexican War of Independence, 31; New Virginia Colony and, 171–172; relations with Europe, 29, 60, 67; relations with Texas Republic, 10–11, 25–28
Mississippi River, 26, 47, 61, 62, 83, 102, 148, 175
Missouri, 25, 159
Missouri Compromise, 13, 134
Mobile, Ala., 8, 34, 38, 40–42, 49, 81, 108, 146, 179; blockade running in, 8, 148–152; Mobile Greys, 65; population in, 109; slave trade in, 114
Monroe Doctrine, 61
Moore, John H., 20
Moore, Van, 160
Murphy, Maria, 161

Native Americans, 1, 4, 7, 12, 134, 135, 152; Aztecs, 64–65, 71, 79; Black Hawk War, 75; in Florida, 42–50, 56–57, 79; in Gulf South, 28, 36, 37, 38, 56, 60, 67, 68, 107; Indian Removal, 38; Indian Territory, 43; in Texas, 18–19, 21, 24–25, 27, 29, 34, 37–39, 60, 110, 124, 125
New Mexico 18, 23; American interests in, 59–60; Texan interest in, 25–26
New Orleans, 7, 8, 34, 38, 39, 166, 168; during Civil War, 148, 149, 150, 154–156, 160; connections to Cuba, 83, 84, 85; cotton boom and, 83, 84; divisions among neighborhoods, 86–87; fears of trade being threatened, 38, 62, 143; filibuster riots and, 100–101; importance to Gulf South, 24, 34, 49, 83, 84, 108–109; military mobilization in, 24, 54, 71, 75, 77–78, 147; New Orleans Greys and, 24; New Orleans Massacre of 1866, 180; populations of, 40, 85–89, 112; relationship with Texas, 24, 33; secession in, 143, 146, 147; slave markets in, 68, 114, 134, 139; support of filibusters, 81, 82, 84, 93–95, 132; threats to commerce of, 84; unionists in, 157, 161–162; as wealthiest and largest city in South, 83
Newspapers, 39, 49, 53, 72, 91, 97, 101, 111, 136; *American Flag*, 65; on defending Gulf Coast, 48, 51; racism in, 74, 77, 79, 141; *Republic of the Rio Grande and Free People,*

Newspapers (*continued*)
65–66; Texan, 20, 21, 23, 126; on U.S.-Mexican War, 54, 63, 65, 77, 79
New York, 49, 50, 53, 84, 85, 92, 170, 174, 178
Nunes, Henry A., 44

Olmsted, Frederick Law, 1, 114, 117, 120–121
Olmsted, John Hull, 1
Oregon Territory, 29, 50, 59
Osceola, 45
Ostend Manifesto, 102–103, 131

Palmer, John R., 65
Pedro II, emperor of Brazil, 174, 176–177
Pensacola: city boosters in, 38, 40–42, 49, 50–54; during Civil War, 161, 180; colonial control over, 39–40; comparison with Galveston, 40; competition with Atlantic Coast ports, 38, 49; congressional appropriations and, 43, 49–50; construction of dry dock, 46–47, 52–55; economic dependence on U.S. military, 38, 40–43, 46–47; fears over British invasion, 37, 49; Fort Barrancas, 39, 42; Fort McRee, 42; Fort Pickens, 42; Gulf Coast canal, 41, 113; improvements to naval yard, 48–49, 50–54, 61; interests by westerners, 36, 52–53; internal improvements to fortifications, 36, 38, 46–49, 52–55; as military outpost, 39–40, 42, 48–53, 55; as part of expansion and defense, 38, 46–47, 49, 52, 54–55; Pensacola Bay and, 38, 39; population in, 40–41; railroads and, 41–42; during secession, 146; during U.S.-Mexican War, 72–73
Perkins, William, 100–101
Poinsett, Joel R., 46–47
Polk, James K., 32, 64, 69; attempts to annex California, 58–59; description of conflict with Mexico, 60–63; 1845 message to Congress, 61
Potsanaquahip (Buffalo Hump), 20
Prescott, Walter, 64
Preston, William, 77–79, 123, 165
Price, Sterling, 165

Quitman, Eliza, 76, 98
Quitman, John, 3, 76, 94–95, 98, 129, 131

Quitman, Louisa (daughter of Eliza and John), 98
Quitman, Louisa (sister of John), 95

Race and racism, 2–7, 11–12, 56–57, 58, 68, 76, 180; Black-white binary, 4, 85; different depictions of Cubans and Mexicans, 64, 73, 85, 92, 104; Mexican War soldiers and sailors, 75–78; miscegenation, race mixing, and "mongrelization," 13, 40, 58, 76, 92, 141; against multiple races and ethnicities simultaneously, 3, 11, 57, 62–64, 68, 74–75, 79, 107, 115, 132, 144, 181; role during secession, 130, 140, 153; role of class, 68, 195n42; views of Mexicans in Gulf South, 19, 22, 32–34, 57, 63, 67, 77, 80, 125; views of Mexicans in Mexico, 59, 63–69, 76; views of Native Americans, 10, 57, 67, 180, 181
Reagan, John, 28, 133
Reconstruction, 156, 164, 167, 180; Redemption and, 177, 180; transnational elements and, 170
Republican Party, 140
Republic of Texas, 9, 10, 50, 61, 90; Congress, 23, 28, 31, 33; imagined views of, 14; independence, 13–14, 17, 24, 143; Republic's problems, 16; senate, 18, 23; as slaveholding republic, 10; southern imperialism and, 11–12; surplus slaves in, 12
Republic of the Rio Grande, 65
Rey, Juan Francisco (Garcia), abduction case, 89–91
Rio Grande, 26, 28, 59, 62; Rio Grande Valley and, 75
Roemer, Ferdinand, 32, 33
Runnels, Hardin, 126, 133
Rusk, General Thomas, 19

San Antonio, 19–20, 26
Sanders, John, 36, 48, 49
Santa Anna, Antonio López de, 12, 16, 65; Anglo racism toward Tejanos and Mexicans, 13–14, 56–58, 69–71; in exile from Mexico, 56; as president of Mexico, 70; return to Mexico, 69–70; during Texas Revolution, 58
Santa Fe Expedition, 25–26, 65

Santa Fe Trail, 25–26
Schmidt, Gustavus, 65
Scott, Washington, 161
Scott, Windfield, and anaconda plan, 148
Secession and secessionists, 6, 8, 126–130, 184n3; criticism of federal government, 124, 127, 130, 132, 144, 145; declarations of causes of secession, 145; expansionism and, 131–141; expansionist fantasies and, 112; expansionist fears and, 126; among Gulf port cities, 54, 55, 57, 92; idea of disunion, 135, 140, 141; transnational aspects of, 130, 141; violence in Texas, 124, 126
Secrest, W., 118–119
Seminole, and Black Seminoles, 4, 54, 118; Coacoochee and, 45; First Seminole Indian War, 37, 38, 40; migration to Mexico, 118; Second Seminole Indian War, 7, 38, 40–45, 48; Wild Cat, 118
Semmes, Raphael, 68, 71–75, 152
Semmes, T. J., 139–140
Shaw, Hugh G., 174
Shawnee, 18, 19; Linney and, 19
Shelby, Joseph, 163
Slavery, 1, 3, 106, 160; African Labor Supply Association and, 136; in Cuba, 4, 83, 92, 136; ex-Confederate colonies and, 172, 173, 180; expansion and, 7, 10, 11, 16, 37, 43, 58, 88, 104, 133; internal slave trade, 109, 113; justifications for, 12, 58; reopening African slave trade, 8, 135–138; slaveholders and, 5, 11, 17, 34, 42, 57, 80, 117, 119, 137, 156, 160, 188n12; slave importations from Cuba, 114, 116
Slemmer, Adam J., 146
Slidell, John, 59
Smith, Ashbel, 138
Smith, Edmund Kirby, 42, 123, 163–167
Soulé, Pierre, 85, 87–88
Southern Convention of 1859, 136
Southern Emigration Society, 174–175
Southwest, 6, 37, 53, 58, 60, 67, 70, 188n12; Mexican cession and, 57
Spain, 15, 22, 28, 31, 39–40, 88, 90, 97, 115, 179; consul in New Orleans, 88–89; romanticized views of conquest of Mexico, 64–65
Spratt, Leonidas, 136
Stewart, Charles, 48

St. Louis, Mo., 25, 65
Sugar production, 10, 15, 84, 89, 108, 174; in Texas, 21–22
Susa, Paulo, 174
Sydnor, John, 110–111

Taylor, Fitch Waterman, 51, 68, 73
Taylor, Zachary, 61, 62
Texas (state): army of, 19, 20, 69; Austin, 20; borderlands, 37, 61, 63, 105, 106, 107, 117, 123, 127; in colonial era, 18, 31; as Confederate refuge, 156, 170; cotton in, 10, 21–22, 30, 33–34, 106, 108, 113, 121, 127; land grants and speculation, 18, 112–113; politics in, 135–136; soldiers of, in images, 4, 26; women in, during Civil War, 159–160
Texas annexation, 64, 66, 76, 111, 181; anti-annexationists, 7, 10, 11, 15, 17–18, 21, 22; border dispute, 56; as bridge between two forms of expansion, 12, 56, 59; contributing to war with Mexico, 50, 56, 58, 62, 67; fears of British intervention, 30, 32–33, 37; joint resolution and, 33, 112; pro-annexationists and annexationists, 11–14, 17, 21, 22, 26, 29–32; *re*-annexation and, 32; sectional politics and, 11, 57; treaty of annexation, 30
Texas Navy, 27–29
Texas Rangers, 21; in U.S.-Mexican War, 66–67, 119
Texas Revolution, 9, 11, 24; Battle of San Jacinto, 12, 16; Battle of the Alamo, 58; memory of, 58
Texas state legislature, 17, 23, 74, 112, 123; Black petitions and, 115; during secession, 142, 145; Texas Preemption Act and, 112
Thrasher, John S., 103
Treaty of Guadalupe Hidalgo, 105, 119, 125, 152
Tyler, John, 29

Union. *See* United States
Unionism and unionists, 126, 130, 142, 144
United States, 2, 4, 6, 130, 148; Armed Occupation Act and, 44; financial claims against Mexico, 60; relations with Texas Republic, 11, 13–16, 23–24, 26 34
U.S. Army: Army of Observation, 62–63; Army of the Gulf, 158; during Civil War,

U.S. Army (*continued*)
  146–149, 153, 154, 155, 158–159, 160, 163; Corps of Engineers, 36, 37, 48, 53; frontier protection, 122–124; invasion of Mexico, 74–79; organization of Texas troops, 75; Third System of Coastal Fortifications, 42; use of enslaved laborers to build fortifications, 42–43
U.S. Congress, 38, 41, 42, 63, 104, 141, 149
U.S.-Mexican War, 3, 35–36, 39, 54–55, 92; American propaganda in, 56–58, 65–70, 77–79; Battle of Monterrey, 76–77; Battle of Palo Alto, 66, 95; Battle of Resaca de la Palma, 66; conclusion of, 78–82, 106, 118; invasion of central Mexico, 70; invasion of northern Mexico, 70, 75; siege of Veracruz, 75, 77; unruly soldiers in, 71; U.S. call for troops, 63, 75; views of soldiers and sailors, 58–59, 68, 70–79
U.S.-Mexico border and borderlands, 3, 6, 56, 59, 106, 118, 119, 120, 122, 160; lower Rio Grande valley, 107; southern borderlands, 116–117, 161; surveying of, 106, 116, 118, 119; Texas border, 61–63, 106, 124–128, 132, 135, 144, 158
U.S. Navy, 4, 36, 38; blockade of Mexican Gulf ports, 39, 54, 59, 62, 68–74, 131; Civil War blockade, 8, 130, 131, 140–144, 147–151, 154, 158, 173; conduct of European ships during Mexican War, 73–74; Gulf Squadron during Mexican War, 61, 72–73; importance to Gulf ports, 41, 46–47; naval yards on Atlantic Coast, 47; presence in Gulf of Mexico and question of enlarging, 61; riot aboard ship by volunteers, 71; use of enslaved laborers, 42–43; and U.S.S. *Constitution*, 72; and U.S.S. *General Taylor*, 44–45; and U.S.S. *Somers*, 69, 72–73
U.S. Senate, 33, 47

Van Buren, Martin, 24; response to annexation, 13, 16
Vasquez, Raphael, 26
Veracruz, Mexico, 60
Victoria, Tex., 21

Walker, Robert J., 11; safety valve theory, 32; support of Texas annexation, 31–32
Walker, William, 131–132
Wallis, George B. and "Arabella," 26
War of 1812, 37, 40, 42; Battle of Pensacola, 37
Webster, Frances, 50
Welles, Gideon, 148
Wharton, William, 13
Whig Party, 121
White, John, 117
Williams, John Lee, 41
Worth, William Jenkins, 44, 45

Yancey, William Lowndes, 136
Yulee, David Levy, 49

UnCivil Wars

Weirding the War: Stories from the Civil War's Ragged Edges
   edited by Stephen Berry
Ruin Nation: Destruction and the American Civil War
   by Megan Kate Nelson
America's Corporal: James Tanner in War and Peace
   by James Marten
*The Blue, the Gray, and the Green:
Toward an Environmental History of the Civil War*
   edited by Brian Allen Drake
Empty Sleeves: Amputation in the Civil War South
   by Brian Craig Miller
Lens of War: Exploring Iconic Photographs of the Civil War
   edited by J. Matthew Gallman and Gary W. Gallagher
*The Slave-Trader's Letter-Book:
Charles Lamar, the Wanderer, and Other Tales of the African Slave Trade*
   by Jim Jordan
Driven from Home: North Carolina's Civil War Refugee Crisis
   by David Silkenat
*The Ghosts of Guerrilla Memory: How Civil War Bushwhackers
Became Gunslingers in the American West*
   by Matthew Christopher Hulbert
Beyond Freedom: Disrupting the History of Emancipation
   edited by David W. Blight and Jim Downs
*The Lost President: A. D. Smith and the Hidden History
of Radical Democracy in Civil War America*
   by Ruth Dunley
Bodies in Blue: Disability in the Civil War North
   by Sarah Handley-Cousins

Visions of Glory: The Civil War in Word and Image
    edited by Kathleen Diffley and Benjamin Fagan
Household War: How Americans Lived and Fought the Civil War
    edited by Lisa Tendrich Frank and LeeAnn Whites
Buying and Selling Civil War Memory in Gilded Age America
    edited by James Marten and Caroline E. Janney
The War after the War: A New History of Reconstruction
    by John Patrick Daly
The Families' Civil War: Black Soldiers and the Fight for Racial Justice
    by Holly A. Pinheiro Jr.
Sand, Science, and the Civil War: Sedimentary Geology and Combat
    by Scott Hippensteel
A Man by Any Other Name: William Clarke Quantrill and the Search for American Manhood
    by Joseph M. Beilein Jr.
A Continuous State of War: Empire Building and Race Making in the Civil War–Era Gulf South
    by Maria Angela Diaz

www.ingramcontent.com/pod-product-compliance
Lightning Source LLC
Chambersburg PA
CBHW021807230426
43669CB00008B/656